Trailing

a

Bear

Trailing

a

Bear

Adventures of
Fred Bear and Bob Munger

Bob Munger

ISBN 0–9645143–0–3

Grateful acknowledgment is made to:
Archery World Magazine, Volume 37, No. 5
September/October 1988, for permission to reproduce the
Fred Bear quotes on the epigraph page and on the back
cover.

Typeset by Sans Serif Inc., Ann Arbor, Michigan.
Printed by McNaughton & Gunn, Saline, Michigan.

*Dedicated to
my wonderful and understanding wife, Phyl,
who watched over our children and
my business during my absence
while on many hunts around
the world with Fred Bear.*

One of the most important things to have on a hunt, besides shooting skill, razor sharp arrows, and your favorite bow, is a good hunting companion. Fred Bear has shared countless campfires with many unique and enjoyable personalities. But there was no hesitation when he recalled his favorite hunting companion. His voice took on a genuine tone of warmth and affection.

"It's Bob Munger. We've gone a lot of places, done a lot of things, been through some real tough hunts including being out six weeks on an ice pack in a tent. He's a good hard worker, he doesn't get discouraged, and he doesn't get cold." Ever playful with those he knew, Fred quipped, "Yeah, he's a hell of a lousy shot with a bow. But he's a hell of a hunter, and has eyes like an eagle."

Archery World Magazine, Volume 37, No. 5
September/October 1988

Bob Munger and Fred Bear were always heroes of mine from the earliest days, attracting me to the mystical flight of the arrow via their spirited and warm personalities every time I saw them with bow in hand. The invitation to join them over many years at the sacred Grouse Haven huntgrounds was the culmination of a bowhunter's dream.

Being able to embrace even a small portion of these gentlemen's human touch and woodsman spirit has made my life that much better. Their humor alone inspired me to pivot always on the positive. I salute Bob Munger and his sidekick Fred Bear, grand gentlemen both.

Ted Nugent, 1995

Contents

Foreword

Bow hunting has been put in the limelight due to the motion pictures that were shown on the "American Sportsman" and the "Outdoorsman" series. I became involved in Fred's company in 1960 as a stockholder, director and later Vice President, and went on many trips with him. Fred and I liked to feel that what was accomplished in hunting films contributed substantially toward the growth of the sport of bow hunting.

In the late sixties, the trend of ecology began to run. Conservation policies were instituted to preserve our game from extinction. Many of the animals that we legally hunted before then were removed from the hunting list. Many seasons were closed on some game animals, and some were put on the extinction list. Education in the schools began reflecting the "Bambi Image". Television withdrew their policies of showing a man shooting an animal. Hunting was not vogue on T.V.

Somehow television has seemed to have maintained the privilege of showing a man killing a man on most any channel during the prime time family hour. I fail to understand this!

Certainly the ecology transformation era has alerted peoples view on hunting, but the new conservation approach that has helped to save so many starving animals, hopefully will help to prolong hunting for the future. I hope the money that has been provided by the hunters will make it possible for future generations to enjoy their American heritage and the tradition of hunting.

Preface

To those who seek adventure, this true story of hunting events should fill one's desires. It is not intended for the faint heart, nor is it for the eyes of the person who does not believe in hunting.

The pages cover a twenty year span during which Fred Bear and I traveled to many lands bow and arrow hunting and making films of our experiences.

Fred, the foremost expert in the sport of bow hunting, made his first films as a company promotion. He later made several for the ABC Television Network.

I have tried to relate some of our most exciting experiences and narrow escapes. Had it not been for our experienced guides this story would not have made it to print. Many events were not without personal danger and a threat to our lives.

We were attacked by two angered polar bears, one grizzly bear and a cape buffalo. All had to be stopped by a gun. I was trapped within a herd of elephants that was a near brush with death.

Equal perils in our travels were the dangerous flying and weather conditions that we confronted.

We logged several thousand miles over the Arctic ice pack and made over one hundred landings on rough Beauford Sea ice. We spent seven weeks in a tent over two hundred miles from Point Barrow hoping to bait a polar bear. We approached over fifty brown bears in our trips on the Kodiak Island chain and the Alaskan Peninsula traveling some five hundred miles of uncharted, remote coastal waters in small boats and skiffs.

We spent nineteen days in the swamps of Marajo

Island in the mouth of the Amazon River to hunt the asiatic buffalo. We confronted most of the worlds most dangerous animals.

We both agreed, there are no more thrilling hunting experiences than to face polar bears, brown bears, grizzly bears, cape buffalos, asiatic buffalos, and elephants with a bow and arrow.

Acknowledgments

I was very fortunate to have had the many hunting experiences, the friendship and the guidance with my lifelong hunting companion, Fred Bear. All of this made my book become a reality.

I owe its completion to my wonderful wife Phyllis, who was patient throughout the twelve years I was assembling the information as she assisted me with its final completion. I am forever grateful for her understanding and tolerance during the times I was away with Fred for months while she assumed the responsibility of caring for our family and watching over my business.

I look back with pleasant thought over the twelve years when we recorded my field notes in our trailer up at our special hideaway on the northern shore of Lake Michigan. It gives me a very good and rewarding feeling of accomplishment.

I would like to give special recognition to wildlife extraordinaire, Charles Denauht, who has contributed so much with his oil painting "Arctic Caribou" of Fred and me, as well as his other artwork in this book.

Children's Statements

The expression, "LIVE LIFE TO THE FULLEST,"so apptley fits my father. Yes, this book for the most part is about the many adventures Dad had following and hunting with his close friend Fred Bear on their many hunting trips. This is about one man's desire and enthusiasm to enjoy the sport of hunting and fishing with his friends and the stories that lingered on for many years. He would return from a magnificent trip in Alaska with Fred Bear where they might have had a successful hunt to find him fly fishing for Blue Gill on Gun Lake or hunting for partridges in the swamps of Barry County. His excitement of telling stories of the fish he caught or didn't catch were sometimes equal or greater than those of a successful BIG GAME Hunt!

Hunting and fishing for my father was an opportunity for him to be outdoors with nature and friends. Yes, this book is about trailing a very famous Fred Bear, and it's about the companionship my father and Fred Bear had with each other. From the famous to people you may not know, it was through hunting and fishing that helped my father develop close friendships with many as well as Fred Bear. To name just a few that I feel this book should be dedicated to, friends who shared the thrill and stories of hunting and fishing with my father are: Harvey Holcomb, Bart Rypstra, Bun Elles, Al Ambroson, Jerry Anderson, Dick Mauch and Ken Jones.

This book would not have been possible without his best friend, partner and wife, my mother. They had a very special love and relationship. They were married on the day after the opening of the Michigan Deer Season. My mother understood that most of their anniversaries would be spent apart as my father hunted in Northern Michigan.

My mother always made sure we had a strong family unit supporting father's hunts and our many shared times together like our family trips and the growing up on Gun Lake. People have said there couldn't be a better met couple with "mutual love" than Phyllis and Bob. After us kids were gone Mom followed Dad to their last moments together. These wonderful journeys took them around the world enjoying sights through each other's eyes. Their most favorite spot was spending 3–4 months on the shores of Lake Michigan in the Upper Peninsula without the comforts of running water, heat and electricity. Their time of walking the beaches and fishing the local streams became their most special of all moments.

"Living their life memories over a campfire on the lake shore." That was my Mother and Father.

—Richard R. Munger

There are so many wonderful memories I have of my father returning from his many hunting trips with his trophies, beard, gifts, photos and, best of all, his wonderful stories. I would sit, wide eyed, as he reminisced about his hunts, I would laugh at his humorous stories, gasp at his many near escapes from danger and always be open to hearing many of the stories, as did his family and friends, over and over again. My father was a great story teller and he loved sharing and reliving his hunting experiences and adventures. As he wove his tales, his eyes would light up and anyone within hearing distance would become a captive audience until the end of his stories. Dad was still telling his stories to anyone who would listen in the hospital, just days before he passed away. This book, *Trailing A Bear,* was his dream and life ambition. It compiles all of the stories of his hunts with his dear friend, Fred Bear. Before Dad died, he made us, his daughters and son, promise that we would have the book printed and published. Now, this book will allow our father to continue telling his stories until the end of time.

—Ann Munger

In my father's last months of life, I remember spending one day in particular with him in a hospital in Grand Rapids, Michigan. He was not well physically, but mentally he still talked of plans for his book. His mind overflowed with ideas, and his enthusiasm for it seemed to be never-ending. On that August afternoon, I recall holding his hand as he lay on a hospital bed. We had a moment to talk, and it was at that time he made me promise that we would print his book if he wasn't able to. We all knew that truly was his last wish.

It's been five years since my father passed away, and I am so proud that my brother, sister and I are keeping our promise to him, and this book is a reality.

I remember growing up in a home where his travels and hunts were a big part of my childhood memories. His wonderful stories, slide shows, native art and artifacts from around the world, as well as the mounted animals, were a way of life for us. In spite of all of these mounts in our home, our father passed along to each of us a respect and love for animals and his love for the out-of-doors!

My father had a special gift of being a great story teller and enjoyed sharing his travels with many. My mother was also his special gift, for he was a lucky man to have a woman who truly shared and supported his passion for hunting. From the days when he was off hunting with Fred on six-week hunts to their last struggling years of poor health, my mother stood by and supported his love for hunting and his endeavors. Even in death, she passed away two weeks after my father.

I dedicate this book to my parents, for their love and commitment to each other. That is my fondest memory of all and their greatest accomplishment.

It saddens me that my children will never hear their Grandpa share his hunting stories with them or be able to go hunting or fishing with him. Yet I am so thankful for this book, that my father's hunting legacy can be passed on to our children and to the future hunters who will enjoy reading about his travels and adventures.

Mom and Dad, I miss you so much,

—Nancy Munger Anderson

I

Our Auspicious Meeting
1951

Fred Bear is the world's top bow and arrow hunter. Who should know this better than I, Bob Munger? I've been fortunate to have had the privilege of going with Fred on many of his big game hunts throughout the world, both as his hunting companion and part time cameraman. I'm the guy who saw Fred Bear do the many exciting things while hunting, that he laid claim to in his book, *Fred Bear's Field Notes*. So I guess by that virtue I'm entitled to tell some "Bear" facts that I witnessed first hand.

Fred Bear's name is a legend in the archery world and like many others have told me, he has also been my idol! Someday I think Fred bear may be as well known as other famous Americans such as Ernest Hemingway. Fred is a true innovator who has probably done more to develop and promote the sport of archery than any other man, living or dead.

I felt that I should call this book, *Trailing A Bear*, as I have travelled thousands of miles with Fred, and trailed

1

him to many lands. To say our first meeting was an auspicious occasion is really an understatement. This meeting took place in 1951 and had to be one of the most unbelievable coincidences that has ever occurred in the woods. I couldn't begin to dream up such a yarn. Had our paths not crossed at this particular spot and time, many events that happened during my lifetime would never have taken place. Because of that chance meeting with Fred, I've met many famous people and gone on many fantastic hunting trips with Fred throughout the world.

I have been an enthusiastic bow hunter since 1940. I'd read and heard a lot about Fred Bear. I'm not a target shooter, so I didn't go to the shooting events that Fred would normally attend. As you probably know Fred made quite a name for himself as a target shooter. Bill Graham of Charlotte, Michigan, a good friend of mine, first got me interested in the sport of archery. I was in the hardware, farm equipment, and sporting goods business; Bill was a sales rep for the Bear Archery Company, one of the first in Michigan. I had taken on the Bear line of bows and arrows and in a short time became interested in trying the sport myself.

Bill received an invitation from Fred to go deer hunting in the northern part of Michigan. On his return, he told me about his exciting times hunting with Fred and asked me if I would like to join him on the next trip.

Two weeks later we took him up on his offer. Bill, my wife Phyl, and I drove up north, arriving before dark at the hunting camp at James Ranch. No other hunters had arrived yet. We were met by our jovial host, Ivan James, a small reddish faced guy with a pot belly and a good sense of humor.

The James Ranch, a privately owned and operated bow hunting club for white-tail deer, was located in the northeast part of the lower peninsula.. The Port Huron Club, a rifle club, bordered the James Ranch just north of the James Ranch.

After the arrival of a couple of other hunters we sat down to a banquet meal, prepared and served by Ivan's wife, Edith. Later we sat around spinning a few deer stories and also got some advice from Ivan: "Don't cross the road and go onto the Port Huron Club property next door when you go hunting tomorrow". We then turned in for the night, and were up before daylight the next morning.

Bill and I started out with wild anticipations. In those days there was a fantastic deer herd in that part of Michigan. Bill decided to hunt in the center of the ranch and directed me to work toward the northern boundary, where I would find a blind that he had built. Following his directions, I went to the north end, found the blind with the help of my flashlight and sat down to wait. During the next hour, I watched a continuous procession of deer migrating north across the road to the Port Huron Club. Among the herd were many large bucks with nice racks, however, none of them came close to me.

Big racks do excite me. I lose my relaxed composure and what little good sense I might possess when I see a big rack. I tolerated this procession for as long as I could. Then after a short deliberation I stepped out to the road to check the tracks that disappeared into the Port Huron Club. Again I spent a short time trying to convince myself that I shouldn't enter this private domain, but I failed. I slowly drifted in that direction. Maybe the wind helped?

Carefully, I directed my stalk into the wind. I went at a slow pace watching for the deer herd that had disappeared in the woods. A half hour passed before I saw a deer. As I picked my way through the tall ferns, I suddenly heard the brush crash off to my right, I froze and knelt to the ground. Looking up, I saw a nice buck bounding toward me.

The autumn leaves had started to fall and the woods was noisy. I was wearing camouflage clothing and I crouched hidden behind some brush and ferns. The deer came up, obligingly stopped, stood broadside and looked back. This gave me my chance to come to a full draw. I aimed and carefully released my arrow. It passed over his back, he jumped, ran just a few feet, stopped and then looked back at me. I put another arrow on the string, and was about to draw down on him when I heard a stick crack

to my right. The buck took off. I looked around expecting
to see another deer, but it turned out to be a hunter. My
first thought was, "Oh! my God it's one of the Port Huron
Club members and he's got me red handed".

The hunter was dressed in camouflage garb, and was
coming directly toward me. He had not spotted me yet. It
was a shocking moment when I recognized the hunter as
Fred Bear from the many pictures I'd seen of him. I took a
deep breath and relaxed as this gave me the drop on him. I
knew it was very unlikely that he was a member of the Port
Huron Rifle Club.

Fred didn't know me and naturally thought I was a
member of the club. Fred had wandered over here, seeing
the same tracks that I'd followed.

He was extremely polite and we had a very jovial conversation. After visiting for a few moments, he asked me if
I had seen the deer he'd been tracking, I told him that I
had, and had taken a shot at it. He asked if I had hit it, and
I told him that I didn't. Then he wanted to know if I had
found my arrow. I said no. He offered to help me find it. He
still didn't really know who I was. We soon found my arrow
buried in a stump. As we stood checking my arrow for any
sign of blood, a crow lit up in the top of a tree near us. Fred
whispered, "Let's take a shot at it". We both shot and
missed. We started to walk in the direction where our
arrows should have landed, we shot on a forty-five degree
angle and were sure we would find them easily. About then,
Fred unknowingly stepped directly on a hornet's nest.
They really started lacing it to us and we retreated post
haste, forgetting about our arrows.

I've often thought, that with all the deer in that area,
how come Fred had chosen to go after my deer? When we
finally got around to introducing ourselves, we both felt a
bit more relaxed. It was a comfortable feeling to find out
that we were both in the same predicament. Fred suggested we continue hunting together. I guess he thought this
would be the best way to keep us from ratting on each
other, about getting lost on the Port Huron Club property.

We worked into the wind, and Fred soon spotted a nice

forkhorn. As we crawled toward the buck on our hands and knees through the ferns, the buck decided to lay down. He laid with his back to the wind and looked downwind in our direction. Fred and I decided to crawl through the high ferns and try to maneuver into a position for a shot. We had no means of communicating with each other, and shortly found that we were both lost from the other's view. Neither of us knew whether to continue or just lay and wait.

We waited some fifteen or twenty minutes. It seemed like an hour. Finally, the buck got up and walked slowly to my right. I caught a glimpse of movement out of the corner of my eye, and saw Fred about forty yards from me, up on one knee, drawing a bead on the buck. His arrow slid over the buck's back, and the buck took off with no ill effects.

We returned together to the ranch house, vowing to tell none of our hunting experiences to our buddies.

Later that day I went out with Bill for the evening hunt. As I have stated, I brought my wife Phyl with me. After Bill and I had left, she decided to try her hand at bow hunting for the first time. I must admit that I hadn't given her much training on shooting a bow. Frankly, I never dreamt that she would even want to hunt. However, I had brought a light-weight Bear recurve and had bought her a license so she would feel like part of the hunting gang.

She took her bow, which I had neglected to string up for her, and stepped out of our cabin in search of some help. She saw a tall lanky bow hunter coming out of the main ranch house. She hailed him down and politely asked him if he knew how to string a bow. She had never seen Fred before that moment. Fred was very obliging and strung the bow for her, but did not reveal who he was. Knowing Fred, he would do this for any good looking gal.

That evening Fred left the ranch to return to his factory at Grayling.

After we met, I would stop in Grayling to see Fred at his factory, on my trips up to the Grayling Winter Sports area. I was a Boy Scout leader at the time, and I would take a group of scouts to the Grayling ski area for the weekend.

Unlucky Archers Can Get Arrows

Dec. 73 1951

Archers who aimed arrows at deer and missed during the recent bow and arrow season can have their arrows by calling at the Port Huron Hunting Club near Curran. Club members Roy and Walter Norton picked up two arrows during the present gun season. Names inscribed on the arrows read: Fred Bear and R. Munger.

Appeared in the December, 1951 issue of The Detroit News.

I'd usually stop and talk hunting with him. Fred took us on tours of his factory.

In December, I was looking through *The Detroit News* and ran across an article entitled, "Attention Archers!". It said that if Fred Bear and Bob Munger would report to the lodge of the Port Huron Club, they could have the arrows back which they had lost while hunting on their private club in October. I cut this out of the paper and sent it to Fred at Christmas time as a sort of Christmas card.

That was the last time, I believe, that either of us ever put our names on our arrows. I had good reason for putting my name on my arrows—because I wanted them back and couldn't afford to lose them—but I never understood why a guy with a warehouse full of tons of arrows needed to get his back.

Had I not bumped into Fred at that particular spot, the drastic changes that occurred in my lifetime would probably never have taken place. Some were good and some bad. Since that first meeting with Fred, I have hunted with him in many parts of Alaska, British Columbia, Ontario, Africa, South America, and several states throughout the United States.

This book is an account of these hunting trips.

II

Bow Hunting the Ice Bear
1960

Several years after I had met Fred at the James Ranch, I went to Alaska with an old hunting friend of mine, Harvey Holcomb, from Charlotte, Michigan, to hunt brown bear on Kodiak Island. While passing through the airport at Anchorage, we saw a huge, life-sized polar bear mount standing on his hind legs, displayed in the airport lobby. This mount looked very impressive to me. Harvey and I decided then and there that the following year we would go after one of these beasts.

We arranged the hunt with Lee Holen, a polar bear guide with whom Harvey and I had hunted moose and black bear. It was all set for the next spring. In March, I ran across an article in a Chicago paper telling how our guide, Lee Holen, and another fellow, on a polar bear shoot, went through the ice in the process of landing their plane. Harvey made the mistake of showing this to his wife. He was immediately cancelled out of the polar bear business.

The next week, I went to Grayling and stopped to see

Fred. I told him that I'd lost my hunting partner and Fred responded, "Well, you know I've always wanted to shoot a polar bear. Why don't we go together?" I was both elated and quite honored to have the opportunity to go hunting with the famous Fred Bear.

We agreed on some preliminary plans, and Fred made arrangements for us to go with Dick McIntyre, Fred's friend from Fairbanks. We planned to hunt out of Kotzebue. However, Fred called me a short time later to say he had heard from Dick that the ice conditions were very bad out of Kotzebue at that time. He suggested that we either cancel our hunt and go up the following year, or go to Point Barrow. Point Barrow was farther north and the ice conditions there were said to be good.

Fred and I decided we wanted to go that year, not the next, and told Dick to set us up with somebody for a hunt in the spring. Dick made arrangements for us to go with George Theile and Pete Merray who were hunting out of Point Barrow. We were also told that George had killed two polar bears with a bow and arrow, so we felt that he was our kind of guy.

I met Fred in Chicago at O'Hare Airport. It takes quite a bit of gear to go polar bear hunting. I shipped my excess luggage as air freight, but when we got to Seattle I had no luggage. Since it was a nonstop flight from Chicago to Seattle, it seemed rather difficult to lose any luggage while in the air. I spent hours with the airlines in an effort to locate my lost luggage and polar hunting gear. I never did find it. Fred said he thought our outfitter, Dick McIntyre, could fix me up with some clothes. This consoled me a little as I was worrying about being the first guy to go on a polar bear hunt in his BVDs.

Fred had lined up free passes with Alaska Airlines on the flight from Seattle to Fairbanks. He planned to make a film for his company on polar bear hunting. He had previously made hunting films to promote the sport of archery and the product he made, bows and arrows, at Bear Archery Company. This also helped to raise his name to national recognition. Fred had agreed to put the picture of the Alaskan Airline's plane in the introduction to the film in return for these free passes and free transportation of our luggage.

We contacted Bill Burke, the public relations man for Alaskan Airlines. He took us to a meat packaging plant, which he had an interest in, and fixed us up with a month's supply of cold cuts. The airlines also sent an escort to show us around Fairbanks, as well as a newspaper journalist who was writing a story on the trip. Fred brought some of his 16mm movies that he had made of previous hunts and showed them on the plane during our flight to Fairbanks.

After the flight time change and the party session on the plane, we were both worn out, but our hosts insisted that we see the city as soon as we landed in Fairbanks. They started with a tour of the bars, hoping to find someone who had recently come from Barrow and who could give us the weather conditions there and some hunting information.

In the first bar we visited, there was a contingent of motley looking characters. Fred suggested we have a little fun with them. We had been playing liars' poker on the plane, so we rigged a little game that we thought might impress the natives.

They were giving us the eye as we were strangers in town. We put a stack of one dollar bills in front of us. On top of the stack, we put a twenty dollar bill. It looked like we were playing with a large stack of twenties. This immediately drew the attention of the surrounding tables. Fred would ask me how my ranches were coming, and I'd ask Fred if his new oil well had come in yet, implying we were from Texas. Before we knew it, we had all the group with their eyeballs popping out, listening to our conversation of lies and watching our card game. Just "good guys" having some harmless fun.

The next morning, we went to Dick McIntyre's sporting goods store, called Frontier Sport Center, and bought our licenses. Dick showed us the polar bear he had on display, and told us about his experience shooting it. This was one of only three polar bears that had ever been killed with a bow and arrow. Dick had seen a bear track with blood in its trail from the air, and followed it for twenty miles. He came upon the bear lying down in the snow. So he landed and killed it with his bow and arrow. Apparently the bear had cut its leg on some sharp ice and had severed an artery which caused much bleeding.

As Fred predicted, I got fixed up with some warm clothes. Dick McIntyre felt sorry for me and gave me some of his clothes. He thought George Theile could fix me up with some fur pants and muckluks among other things I'd need when we got to Barrow.

We took off the next day about three o'clock from Fairbanks to Barrow in an old C-46 operated by Wein Airlines. There was Fred, myself, the pilot and co-pilot, and one hostess—a good looker. The seats had been removed to make room for freight. All the luggage was lashed down securely with ropes.

As we flew over the Tannana River, we noticed a small plane spraying a black substance on the ice on the river below. The pilot explained it was coal dust which helped melt the ice so it would recede slowly and not cause a flash flood in Fairbanks.

We crossed the Arctic Circle and upon doing so, Fred and I were awarded certificates with our names inscribed on them. The pilot and co-pilot each signed them as souvenirs of the trip. The trip is a six-hundred and fifty mile flight which took us up through the Brooks Range. As we approached the mountains, instead of flying at a high altitude, the pilot flew low through the passes.

Fred and I were invited to go up to the pilot's quarters where we had a real good view of this fantastic snow covered mountain range. We flew through the Anaktuvuk Pass, which the Eskimos and Indians use to travel through to the north slope. This is also the pass through which the huge caribou herds migrate each year. The small native village of Anaktuvuk is located here and we could see the Eskimos waving at us as we flew over.

From this point on, the countryside flattened out for

the next one-hundred and fifty miles, from the air it looks literally as flat as a pancake. The tundra below was covered with snow. There were no trees or evidence of any vegetation. This is called the land of oil drums. The Army, Navy and Air Force built and utilized early warning systems here and at Point Barrow. White Alice and the other radar equipment had been built during the war. In the process of supplying the area, the military dumped thousands of drums along the way. You could actually see an oil drum several miles away when you were at ground level.

The flight lasted about three and a half hours. I will always remember the parting remark the hostess made when we landed at Barrow. Apparently she had some misgivings about us tackling a polar bear with a bow and arrow. As we parted she simply said, "Be brave". Fred gave her one of his postcards with his picture on it.

The quonset terminal was filled with Eskimos and natives from the Barrow area. All of them had come out with their dog sleds to meet the plane. This was before the days of the snowmobile. We, of course, weren't too hard to find, being the only two passengers.

A fellow in a huge wolf parka came up and introduced himself as George Theile. George is half Eskimo and had been a bush pilot in the Arctic for many years. He had flown many rescue missions and had quite a reputation for being a topnotch pilot, and a good polar bear hunter as well. He was the only man that we knew of, who had shot two polar bears with a bow and arrow, without a backup.

The Eskimos gave us a ride into the village in the freight truck, which also carried the mail and our gear. We passed through a little group of huts on the way, a settlement called Browersville. There was a native supply store there owned by a man named Brower. He was reported to be the only Eskimo millionaire.

It's about a half mile between Browersville and Barrow. The road goes across a frozen lake. Small planes use this lake as their landing field. There were a dozen ski-equipped planes there. Looking south from where we had come and north toward the ocean, the shoreline seemed the same, except toward the ocean there were huge pieces of ice, some fifteen miles away. The ice was fused to the shoreline for ten or fifteen miles out, then there was a break, or lead, as it is called. From there out was the ever floating pack ice.

The best way that I can describe the weather in Fairbanks and the weather when we got off the plane at Barrow, is to say it's like opening up your deep freeze, jumping into it and shutting the lid. The temperature was twenty degrees below zero when we arrived. Fred and I didn't waste any time putting on heavier clothing. This was the month of April when the sun barely sets throughout the twenty-four hour day. We could actually read a newspaper outdoors at midnight it was so bright.

They took us to the Top of the World Hotel, the only hotel in the little village of nine hundred Eskimos. It had quite a layout but I don't think Hilton will ever buy it. The hotel was a crude wooden structure the size of a small schoolhouse, the lobby was no bigger than a small living room. The building was unattended and the door locked. We had to go across the street to pick up the key at Al's Café, the only eating place in town.

For two weeks, Fred and I were the only occupants of the Top of the World Hotel. There were four rooms, each had two single bunks. We found it was impossible for Fred and I to share a room because of the small area left after we got our gear into it. So we each selected our own individual "suite".

There was an old oil heater in the back and an Eskimo came in once a day to check the oil and bring us ice. The only drinking water came from a twenty-gallon garbage can in which they put blocks of ice to be melted on the stove. This ice was cut from the fresh water lake and brought by dog sled to the hotel. It was Barrows' only water supply. All of the houses had a pile of ice for this purpose.

Luxuries at the hotel included chemical toilets and electric lights. There were no rugs on the floor and you would think insulation had not yet been invented. We slept with most of our clothes on in down-filled sleeping bags in order to keep warm.

The village of Barrow is a very interesting native village. There were no thoughts of it ever being a town when it was built. The only road that was reasonably straight was the one which went down through the middle of the village. The rest of the roads crisscrossed in between, throughout the village.

Fred and I spent several pleasurable days wandering around the village, looking at the Eskimo's equipment, talking with them and getting acquainted. Because George was half Eskimo, we were accepted a little better than if we had a white outfitter. Yet the Eskimos did not accept us with open arms. They were rather shy and reluctant to talk at first, but through George's contacts, we were better accepted than some of the other hunters who came later.

The Eskimos had their skin boats in production, preparing for the coming bowhead whale season. Fred and I hoped to film the killing of one of these huge whales after we finished our polar bear hunt. There are years in Barrow when not a single whale is killed. Other years, there might be a dozen killed. Even back then, a large whale was reported to be worth $10,000 to the Eskimos in food and oil.

In front of the village of Barrow, on the ice pack, there was a large black spotted area that Fred and I were curious about. We walked out to investigate and found oil drums filled with the sewage and garbage collected throughout the winter by the Eskimos. They haul these out about a half a mile on large sleds. When the ice recedes in the spring, melting away from the shoreline, the garbage floats out to sea. This works most of the time, except one year an onshore breeze blew the ice, garbage and sewage back to shore and dumped it right on the main street of Barrow. I'm glad Fred and I weren't there that year.

The Eskimos had all kinds of things stored around their houses, and not in too neat a fashion. There were walrus tusks and skulls, skin kayaks, seal hunting equipment, caribou hides, antlers and all kinds of trash. The roof seemed to be the favorite spot on which to throw things. Some of it looked as if it had been there for years. Well, we had a great time going around and looking at these things that were all new and interesting to both of us.

In the evening, several other polar bear hunting guides would come over to the hotel. Having heard that Fred was in town, they were interested in meeting him. We would stay up practically all night spinning yarns about our many hunting experiences. We even became dubious about whether or not we wanted to continue our bear hunting expedition after hearing some of their wild stories.

Early the next morning we went across the street to Al's quonset hut café. This place is well worth describing. The entrance was tunnel-like, built of wood, perhaps twelve feet long. It was coated solid with ice a foot thick on both sides, ceiling and the floor. This formed when the steam, coming through the front door, hit the subzero air.

As we entered the cafe we noticed an Eskimo gal, probably in her 20's, dressed in a fur parka, sitting at a corner table. Fred and I were the only other customers at that early hour.

After Al took our order, the Eskimo gal started up the juke box, then shuffled over to our table and sat down across from me. She apparently had been on an all night binge. She looked me straight in the eye—the best she could—and said, "Yuv got the most beautiful blue eyes I've ever seen". Fred, of course, chimed right in and agreed whole heartedly with her. She reached across the table, grabbed my hands and said, "Let's dance Blue Eyes". Fred told her what a good dancer I was and tried to force me to prove it. I might have agreed to go along with this—mostly to please Fred—but when she bent over the table I spotted a little papoose tucked in the rough of her parka. I also got a sniff that told me the kid wasn't wearing pampers. Frankly, I had one hell of a time fighting her and Fred off in their persistent attempt to "Lawrence Welk" me around the room.

I tried to sic her on Fred, but she had a thing about

blue eyes. From that day on, according to Fred, my name has been "Blue Eyes". Every letter was "Dear Blue Eyes" or "B.E.". It caused me considerable discomfort and embarrassment throughout the years as Fred's favorite joke to bring up at a cocktail party. I still don't know whether my wife believes Fred's version of the event or mine.

We got acquainted with Al, the café owner and cook. His specialty was reindeer steaks. Fred and I had reindeer steaks everyday during the time we were in Barrow.

There was a door in the rear of the café which Fred had to investigate. A dim red light bulb hung from the ceiling with a cardboard sign attached by a string. The sign read, "No Kissing". The young Eskimo kids came to dance at the café. A pinball machine sat in the corner. To operate it, you simply picked up the glass and replaced the balls when the game was finished. Fred and I got pretty good at pinball before the trip was over. A pool table also sat in another corner.

Fred had made arrangements for a camera man to come along on the hunt to take the movies. For some reason or another, the guy never showed. This, more or less, left me to be the camera man. I knew nothing about operating a movie camera, so Fred gave me a series of lessons. We went through many practice sessions. The camera was an Eastman K-100 16mm, mounted on a gun stock. There was also a sequence camera on the end of the stock which could take a series of still pictures in rapid succession. This could be set on automatic so it would rip off twenty shots of film in a matter of seconds, or it could be set manually.

I operated the movie camera with my right hand and the sequence camera with my left. I could also see all the action through the lens of the movie camera while filming. I found that when a bear is only twenty-five yards away, he looks a hell of a lot bigger. It got a little exciting sometimes and was hard for me to remember to run both cameras at once. I always hoped I had learned my lessons well and the films would turn out okay. Fred checked the light and speed settings before every stalk, so all I had to do was tag along and operate the cameras.

We both learned a great deal during the next two weeks about shooting film in the Arctic. The Arctic cold posed many problems for operating a camera. There was so much light on the white snow reflecting back into our faces, we had to use filtered lenses. Even then, we had to tape all the seams on the camera so the light couldn't get inside. Fred made a quilted jacket for the movie camera, like a regular down-filled jacket. It had four pockets into which we could slide hand warmers. With temperatures down to thirty-five degrees below, we had to keep the camera warm in order to have it operate properly. Otherwise, it would slow down or the batteries would freeze.

Fred and I were actually a little late in arriving at Barrow. George and Pete had lined up some other hunters while waiting for us. This gave us more chances to case the town, talk with the Eskimos, and practice with the camera, which was good.

We took the camera about half a mile out on the ice and did a lot of shooting. I filmed Fred walking across various ice formations and spent several days getting prepared for our hunt. On Sunday, we attended the Church of God. This was Easter Sunday, the Eskimos came in their best regalia and beautiful parkas. Even the kids had fancy parkas. The old wooden church was a small structure, with a pot bellied stove and wood benches.

A minister flew in from Fairbanks to conduct the service. Since he could not speak the native tongue, an old time friend of George Theile's translated for the congregation. He translated one sentence at a time before going on to the next one. His name was Ned Nesunghia, an Eskimo in his late 70s. Nobody removed their parkas or mittens during the service. It was a very impressive and interesting ceremony, at least it kept us awake.

At last George and Pete were ready to take us hunting. All the townspeople were interested in Fred, for some of the Eskimos used bows and arrows, as well as spears and harpoons. A contingent of natives followed us daily. They were at the airstrip both upon our leaving and our return. They accompanied us back to the hotel with about a dozen kids tagging along.

We went over to Al's place for breakfast the next morning. Fred set his camera gear outside the front of the café. If he had taken it in, then brought it out again, it would have steamed up and frozen.

During the course of our breakfast, the man who had brought us in on the truck from the airport wandered in. It was pretty cold that morning, probably twenty-five degrees below. He said he couldn't see through the frosted windshield very well and had run over something near the road in front of the café. He added, "It looked like it might have been a camera!" Fred jumped to his feet and ran outside to salvage what was left of his precious equipment. He returned shortly with a kind of chicken grin on his face. The camera equipment was safe. It was the first time we realized that Eskimos have a sense of humor. This incident seemed to break the ice a little.

After breakfast we walked to the plane, which was waiting for us on the lake. Since the lake was the only smooth surface near the village, it was used as a landing strip. George and Pete had been down there before us, getting the plane ready for take off. They put a canvas sleeve over the propeller blade which flared out at the bottom, making a sort of teepee. Inside of this they put a large salamander, or gasoline fire pot, something like plumbers use to melt their lead. This heats up the engine so it can be started. The night before, they had drained the oil out of the crankcase and taken it home with them to keep it warm on the stove.

When the engine was heated, we went back and picked up the oil to put it in the crankcase. There were several 50 gallon drums of gasoline beside the plane, used for tie downs. We pumped the gasoline for the plane out of those drums with a small hand pump. This was a real cool task.

Fred and I were appointed as the rope team. A rope is used to saw off the frost on the wings. Fred had one end and I had the other. Many times we took an ice spud and broke the skis loose from the ice where they had frozen during the night. Then we would have to push the plane to get it started because the skis were still sticking to the ice.

After gassing the planes, we put several extra five-gallon cans of gas into Pete's airplane. We finally lifted off about a hour and a half later. Fred and I flew with George in his Piper family cruiser, Pete followed with the load of gasoline in his super cub. George made radio contact with the tower, the Arctic Research, telling them where we were going. This is a safety precaution.

Sometimes we would fly out over one-hundred miles, flying real low—perhaps two-hundred feet over the ice—to locate bear tracks. When we wished to return, we'd climb to about six-thousand feet and radio the tower so they could get a fix on us and bring us straight back to Barrow.

Whenever we crossed the first lead, we could see whaling camps in the distance with several tents located on the edge of the lead. We tried to stay away from these camps, because the airplane noise might scare the seals or whales the Eskimos were trying to harpoon. We didn't want the Eskimos mad at us.

The greatest risk in hunting polar bears is really not the polar bears, but the flying. Particularly when hunting with a bow, you have to make many more landings than when hunting with a rifle. You can shoot a polar bear at a long distance with a rifle and not have to take off again. But when you have to get within thirty or forty yards of a bear, it takes quite a few landings every day to accomplish this.

The uncertainty of not knowing whether the ice was thick enough when we sat the plane down, left Fred and me with more than a little apprehension. We noticed that as soon as we landed on a spot that was smooth, George and Pete would taxi the planes onto thicker ice. The takeoffs and landings were very exciting, as was the low level flying. One who was susceptible to air sickness would have quite a problem, because when they start tracking a bear, they tip the plane right and left putting the wing tips down so they can see directly below them. It's like riding a roller coaster. Fortunately it didn't bother Fred and me. I guess we were too cold to get sick.

We checked the thermometer that was taped onto the wing strut, it was twenty-three degrees below zero the morning we took off on that first flight. After flying twenty miles, we came to the pressure ice where the first break was a towering jumble of huge blocks of ice. Some of the piles were seventy to one hundred feet tall. They were caused by the grinding of the pack ice against the shore ice.

In the back seat, the frost was so thick on the windows that Fred and I could hardly see out. George had a heater hose connected to the manifold, which he used to fan the windshield to keep the view clear. Once in a while he'd become benevolent, pass some heat back to Fred and me, and let us get a little of that warm air in our faces. It sure felt good.

About thirty miles out we found an open area of bluish-black water. There we could see two large bowhead whales sounding and spouting. These whales are about eighty feet long and weigh up to eighty tons. Along these leads is the best place to hunt polar bears because the seals inhabit the open waters. The seals perch on the side of the ice just about the same as turtles sitting on a log. The polar bears sneak up and catch them, seals are their main source of food.

The contour of the ice is part smooth and part rough with lots of pock marks. Fred and I imagined it probably was like hunting on the moon. The tracking plane we were in flew one hundred to two hundred feet above the ice, seeking out fresh bear tracks. Some days it was impossible to find tracks on the ice, the wind-blown snow made them invisible. But when the snow was fluffy, we could easily spot the bears' large footprints. The snow in the Arctic is made up of very fine particles, not large flakes like it is in the lower "48".

When we spotted a polar bear track, we followed it the best we could. Sometimes we followed it for twenty-five or thirty miles before we either came up on the bear or lost it.

By diving down and looking over a bear, George could tell us the size of it; he would ask Fred if he wanted to give him a go. Usually George was a joking character, but this was serious business for him. As soon as he started hunting and tracking a bear, he never would say a word until he saw a bear.

The first bear we saw was about an eight footer, George suggested we forego this one. Fred had explained to George the first time we had gotten together that he wanted a large bear. He said that he would pay George one-hundred dollars an inch for every inch over a nine-foot bear. Naturally, George was hopeful that Fred would get, at least, a ten-foot bear—length of hide plus width, divided by 2, determines the size of the bear.

Hunting polar bears with a rifle is a pretty simple feat and not very sporting. With two airplanes and two guns, the bear doesn't have much of a chance. He has no place to go and the planes can sometimes land right beside him. It's almost like betting on a bull in a bull fight. As a result, *Boone and Crockett*, a number of years ago, removed polar bears from the record books if they had been taken by airplanes and recorded only those that were considered a fair chase by using dog sleds.

It was very poor tracking this particular day. The wind was blowing the drifting snow, we decided to land, have lunch, regroup and talk things over. We gassed up the planes, ate our sandwiches and took off in an easterly direction where George had seen quite a few bears the week before.

We flew about twenty-five miles and found a good sized bear track. We followed this for probably ten miles and came to some very thin ice and open water. We approached the ice, saw the bear walking along the ice near the open water and looked him over. Diving down on him, we saw that he was a huge bear. Fred said he would gladly settle for him.

The bear was heading toward the open water. As he approached the thinner part of the ice, which bordered the heavy pack ice, he broke through. To our amazement, rather than trying to fight the ice, he swam under it. The ice was clear, and I took pictures of his progress. He would go about twenty yards, bang his head against the ice, break it, come up and get a breath of air. Then he'd dive down and take off again, come back up and do the same thing, always looking toward the open water and heading out to it.

There was probably a mile of open water before he was able to come to the next floating island of ice. George suggested we land. The ice was jumbled up in huge blocks, approximately forty feet high where it bordered the open water. Landing back quite a ways so the bear wouldn't see the airplane, we prepared to stake out the ambush. I took the camera, and threw a Weatherby rifle across my back for personal insurance. Fred got his bow set and George led the way toward the huge towering wall of ice. George climbed up and peeked out over the top; he could see the bear was coming directly toward us. The wind was in our favor. George checked again and we had moved two-hundred yards to left hoping to intercept him. We waited a few minutes, George peeked over the top again and whispered, "The bear is coming directly at us."

We could see nothing except the huge block of ice, like a big snow drift. Fred, of course, was the number one man in front, I was behind him with the camera and George was off to the left of us just a little bit to the rear, so he would not appear in the picture.

The wind died down, we could hear the bear splashing as he climbed out onto the ice, on the other side of the towering block. Fred and I had on white camouflage outfits, but George wore a wolf parka. As soon as the bear reached the top, about sixty feet away, he spotted us, stood on his hind legs and looked us over. All I could think of was the picture I had seen of King Kong standing on the Empire State Building. He looked like he was fifteen feet tall.

I started the camera, Fred began to pull his bow back, when to our shock and amazement, George hollered, "Don't shoot!". The bear dropped to all fours and took off across the top of the large chunks of ice. Fred asked George why he had told him not to shoot. George explained that he wanted the bear to go past us, then have Fred shoot him. George said if Fred shot him on top of the ice, he would have whirled, gone back into the open sea, and the salt water entering the open wound would kill him. The bear would have sunk and we would have lost him.

We hurried, the best we could, down the edge of the ice ridge. I had taken off my heavy mittens to operate the camera, and I quickly learned an important thing. Mittens should have a leather lace tied to them so they can hang around your neck. Then when you take them off and leave the area, the mittens will go with you. My hands were badly frostbitten because I dropped the mittens when I started the camera. All the skin on my fingers, on the palm side of my hand, peeled in a few days.

It is very difficult to run when the temperature is so low. The cold air gets into your lungs causing a burning sensation in your chest. Fred has had emphysema for some time, I'm sure it was harder for him than it was for me.

The bear came out into view again, but was too far away. We stopped the chase then. Naturally, we were all disappointed things turned out as they did. We had a wonderful opportunity and it got away from us. Fred was really disappointed and upset. I had looked right down his arrow and it was aimed straight at the bear's chest. It would have been a real break if he had been able to shoot that bear so early in the hunt. It would have saved us two more years of struggle.

As we stood talking, I started looking for my mittens. I found them back some two-hundred yards. My rifle was across my back and as I turned around to look for my mittens, Fred said, "What's wrong with your gun?" Somehow I had managed to twist around and release the clip holding the cartridges. They had fallen out onto the ice. Fred gave me the business about being a real good backup. I not only lost my mittens, but I was carrying a gun with an empty clip. We went back to the plane.

Incidentally, George's first function when he lands is to take the tarp out and put it over the engine to keep it warm, not knowing how long we'll be gone. One aspect of bow hunting is, that it takes you time to accomplish the feat. You might be away from the aircraft for an hour or more. The wind direction might also switch. George could choose a north and south runway, suitable for landing into the north wind. However, after an hour or so, the wind might switch around and come out of the west. This makes a cross wind take off and adds considerable length to it. Usually, at the end there are huge blocks of ice. Many times when we successfully slid over the top of these we would pat George on the back.

We flew around for another hour. George decided that it wasn't worth our time to stay out there any longer. We headed back to Point Barrow. We climbed to six thousand feet, got a radio fix, kept a course toward the little village. It's a beautiful sight to see those little black dots appear on the horizon, knowing we had hit the mark and were going to make it back to our destination.

For something to do that evening George suggested we watch the evening flight come in from Fairbanks. Every Friday night this flight, caller the "Booze Bomber," would arrive at six o'clock. Barrow was a dry town and didn't allow the sale of any alcoholic spirits. The natives made arrangements by radio telephone to Fairbanks and ordered their booze to be sent on the flight to Barrow.

We went down to the quonset hanger on the airstrip, it was fascinating to see all the dog sleds. There were probably fifty sleds scattered around, all waiting for the Booze Bomber. They unloaded the plane, carried the cargo into the terminal building, and brought all the bottles packaged in paper sacks. They would call out a man's name and he would step forward, pay for a sack package, and take it with him. One real thirsty guy toasted his order as soon as he left the hanger. Friday night is a wild night, but not as bad as Saturday. They order enough to last for several days. A saying in Barrow is that "every night is Saturday night except Saturday night, and that's New Year's Eve." Fred and I usually stayed in our rooms on Saturday nights.

The next morning we started out about eight o'clock.

During the night we'd had some strong winds. It was blowing offshore in the morning. As we headed out, George said, "We're going to have to go west a ways. We don't fly over open water." We couldn't see any ice at all after the first lead. There was an opening, that probably was sixty miles of open water, that George didn't intend to fly over with a single engine. So we started flying west towards a native village called Wainwright, one-hundred miles from Barrow. A rifle hunter who had brought in many bears said they came from Wainwright.

Fifteen miles out of Barrow, George dove down on a marker, explaining that this small marker was in memory of Will Rogers and Wiley Post who had crashed at this spot in August 1935. The story goes that their plane rose off a small lake, banked and then plunged into the ground, killing both men.

After traveling about forty miles, we came to a large bear track. We followed it for nearly a half an hour and finally came upon the skinned carcass of the dead bear.

We went back to Wainwright and had some deer burgers at a little Eskimo hut. Sitting near the entrance of this little quonset building were large barrels of Arctic fox pelts, and claws and wings from the Arctic snow owl. I do not think the tablecloth had been washed since the previous spring. It stuck to our elbows when we tried to leave.

We hunted on the way back to Barrow, but only saw one small track. The next day, weather conditions improved and we went northeast of Barrow where the ice looked pretty good. George spotted a good bear track in some real rough ice and tracked him for several miles. He would lose the track and circle around. He succeeded in making me and Fred a little sick weaving back and forth and twisting around.

We finally saw the bear lying down. He looked like a pretty good-sized animal. George thought the bear would probably stay right there, so we landed within two hundred yards of him. The bear never moved. George jumped out with a rifle first, just in case the bear might attack the airplane. They have been known to tear up an airplane, but this one was content to just stay down and look at the plane.

Fred got his gear and I got my equipment ready. We covered the airplane engine and started toward the bear. We got within one-hundred yards of the bear, but I couldn't do much with my mittens on. By then, I had some thongs tied on them so I just slipped them off and took hold of the camera, not realizing that my bare hands against the aluminum on the camera would be a disaster.

We approached the bear, and he never looked at us— he purposely looked in the other direction. He acknowledged the fact that he knew we were there because he made a hissing noise with his nose. Fred said later he didn't like that business of the bear not looking at us. When we got within sixty yards of the bear, Fred pulled one mitten off with his teeth and took a shot at him. The arrow went just over his back, the bear leaped to his feet and ran. We turned to go to the airplane, I noticed Fred had a front tooth missing. He had a tooth mounted on a peg. It was so cold that when he bit down on his mitten to pull it off, the tooth stuck to it. We never found the tooth. I wound up with a bad burn on the fingers of my left hand, again. All the skin came off within a few days.

Back at the plane we decided we'd have lunch before taking off. The only problem was that George forgot to bring lunches. "Well," he said, "just a minute, I think we've got something in here." He scrounged around in the back end of the plane and found a couple of sandwiches he'd had there for several days or weeks for previous hunters. They were frozen like bricks and we had a miserable time trying to chew them. We couldn't tell what kind of sandwiches they were. I was trying desperately to bite through what I thought was a dark piece of meat, it turned out to be a ripe olive with the pit in it.

That afternoon we spotted a fairly good track which we followed for some time before spotting the bear. We made several landings, but the bear always shied away from us, we weren't able to get within eighty yards of him. As a result Fred didn't shoot. On the way back to Barrow, we spotted another bear lying on the ice pack looking down into a seal hole. George thought this would be a pretty good chance, because he was concentrating on something else and wouldn't pay any attention to us.

We landed half a mile away and sneaked up on him. When we were within forty yards of the bear Fred took a shot at him. There was a big block of ice about three feet behind the bear. Fred was using arrows with orange feathers and placed the arrow on the ice just about an inch over the bear's back. He was disgusted with himself. The bear never raised his head, apparently he didn't hear the arrow. Fred put the second arrow about an inch from the first one. This time the bear heard it. He looked up, saw us and took off with leaping jumps disappearing over the pressure ridge.

Again, Fred was disgusted. I asked him on the way up if he was in good form. He said he'd shot a half a dozen arrows. Previously Fred had told me that shooting a bow is like riding a bicycle, after you once learn how to do it you never forget.

Fred was disheartened by the fact that he had muffed a real good chance. I told him if Arnold Palmer wore all the clothes he had in his closet to play golf, he probably wouldn't par every hole either. Hunting under such conditions was almost unbelievable. Our fingers immediately turned from hot to cold when we took off our mittens and we had to wear lots of bulky clothing. We wore long underwear and heavy jackets, over these we wore our white camouflage suits. Fred had to tape the wrist of his suit, because it was so bulky the bow string would hit it. Everything operates differently at twenty-five below zero.

We took off and headed back to Barrow, hoping that a better day would come. Again, as it happened every day, there was a group of Eskimo kids waiting for us, maybe a dozen of them. They followed us up through the village, tagging along, asking a lot of questions about what we did that day.

That night after dinner, we walked around the village a bit. At one house, several little sled dog puppies were tied to stakes and we took some pictures of them. Then we went down to the supply store, a combination hardware and general merchandise. On sale were bronze whaling guns which have a dynamite delay charge in them. They were made in Pennsylvania. The Eskimos used them to harpoon whales. We came across a little gift shop run by an Eskimo and bought some ivory carvings and souvenirs. It had been a long day. We stopped in at Al's Café for a cup of coffee and listened to the juke box. The tune, "Wild One", by Bobby Darin seemed to be the only record they had. We heard that tune every day after we finished the hunt as it was always playing when we were in Al's Café.

Fred asked one of the Eskimos to make a pair of caribou-hide mittens. They were quite beautiful, but when they got wet they smelled like urine. During the tanning process the Eskimos put urine on the hide and chew it with their teeth to make it soft. Fred and I made a rule never to kiss Eskimo girls who had been tanning hides.

The next day we headed to where we had last seen tracks the day before, but lost them. There had been a soft snowfall during the night and George thought it would be good tracking. We were flying along smoothly when suddenly there was a loud explosion in the plane. All three of us jumped. Fred had leaned his bow up against the front seat of the airplane and George had placed the heater hose next to it. Fred was taking a little nap and hadn't noticed the heater hose next to the bow. The heat from the hose melted the tip of Fred's bow. The laminated fiberglass recurve tip gave way and the string broke, making the noise. This was probably the first time anybody ever had a bow melt when hunting polar bears at twenty below zero. This should be in the *Guinness Book of World Records*. Of course we had to return to Barrow and pick up another bow. I told Fred, "They don't make em like they use to!"

We flew out one-hundred miles northeast of Barrow the next afternoon, and spotted a huge bear at about three o'clock. It was stretched out flat on its side, sound asleep, with all four legs extended just like a dog taking a snooze. We landed downwind from him and proceeded to make our stalk. The wind had died down and it was very quiet. As we approached the bear, we noticed that we were making quite a bit of noise. The snow beneath our feet was squeaking because it was so cold. We were fearful the bear might wake up and see us, but he didn't. We got close enough so we could hear him snoring, see his breath and the steam coming up from his nose. Fred got into position about twenty-five yards away. He had an open shot except for the little ice ledge directly in front of the bear. Fred had to just miss this ledge in order to place an arrow in the chest cavity of the bear.

I started the camera and Fred released an arrow. The feather clipped the ice in front of the bear and ricocheted off and slid over his back—a clean miss. The huge beast awakened, whirled and ran off before Fred could take another shot.

Again, Fred was muffed at himself. We returned to the plane to have our lunch, took off after a short break and headed straight north. About forty miles out, we found a large boar and a sow together. George dove down on them and they separated. The boar stood on his hind legs, he looked as if he was going to take a swat at the airplane. He was rather unhappy that his romance had been broken up. The sow took off and ran in the opposite direction. The boar continued down a pressure ridge that looked like a huge stone fence row. We followed him for several miles; he began to amble along at a slow pace. Every once in a while, he laid down and looked up at the plane, rather disgusted that we had arrived on the scene.

George sized up a good place to land and set up an ambush. It was apparent the bear was going to continue in that direction. We landed and started down the pressure ridge, not knowing which side of it the bear would appear. He might cross over and meet us on the other side. This presented a problem, because we didn't want George between Fred and the bear. George should be off to the side of us, in position where he could protect us if the bear charged. I also didn't want to be between George and the bear.

We proceeded cautiously up the ridge. George motioned that he had seen the bear and that Fred should step over to his right. The bear had laid down. We could see his hindquarters sticking out. George whispered to Fred to put an arrow into his rump and that when the bear turned to fight the arrow, Fred would have a chance for a good shot. Fred put the arrow exactly where George had suggested, it buried deep into the bear's hindquarters.

The bear whirled, saw us and made his charge from about twenty-five yards. George was quick to handle the situation. He fired his .300 magnum into the bear's chest, the bear staggered but kept on coming. George fired a second shot into the bear, it still kept coming. By this time, Fred had managed to get another arrow on the string and took a second shot. The arrow hit the bear in the chest. He was still coming toward us when George fired a third shot. This time the bear collapsed. Fred and I were ready to collapse too! He died less than ten paces from us.

We skinned the hide out, took some pictures, then taxied the plane up as close as we could. It took the three of us to lift the bear hide and hindquarters into the plane. George guessed the weight of the bear to be about twelve-hundred pounds.

Fred was sadly disappointed that he took his polar bear with a bullet in him. We had come so far, spent so much time the previous ten days landing on the ice pack, making many tries for a bear and then had to put a bullet in it. It almost seemed too much to bear.

As George headed the plane back to Barrow, he repeated several times he was sorry he had to finish the bear with his gun. Fred and I both agreed it was a necessary act.

Two days of hunting season were left. I planned to go out the next day with my rifle and take a bear, but the weather was bad when we woke up. It was impossible to go out, so we stayed around the hotel. Fred bought a Kayak from an Eskimo. We had seen it on the roof of his house and Fred asked him how much he wanted for it. He said, "What were you planning on paying for it?" Fred answered, "I was thinking of $125." The Eskimo said, "I was thinking of $150." Fred bought it and shipped it back to his museum in Grayling.

I wanted to get a good-sized bear and have a life-sized mount made for display in the sporting goods department of my hardware store. The weather cleared the day after so we took off. Fred agreed to be cameraman. It was sort of like the last half of the ninth inning for me, and I had little hope of finding a bear in that short time. We were leaving the next morning.

I flew with Pete, Fred flew with George. When we got out about forty miles we hit a good track. We trailed it for thirty miles and found a large bear shuffling along in the snow. I decided to make a try for him, and Pete landed. The bear was headed in our direction. We stationed ourselves behind a huge block of ice. In ten minutes, he came shuffling by about one-hundred yards from us. Apparently, he got a sniff of us because he stopped and looked in our direction. This gave me a good chance to get a shot at him.

I was all ready and had him in the scope. When I squeezed the trigger the impact of the bullet knocked him flat on his side. To my surprise, he jumped up and ran out of our sight into the rough blocks of ice. George flew fifty feet over us with the window open and hollered. We could barely hear him over the engine noise, but we thought he said the bear was still alive. This meant that Pete and I had to go in the ice cluster and "dig" him out with the rifle barrel.

We didn't know whether he was twenty or one-hundred yards from us. As we rounded a large chunk of ice, I saw him about sixty yards away. He was lying down, but his head was up. The second shot finished him. It wasn't long before George and Fred came up as Pete and I stood admiring the bear. Fred said to George, "Isn't that just like a damn rifle hunter! He dropped him right in a hole where there's no light to take a picture."

We skinned the bear out and taxied Pete's plane up as close as we could. After loading the hide and hindquarters in the plane, we took off for Barrow. I could hardly believe that I had gotten my bear, and in only two hours. It was more than I had anticipated!

There is quite a contrast between hunting with a rifle and hunting with a bow and arrow. Fred had been chasing bears for two weeks, making many dangerous landings. He's had a number of opportunities, but was going home empty handed.

We took the bear hide to an Eskimo woman who, with a skinning knife called an ulu, took the fat and grease off then dragged it out onto the ice. After chipping a hole in the ice, she dropped the hide down through it on a rope so it could soak. This drew out the blood. Then she brought it up and laid it flesh down on the snow. The hide was covered with snow and left there for the night. The next day she dried the hide by fluffing the hair with fresh snow. After all this was done, we shipped it to my taxidermist, Jonas Brothers in Seattle.

George suggested that we turn in our commercial Wein Airline tickets and fly back to Anchorage with him and Pete. They had to take the planes back as the polar bear season was over. We were their last hunters. They said it wouldn't cost us anything except gas and offered to show us some country that few white men had ever seen.

We decided to take them up on their offer. The weather was bad the next morning, but around 1 p.m. it cleared up. The wind was extremely strong, it must have been blowing at least sixty knots. It was so gusty the boys were afraid to light the heaters.

On our flight to Fairbanks, the weather was marginal, so we flew just above the ice in the rivers. George and Pete talked back and forth over the radio. George would say, I think we could go up "such and such" river and turn to the right; we could follow that up and cross over at "such and such" pass. They fly by "the seat of their pants", and don't have any navigational aides besides a compass. They just zigzag through the mountain range.

At one time when Pete and I were behind George and Fred, the snow was so bad that at two-hundred yards, the plane ahead completely disappeared from view. We had to land and wait until the snow subsided.

As we flew into the Brooks Mountain range, the rolling hills gradually got higher and higher. We could see the snow-covered jagged peaks in every direction as we climbed to the crest of the mountain. What a beautiful view, but what a hell of a place to land an airplane. Looking down in the valley we could see Eskimo dog sleds full of firewood. Pete said the Eskimos were coming from an area where timber was scarce—about fifty miles to the south.

When we left the Brooks Range, the weather improved a hundred percent. Closer to Fairbanks, it seemed balmy and I noticed that there was no snow on the ground. Since the plane had skis, I asked Pete, "How are you going to set this thing down on the bare ground?" He told me that during the winter, they bulldozed the snow off the end of the main runway at the airport. It melts, making a slushy spot suitable for landing. He set the plane down gently in the mud and slush, we slid to a sudden halt. Pete warned me to secure my seatbelt because it was going to be an abrupt stop.

We landed half a mile from the terminal. Fred called a cab to take us downtown, and we dropped off the bear hide at McIntyre's Sport Center for shipment to Jonas Brothers in Seattle. Fred and I ate the best steak dinner that we had had for weeks. We took off for Anchorage the next morning.

Reflections

I have a lot of respect and confidence in these guys who risk their necks under what has to be some of the world's worst flying conditions. But as the pilots say, any time you can walk away from it, it's a good landing.

Often times when George spotted a bear, he would let down to about twenty feet off the ice and fly over the bear to give Fred a good look. This is getting pretty close to the ground, particularly if the wind gusts are bouncing the plane around. We were reminded of the story about the game management plane that swooped down to shoot a bear with a tranquilizer gun. Strong wind gusts dropped the plane and the plane's prop cut off the bear's head. The plane was forced down, but no one was hurt.

The use of airplanes for polar bear hunting has since been ruled illegal in Alaska.

On one occasion, our plane was caught in a gust just as George was touching down. The wind forced the skis to touch a few feet too soon and we heard a loud crash. After we skidded to a halt we found that a block of ice had claimed our tail ski. George wired it back on to get us back to Barrow. Many good pilots got too interested in looking at the game when making a tight banking turn, lost their air speed and crashed—lay buried today. You generally didn't walk away from one of these landings.

On occasions, I would fly with Pete in the cover plane that trailed George. We would fly probably five hundred feet off the ice. Sometimes we landed first when a bear was spotted. We would stay back a half mile, so the bear did not see the plane. Pete would let me out with the camera gear and my rifle, and then take off to keep the bear in view.

I don't mind telling you it's a spooky feeling to be alone on the ice pack, some one-hundred miles off shore. It was comforting when George and Fred set down and joined me. Losing one or two men and planes every year was not uncommon during the polar bear season. I thought many times of my friend Tony Sulak who was in a plane that broke through the ice on a landing. Tony swam to good ice and lived to go back again, but the pilot of that flight drowned as his plane slowly sank. Lee Holden also went through the ice, but managed to get his hunter and himself back to shore by walking some fifty miles on the ice pack.

III

Big Head
1960

Upon returning from Fairbanks, we spent a couple of days in Anchorage where Fred picked up our bear licenses. The salesman in the sporting goods store, Chuck Keener, had previously worked for the Department of Fish and Wildlife of Alaska. He asked us if we wanted to go black bear hunting the next day. Fred and I jumped at the offer.

Chuck took us south of Anchorage, near the Portage Glacier. We climbed a couple of small mountains but we didn't see any black bears. However, we did hear some good tales, since Chuck was full of stories. Working in sporting goods he learned there are two types of gun shoppers: the "tooth pickers" and the "whistlers". Chuck explained, the "tooth picker" is the guy who has a few minutes after lunch, and being a gun nut, he strolls in the store and wanders around. Having just had lunch, he comes in sucking on a toothpick. He doesn't ask any questions, just looks over the guns and then politely leaves, still picking his teeth and munching the toothpick. The "whistler" is a guy who comes in after work, examines the guns and finally gets the courage to ask the price of one. When told the price, he whistles and makes a beeline for the front door."

Fred and I went out for dinner with Chuck and he told us about the time he was out photographing moose. There was snow on the ground and he was loaded with camera gear. He and his partner soon spotted a cow and calf and slowly walked toward them. However, when they tried to shoot a close up, the cow took offense and charged. Chuck's partner ran faster and made it first to the nearest tree, which he quickly climbed.

Chuck was shedding camera gear as he ran, with the cow moose closing in on him, while his partner was safely perched in the only tree in the area. He hollered to Chuck, "It looks like there's a hole in the base of this tree, jump into it!" Chuck did, and the moose came up and bumped the tree. Suddenly, Chuck scooted out of the hole. His partner yelled "Get back in there!" Chuck called back, "I can't there's a bear in there!"

We had been listening attentively, to the build-up of this tale, but after the punch line we knew we'd been had. Now Fred is a great story teller himself, so he added this yarn to his collection. Since that dinner with Chuck, he has told the tale many times, using me as the goat. He also made a record, narrated by Curt Bowdy, that tells the same story, again having me get in and out of the hole. People continually ask me what happened, and I tell them the bear ate me up.

After that entertaining dinner with Chuck Keener, we flew to Kodiak the next morning to get down to the serious business of brown bear hunting. Fred and I went to see an acquaintance of mine, Mr. Knutsen, who ran a sporting goods store. We swapped a few yarns with him and he invited us to his home that evening to see the movies he had taken on numerous hunting trips.

That afternoon, we went to the boat harbor to find Ed Builderback and the *Valiant Maid*, a fifty-seven-foot purse seiner and a very seaworthy boat. Harley King, a friend of Ed's, was the first mate. Ed had made arrangements for us to leave the next morning. We left the *Valiant Maid* to go after supplies, and then went out for dinner.

That evening, Ed, Fred, and I went to Mr. Knutsen's house to see the movies. Halfway through the films I heard a loud snoring noise in the background. I turned my head and was shocked to find that Fred had gone to sleep. I thought this was a very impolite thing to do, especially when a fellow offered to show his exciting bear movies. I guess Fred was just pooped out after our long day.

We started out early Monday on the *Valiant Maid*. Our course took us around the north end and down the western shore of Kodiak, where we landed and began scouting for bears. This time of year brown bears leave their dens which are near the tops of the fifteen-hundred-foot mountains. Much of the snow-covered areas have no brush and the bears can be seen clearly against the white snow. It's also easy to follow their tracks after they wallow through the snow with their eighteen-inch paws.

We found a few bear tracks, but no bear. The four of us climbed further, found a good vantage point, and sat there for an hour or so glassing the area. Finally, we spotted a bear quite some distance up the side of the mountain, which we studied through our binoculars. Suddenly, Harley broke the silence, exclaiming, "Hey, that's the funniest looking brown bear I ever saw! He's got a long tail!"

On closer observation, we realized we had spotted a red fox. In the position it was standing, it did look something like a bear, but as it turned around we saw its long tail. Fred gave Ed and Harley a hard time over this.

Harley and Ed went ahead of us back toward the boat, but Fred and I chose a short cut through some thick alder brush. As we were working our way through it, we heard a rifle shot so close that it nearly deafened us. Ed hollored, "He's coming your way!" Fred and I turned pale and didn't know what the hell to do. We expected to see a big brown bear come charging at us. Just then out stepped Ed clutching a rabbit he had shot with his 300 calibre rifle. That was the most exciting rabbit hunt I'd ever been on. Ed doesn't normally do things like that, but on the spur of the moment he thought he'd have some fun with us, and pay Fred back for riding him about the fox they spotted.

As we started down the bay in the *Valiant Maid,* there was an orange marker in the water. Ed told us this was common practice. Ed explained that it was a crab pot, and suggested we look to see if there were any crabs in it. The cage-type king crab pots are made of three-fourth inch pipe and covered with wire mesh, approximately three feet high and six feet in diameter. Upon lifting it up with his power winch, he found it had eight huge king crabs in it. We took out four of them, then feeling a bit guilty about the theft, we put a bottle of whiskey in the pot and lowered it down. Continuing our cruise toward Kodiak Bay on the southwest end of the island, we discovered an abandoned cannery, which had been closed for years. Ed wanted to take a look at it so he tied the *Valiant Maid* up to the old wharf. We were surprised to see a man and woman coming out to meet us. They were the caretakers for this old herring cannery which had closed when the herring market fell apart. They invited us to their house, where the woman had just finished baking some pies. Ed offered to trade a rabbit for a pie. His offer was accepted and we got two pies for one rabbit—a pretty good deal.

She told us about their pet brown bear, Chester. He was a good-sized bear and had been coming to the house for handouts since he was a cub. Chester would come right up to the door and let her feed him by hand, but she was the only one who could do it. She told us that if her husband started to walk down to the cannery, and the bear saw him, he would chase him into one of the old buildings. It seemed like good fun to Chester, but was quite a dangerous game of tag for the caretaker. The lady was quite concerned that Ed might spot "Chester" and want Fred to shoot him.

After our visit, we continued down the south side of the Island. As we idled along, I needled Ed about the time I hunted with Park Munsey, a famous guide, who lived in

Uyak Bay. I happened to have with me a book written by Munsey about brown bear hunting. So every time Ed told us how he would do this or that when brown bear hunting, I'd counter, "That's not the way Park Munsey said he did it." Ed became quite miffed. All afternoon Fred and I kept bringing up Munsey's name. In Ed's mind, we created quite a bit of antagonism toward him. We began to hope we wouldn't run into Munsey, as Ed threatened to tie into him if he ever saw him.

The next day we cruised past Munsey's house, and as we approached the end of the bay we saw a skiff coming towards us. I put my binoculars on it, and sure enough, it was Park Munsey. I suggested to Fred that we invite him aboard for a drink for old times sake. After some coaxing, Ed finally agreed.

When Munsey's boat drew near, we stopped, and I hollered for him to come aboard. He had a hunter with him, and they had just taken an eleven foot brownie. Fred and I stood back waiting for sparks to fly, but everything went smoothly. I guess Ed's bite isn't as bad as his bark. We had a good visit with them, and then set out for Larsen's Bay.

As we cruised along the shoreline, I scanned the beach with my binoculars and spotted a bear lying near some high grass. We shut the engine down and put the skiff overboard. Fred, Ed and I went ashore to have a go at him. It looked like the bear was in a convenient spot for us to sneak closer through the tall grass so Fred could get a shot at him. The wind seemed to be in our favor, too.

We spent twenty minutes circling around to get in the right wind position and come up on the bear from the rear. The bear was stretched out on some rocks, apparently sleeping soundly. We crawled on our hands and knees until we were forty yards from the bear, so close we hardly dared whisper to each other. Ed raised up slowly, and studied the bear through his glasses. Suddenly, he stood up and yelled, "Hell! That bear is dead!"

Fred cried, "What?" But sure enough he was. Someone had already taken a pot shot at him and killed him. Here we had pulled off the greatest stalk of our lives, only to sneak up on a dead bear!

Not wanting our day's work to be in vain, we skinned the bear and carried the hide back to the boat. It measured eight and a half feet and was in good condition. Later, Fred had it made into a rug for his den. We continued on to Larsen Bay and tied up at the king crab cannery dock.

The next day we took a tour of the cannery and surveyed a huge cage of live king crabs. They had been caught in crab pots and transferred to a large holding pen, alive, like cattle in the stock yards. The water in the pen was six to eight feet deep, and there were hundreds of large king crabs crawling around in it waiting to be processed for shipment to Seattle. It seemed strange to us that we couldn't go into a restaurant anywhere in Alaska and order fresh king crabs. They were all frozen, shipped to Seattle, then sent back to Alaska. And they didn't taste like the fresh ones Fred and I had caught in our own crab pots.

The next morning, we wanted to make a run across the Shelikof Straits to the Alaskan Peninsula, Ed thought it was too windy and urged us to wait at least a day. Instead, he suggested that we jump in the skiff, go north a few miles, then hike over a mountain range to the Karluk River in the valley. That area was reported to be good bear territory and was also famous for large rainbow trout.

It took two hours to hike over the mountain. After our three mile hike up the mountain side, we topped out and discovered a beautiful valley with the Karluk River racing through it. The river flows out of Karluk Lake to the ocean, and the rainbow trout travel from the big lake to spawn in the creek.

I couldn't wait to give them a try. I had a spinning rod with ten pound test line. With the second cast I hung onto a real good fish. It took me fifteen minutes to play him in the fast running water. When I got him to where I could see how big he was, I wondered if I could land him without a net.

Ed offered to help, and came over to take hold of the line and jerk him in, but I hollered, "Let me land him!" A fish meant absolutely nothing to Ed, but to me it was a trophy. I finally managed to beach him and he weighed fourteen pounds, big enough to have mounted. I caught several more smaller fish.

While I fished, the others glassed the mountains around us, but didn't see any sign of bears. Then Ed recommended that we head back in order to return before dark. On the hike back, Ed kicked out a rabbit and suggested to Fred that he pull a stalk on it with his bow. Darned if he didn't pull the trick off and spear the rabbit. So we had fried rabbit and rainbow trout for dinner that night.

Ed checked the weather and thought we could make a run across the Skelikof Straits around midnight, but it didn't turn out that way. We finally started out around eight a.m. the next morning and had a rough choppy ride across the straits. These straits have the reputation of being one of the roughest bodies of water in Alaska. The Japanese current flows from the south and the winds kick up huge waves to make for a rough ride across the sixty mile stretch of open water.

That evening we pulled into a small harbor that was sheltered by a towering mountain to the west of us. We ran the *Valiant Maid* within sixty yards of shore, threw out the anchor, then backed off. The wind was coming off shore from the mountains and Ed felt this would be a good spot to tie up for a few days.

On the way across, Ed told us about the sad experience when his brother was killed here in the Peninsula. Ed and his brother had worked as a team during the salmon season. His brother flew a Super Cub on floats, and Ed ran the *Valiant Maid*. From the air you can see the salmon schooling. They make big circles, going around and around, working their way slowly up the beaches till they find the cold water of a stream where they can run in and spawn. Ed's brother would fly out with the Super Cub and spot the schools of salmon, then contact Ed, who would then cruise to the area and seine them. He claimed that sometimes he'd catch as many as two thousand fish out of a school. At that time the market was bringing around one dollar per fish.

After they had finished their work for the day, Ed's brother said he was going to fly over to an inland lake and fish for some rainbow trout. He didn't return that night. Ed went looking for him in the morning and found the plane wrecked, with his brother in it, dead. He had hit a tree on take off.

We made a short reconnaissance trip ashore, and found a number of floating rocks. These came from the Mount Katmi Volcanic Range fifty miles north. The volcanos in this range erupted in 1912, throwing these rocks in the water. They float and drift just like wood.

Another interesting thing we found on the beach were many clear glass Japanese floats. These are large round balls, anywhere from the size of a baseball to a basketball, made of heavy thick glass in various colors. Japanese fishermen used them to hold up the tops of their nets. Sometimes in high seas and heavy winds, they break loose and wash ashore, where they become sand blasted and lose their transparency.

The Alaskan Peninsula is where most of the bad weather is born, from Atu all the way up the coast. The wind is very strong all the time. We had a number of days when the winds blew so hard that Fred didn't feel he could shoot an arrow straight. The strong gusting winds swept down over the cliffs and blew the *Valiant Maid*, causing the anchor to drag. We'd have to start the engine, run in, pick up the anchor, then anchor all over again.

I used to lay in the bunk at night and wonder what would happen if we blew loose like we had done several times before, and Ed wasn't able to start the engine. We'd probably have wound up in Hawaii or Australia. I'm not much of a sailor anyway and I'm kind of an ol' worry wart. I spent many hours wide awake worrying about those terrific winds.

We glassed the snow capped slopes high up the mountains in search of bear tracks. Just below the snowline we spotted a boar and a sow. We watched them for about an hour. When they laid down, we loaded the skiff and took off for shore. The mountain range ran north and south, and the wind came over the top of the mountains, which made it feasible for us to make stalk.

It was no easy task to climb those mountains. The alder brush was so thick in places that we had to twist and crawl to get through it. The hip boots I was wearing—a must—didn't make it any easier. Water trickled through most of the open areas, making a muddy substance that ran down the mountain side. It was slippery, and I slid back with almost every step I took. The mid-day sun melted the snow on top of the mountain, and water splashed down in torrents by afternoon. With all these obstacles, it took us over an hour to work up to the area where we had seen the bears.

Ed spotted the bears, both now standing one hundred yards up the mountain. One of them was looking in our direction, and watched us for several minutes. Ed told us to be still. We remained motionless and finally after ten minutes of agony the bears strolled off. We later concluded that even though we were concealed in the thick alder brush, the aluminum on the movie camera might have flashed in the sun and attracted their attention. After this experience we taped the aluminum on the camera so it wouldn't happen again.

Slowly we approached the spot where the bears had disappeared, now some eighty-five yards away. To our right was a huge pyramid of shale. On the left was a huge drop-off of perhaps one thousand feet—nothing but thin air. There was a little trail, or ledge, next to this thirty-foot shale pyramid. Fred thought if he and I could climb it, we could peek down over the other side, to where the bear had disappeared and get a close shot at him.

We started to crawl up the forty-five degree angle pyramid and found that it was all loose rocks, like a fine coal pile. We were slipping and sliding. Fred used his bow as a crutch. I went on my hands and knees with the camera strapped over my shoulder. There was no vegetation to hang onto for support. When Fred and I were about halfway up, we saw Ed tiptoe around the trail on the down side of the pyramid, to see where the bears had gone. All of a sudden, Ed came back in high gear, stopping to our left, behind and below us. At about twenty-five feet, he whirled around and had his 300 up to his shoulder ready for action. Then the huge brown boar, which we later labeled "Big Head," stepped out twenty feet from Ed and started towards him. Ed had almost run over him when he went around the rock ledge and the bear followed Ed's retreat. I don't think he smelled Ed, but he didn't know what he was. Ed figured he had come close enough, and hollered at him, "You bastard, if you take one more step, you're a dead bear!" He then said, "Shoot him, Fred."

The bear responded to Ed's command, but Fred was so busy hanging onto the side of the mountain that he could not get his bow into shooting position, and besides he didn't dare let loose of the mountain. The bear wasn't over fifteen yards from Fred, standing looking at Ed, broadside below us. I was having the same problem hanging on to the heavy movie camera and leaning into the side of the mountain. I too, didn't dare to let go of the terra firma. If I had slipped I might have been riding the bear, or the wind one thousand feet down into the canyon below.

The bear turned momentarily and looked at us. Fred had a perfect shot at the monster, but he just didn't dare let go of the mountain for a shot. The bear again looked back at Ed, who had his 300 trained on his nose. All at once the bear let out a large "wuff," whirled, and shuffled back in the direction he had come from. Ed sneaked down the trail, and saw him disappear in the alder brush.

I believe he was the largest brown bear that we ever saw. What had Fred and I done to deserve this? After all that work, and a perfect target, we couldn't shoot at it with bow or camera.

Catching our breath, we went back down the mountain to the *Valiant Maid*, in a very tired and disgusted mood. I can still see that bear standing there glaring at us.

The next morning we were up bright and early and took the skiff down to the north end. We had seen some bears in this area the day before when we were up on the mountain. We came to a long, narrow bay that seemed like a good spot. About a mile away, at the end of the bay, I spotted a brown object that looked like a good bear. Ed put his binoculars on it and gasped, "My God, that's a horse!" We could hardly believe it. Ed told us that some years past a prospector had done some mining in the area and obviously had left the animal there.

We worked into the area trying to sneak up on the horse, but when we were a hundred yards from it, it saw us. I whinnied like a horse, and to our surprise, it trotted toward us. It was a beautiful chestnut brown with a black tail so long that it dragged on the ground. His gloss black mane looked like it was two feet long. The horse must have been on that little brush covered peninsula for years, ever confronted with the danger of bears. I'm sure it must have spent many restless nights.

Ed was real excited about the critter and thought we should try to get friendly with the horse so he could rope him. Ed wanted to put him on the *Valiant Maid* and take him home. The horse would have no part of it, however, and disappeared off in a gallop.

The next day from the deck of the *Valiant Maid*, we glassed a meadow that sloped up the side of the mountain and down to the beach. Ed wanted to climb up and take a better look at it, so we ran the skiff to the beach. Ed suggested that Harley King and I sit in the skiff while he and Fred went to look things over.

There was hardly any room between the bow of the skiff and the side of the mountain. There was six feet of rocky beach, then a sheer cliff. Ed and Fred climbed around to the right of the rocky mound and disappeared. They hadn't been gone but a few minutes when we heard the brush crack to our left. Looking up, we saw what I thought was a small bear coming toward us. The rocks came down to the water's edge, and if it kept coming, it would have to pass us about six feet from the skiff. Harley grabbed his gun, and I got as far back in the skiff as I could. The bear turned out to be a huge wolverine. He came skipping along and didn't see us until he got right to the bow of the skiff. He then ran directly past us and up the beach. This is the closest I had ever been to a wolverine. My bow was back on the *Valiant Maid*. I think I could have rung his bell.

On the way back to the *Valiant Maid*, we saw a small island with a couple hundred sea lions basking in the sun on the rocks. Ed suggested I go ashore and shoot one for my museum. Fred wanted to shoot some footage for his movie. The rocks were probably a hundred feet tall. We went around on the east side where we could beach the skiff without the sea lions seeing us. The spot where we beached the skiff happened to be the path the sea lions used to slide down from the high cliffs to the water. Ed cautioned us to stand to one side and let the lions slide by if they came close to us. "Those buggers really have a set of teeth," he said, "Normally they won't come after you, but if you corner one he will stand his ground and fight." We both believed him.

We started up the slippery, slimy mess. This place had been their home for many years, and all the rocks were paved with their slick droppings. Some of the sea lions came shooting down this little valley, sliding into the ocean, passing within ten feet of us. All of them were grunting, growling and making a snarling noise. They were also very smelly.

We worked our way to the top of the cliff. This gave us a good vantage point to film the sea lions that were basking on the other side of the island. About seventy-five of these huge beasts were directly below us. A large bull weighs over a thousand pounds. Their whiskers are about a foot and a half in length. Fred got some pictures and I decided against shooting one. We went back to the skiff and headed for a protected cove for the night and hit the sack.

About four o'clock the next morning we were rudely awakened by the *Valiant Maid* pounding real hard, we were adrift. Everybody got up and we look in the anchor as Ed ran the *Valiant Maid* closer to the huge bluff within sixty yards of shore. The waves were so high that the *Valiant Maid* was pounding up and down at least ten feet. The skiff, trailing behind the boat, was held by a three-fourth inch rope. This broke and the skiff started drifting to the other side of the bay. It was probably a mile across to this arm that curled around to the south of us. Fortunately, the wind was blowing in the direction of the arm of land, rather than out to the open sea. Ed quickly put the other skiff overboard.

The forty-horsepower engine was in the skiff that broke loose, and Ed was in the other skiff with just a pair of oars. He was bounding around out there in that rough sea like a ping pong ball, and sometimes we could hardly see him. We watched with our glasses until he made it safely to the shore. We could see him standing there on the beach in his rubber parka, blowing on his hands and waving his arms to get warm. After a half an hour, we were beginning to worry about Ed. He was trying to get the engine started on the skiff and had to physically hold the bow into the wind in the pounding surf with one hand and crank the engine with the other.

Finally, we saw a puff of smoke and he jumped in the skiff and started out toward the *Valiant Maid.* He was throwing white water out in front of the bow, and sometimes when he hit the crest of the six- to eight-foot waves, we could look right underneath the skiff. Fred and I concluded this was one of the most heroic rescues at sea that we had ever witnessed.

As Ed came up to the side we threw him a line and secured the skiff. It was very cold that day, with the wind blowing over sixty knots. Ed was soaked, nearly frozen, and actually blue in color when he got on deck. We never did get the other skiff, nor do we know what happened to it. It must have been blown out to sea.

We stayed there for another day because it was so rough and the wind was still blowing strong. We remained inside the cabin except three times to reset the anchor. Most of the day we spent writing letters and making preparations for the following day. It seemed good to take a day off and not have to climb those damned mountains. For dinner that night we cooked razor clams and seal liver, and reminisced about meeting up with old "Big Head," and shot him two or three times over a cup of coffee, beer and bourbon. If things had been just a little bit different, the hunt would have been over by now.

The next morning we went north to another area called Qualla Bay. The wind was blowing real strong again. In fact, when we came up to the edge of a huge cliff that went back to the west, we found that the wind came in from both sides. The cliff was like a big flat iron out into the ocean, the strong winds sweeping down in swirling gusts. All of a sudden, Ed hollered, "Hang on boys, here comes a 'willy wally'!"

The *Valiant Maid* was fighting the head winds in a heavy sea, and visibility was poor. Fred and I didn't know what a willy wally was, so we quickly jumped into the cabin. Through the spray we could see what looked like a water spout coming directly at us about a hundred yards away. There was no time to turn or do anything to get out of its path. When it hit, the *Valiant Maid* creaked, rocked, groaned and shuddered. Then it was gone, almost like a tornado, but a big spout of water. We stepped onto the deck and to our surprise the deck was strewn with small fish about eight inches long. They were some kind of herring that had been sucked out of the sea. We picked up enough of them to have a fish fry for supper.

The wind kept blowing strong all day. We went ashore once and did see one bear, but Fred concluded that he couldn't throw an arrow in that strong wind. The hunting was scrapped until the next day. We went back to the *Valiant Maid*, laid around for the rest of the day, and ate some king crabs.

The wind was still blowing the next morning, but we thought we'd go ashore and at least check on tracks. We didn't know if we could shoot an arrow, but we thought we'd check things out. After glassing the area and not seeing anything, Ed figured we should climb up on a high bluff; from there we could look over into the next valley on the side of the mountain to the north of us.

Ed led the way and took off in a running gait up the mountain, running with a pair of hip boots on. I followed him, and of course, he gained seventy-five yards on me in the first two-hundred yards. Fred was behind me—probably seventy-five yards. We took our time climbing through huge boulders that were cropping out all around us. We could only see a few yards in all directions because of these huge eight-foot-high rocks.

I had stopped to catch my breath when I heard a horrible noise coming from above me, I could hear rocks sliding. My first thought was, here comes a brownie! But before I could make a move Ed came flying past me about thirty miles an hour, running down the mountain. I was standing behind a boulder and he didn't see me. I thought the next thing I would see would be a big brownie chasing Ed, so I quickly crouched down out of sight. Looking out, I saw Ed stop where Fred was, pointing to the beach. There stood a huge brownie that had come out of the alder brush and walked up to our skiff. I must say that I was relieved, I worked my way down to Ed and Fred.

We decided that we should sneak down and try to get a shot at him, but the bear kept moving. He looked at the *Valiant Maid* and then at the skiff. I guess he didn't like what he saw so he turned and started south around the mountain.

We hurried down to the skiff and went around to the other side of the point. We spied the bear, but he was going along the other side of the mountain and looking back at us. He must have been a little suspicious that we were after him or something wasn't right. We started back to the *Valiant Maid* and got our engine caught several times in a huge growth of kelp near the shore. These have large-stemmed leaves three inches wide, with a six-inch ball on the root end. Fred and I stretched one out on the beach and it measured over a hundred feet long. When these become amassed in the water, it's best to go around them. Ed thought that he could grind them up, but we suddenly found that the engine was clogged and stuck. They grabbed that forty-horsepower Mercury outboard engine like an octopus. We had quite a time working our way out of that kelp bed.

By the time we got back to the *Valiant Maid* it was around six o'clock and the wind had died down some. It was still light enough to see for awhile, so the four of us glassed the mountains and the bay area to the north of us. Ed soon spotted a bear on the beach, on the north side of the wide bay, about a mile from us. It wasn't moving, and looked like it was feeding on some kelp. We had a brief conference to decide what we should do. The sun was sinking over the tops of the mountains, and Fred said, "I doubt if there is any chance to get a picture." Ed answered, "Ya, and it would be a lot easier for two of us to sneak up on him than four of us." So Fred decided that Harley and I should stay with the skiff, and that he and Ed would go after the bear.

The beach was littered with huge logs on the shoreline that fringed the alders. This made a good spot for Ed and Fred to walk and to pull a sneak on the bear. I was amazed at the endurance Fred had at his age. Ed walks at a real fast gait, and Fred practically had to trot to keep up with him. It was a long way to go over the rough rocks, and they had to hurry in order to get to the bear before it got so dark they wouldn't have a chance.

Harley King and I sat on the skiff and watched with our binoculars. We couldn't get the full benefit of the whole exciting hunt, but we did see Fred shoot the bear and the bear running. It looked like he ran towards Fred and Ed. The wind was in the wrong direction so we couldn't hear if a shot had been fired. After the bear disappeared in the alder brush, Harley and I jumped into the skiff and ran down there to join them. Fred had a wide grin on his face and said he thought he had the bear. He was standing in the area about where the bear had been, and pointed out just what had happened.

Fred and Ed had sneaked down from the alders and into the driftwood and kelp lining the beach. Unknowingly, they had taken the same path the bear used to get to the kelp. The bear was pawing in the kelp and standing broadside when they arrived. Fred whispered to Ed that he would like to get a little closer.

Ed said, "Okay. You go, I'll stay." Fred said he wasn't sure what this meant, but he kept sneaking toward the bear. At twenty yards from the bear, Fred stopped by a large log. Fred removed his 44 magnum revolver from its shoulder holster and laid it on the log. The wind was blowing from the bear to Fred. The surf was pounding. Everything seemed to be in Fred's favor, and he shot at the big brownie feeding in the kelp with his head down. Ed was just a few feet back of him and to his left. When the arrow struck the bear behind the shoulder, he whirled, and came after Fred.

Fred grabbed his gun, and was ready to shoot when Ed shouted, "Don't shoot! He's a big one!" Ed didn't want Fred to put a bullet in him so he couldn't be considered a bow and arrow trophy. When the bear heard Ed he reared off to the side, passing them by only five paces, and disappeared in the alder brush.

The four of us started working into the alders. Ed walked up a high ridge off to the side where he could look down into the alders. He signaled to us that the bear was down over to his right. Fred, Harley and I started to walk in that direction. Ed was throwing rocks at what he thought was the bear to see if he was still alive. There was no movement, so he directed us to go in. We had gone into the alder brush about a hundred feet when Fred glanced off to his left. This was the opposite direction from the one Ed had indicated, and there lay the bear not forty feet from us. He was on his back, his legs extended out. Ed had been stoning a pile of rocks that looked like a bear.

Fred was real pleased about this huge bear. We were pretty sure it was the biggest one that had ever been taken with a bow and arrow. It was too late to take any pictures, so we decided we would come back the next morning and get some good pictures in the daylight. As we stood on the beach talking, I looked up on top of the cliff, probably five-hundred feet above us, and there stood a huge bear silhouetted against the sky line. He looked as big as the one Fred had just shot. We returned to the *Valiant Maid* tired and happy.

Ed woke us up about three o'clock the next morning in total darkness. The boat was beginning to heave just a little, and Ed said, "If you want to get that bear skin and skull, you better go to shore right now." The winds were switching around and it looked like we might be in for a real rough blow. Fred, Harley and I loaded up our camera gear, flashlights, rifle and axes, and put over the side into the skiff. The big waves were already beginning to swell and pound on the beach. Harley took his rifle, which pleased me.

When we hit the beach we all got wet because the waves were so high. We pulled the skiff up the best we could to get it out of the water. It was difficult to keep the salt water out of the camera, even carrying it in a plastic bag. We started up through a real black and spooky bunch of alder brush, not knowing whether there was one bear or two. Harley told us that these bears are cannibalistic and will eat one another. If the huge bear we had seen on top of the mountain had come down and found Fred's bear, perhaps he would lay claim to it, and might be just a few yards from the carcass, guarding his find. None of us relished the idea of going in there.

A misty rain started as we worked our way in. We had a couple of flashlights, and finally located the bear. Using the axe, we trimmed all the alder brush out of the way, taking turns holding Harley's gun. It was pitch black and we thought we could hear something walking near us. If a bear rushed us, I doubt if Harley could stop him in the dark. It was quite exciting, to say the least, but fortunately no bear appeared and we were able to get some real fine pictures, using flash bulbs with our cameras.

It takes quite a while to skin a bear that size when you want to have a life size mount. The knife must be sharpened many times because the hide is so tough. Care must be taken not to make any bad cuts that would have to be sewed up by a taxidermist.

We finally got the bear skinned out and packed in on Harley's back pack. Later we learned that it weighed 175 pounds. I took the rifle and cameras and started back. When we reached the skiff the first faint rays of light were beginning to break in the east. The surf had picked up and we had quite a time heading the bow of the skiff into the wind and getting it loaded. After taking on lots of water, we finally pushed off and made it back to the Valiant Maid. Ed had the Valiant Maid warmed up and we struck out through the white pounding surf.

This trophy was a timely reward after failing to get his polar bear up on the arctic ice pack. Fred had spent a lot of time and effort to get this monster, but he said the reward had been worth it. We laid the hide out on the back deck, and Harley spent the next day fleshing it. Fred and I picked at the skull to get all the meat off. The skull is the only recognized measurement acceptable to *Boone and Crocket*. The length and width of the skull, when added together determines the size of the bear. It doesn't make any difference how much the bear weighs, or how long it is, or what the height or length might be. The skull measured twenty-eight inches, and we were sure he would make the *Boone and Crocket* as well as number 1 in *Pope and Young*, the archery record book. We later found he had made *Boone and Crocket* and did make #1 in the *Pope and Young*.

It took us about five hours to make the run back to Kodiak, where we spent the rest of the day. It was raining as we pulled in. Fred and I walked up from the docks to the town to make a radio phone call back to our poor waiting wives and let them know we were still alive.

Fred asked Ed, "How much do I owe you?" Ed replied, "I don't know."

I don't know about you guys but I had one hell of a good time. Whatever you feel it was worth. I never did know what Fred gave Ed. Before the hunt Fred said it won't cost you anything if you go along and take pictures for me.

This sounded like a good deal? All it cost was a modest bar bill. A small tab for such an exciting trip.

The city of Kodiak had dirt streets in those days, with

wooden curbs and gutters. As we were slopping along in the rain, Fred looked down, and there was a twenty dollar bill floating down the gutter. He picked it up, and directly in front of us was a bank. Fred said, "My God! That bank must be leaking!"

We called home and found out that everything was O.K., and told our wives we'd be home in a couple, three days. We took the next flight out of Kodiak to Anchorage, and I flew directly home from Anchorage by way of Chicago. Fred had to stop at Juneau and talk with some game department people. He then took his bear hide and skull to Jonas Brothers in Seattle to have it made into a life-size mount that would stand over eight foot on its hind legs. He may not have been as large as old "Big Head" but one hell of a trophy for a bow hunter, and number one in the book.

IV

Return to the Arctic
1962

In 1962, I again met Fred at O'Hare Airport in Chicago, for the start of our second polar bear hunt. As indicated in chapter II, Fred was unsuccessful in 1960 in getting a bear without a bullet in it. He was still determined to get the job done and complete the filming we had started. We took Northwest Orient Airlines to Anchorage where we transferred to Alaskan Airlines and on to Fairbanks. At Fairbanks we ran into Mary Klineburger, the wife of our friend, Bert Klineburger, who, with his brothers Cris and Gene, owned Jonas Brothers Taxidermy in Seattle. The Klineburgers were also friends of George Theile, our guide, and his wife Gail. We learned in talking with Mary that our other guide, Pete Murray, was going to take his wife, Rene, on the hunt for a few days, Gail Theile was also going along to try for a polar bear.

We settled in at the Fairbanks Inn, then went to Dick McIntyre's sporting goods store to pick up our licenses.

Dick invited us to the Rotary Club luncheon where he was showing pictures of his recent trip to Africa.

Somehow Fred managed to lose his glasses while we were there. We went to the dime store where he pawed through a large selection of reading glasses selling for a buck a piece. After ten minutes of trying on glasses, he found a pair that he thought he could live with. Years ago, he had bought a pair of prescription glasses from an optometrist, and lost those too. He gave up purchasing prescription glasses and decided to buy his glasses at the dime store. I bought a pair for myself too, but found they just about pulled one of my eyeballs out of its socket.

Our hunting party boarded the Wien flight to Barrow the following morning. At the end of the flight I took a picture of our hunting group when we got off the plane. To look at it, you would think we might not have had polar bear hunting in mind, and we hoped that our wives wouldn't take offense at this coeducational hunt. The two guides, their wives, Mary Klineburger, Fred and myself looked like quite a racy group.

Things were pretty much the same at the old Top of the World Hotel. Fred and I even occupied the same rooms we had used two years previous. We met a lot of our old friends, guides and other polar bear hunters and had a big yack session that went deep into the night. In spite of the miserable experience the time before, it was good to be back, ready to meet the challenge once again.

Barrow had begun to go modern. There was even a new bank which looked like a house trailer built out of wood and perched on large sleigh runners. You could have hooked on to it with a truck and dragged it out of town. But inasmuch as there was no road and the nearest town was six hundred and fifty miles away, they didn't have to worry about somebody stealing it. I have heard since, that it burned down a couple of times.

The next morning we called on our Eskimo friend, Al, who ran the restaurant, and ate one of his famous reindeer steak and egg breakfasts. We learned that a new combination grocery and candy store opened since our last visit.

The snow was covered with candy bar wrappers. The entrance of the store resembled a tunnel, with a large freezer on one side. I lifted the lid and found it was full of fish. They were ling cod which are caught through the ice, off shore of Barrow and sold for dog food.

George and Pete joined us that evening for dinner at Al's Restaurant after which we all went back to the hotel. Fred, quite tactfully, mentioned that he wished George would hold off a little longer with his backup rifle, hinting that he might have shot too quickly on the previous hunt when the bear charged us. This didn't set too well with George, who glared at Fred and said, "You take care of your end of it, and I'll take care of mine."

The next day a man from Arctic Research contacted Fred. He wanted Fred to show his hunting movies to the people at Arctic Research's headquarters in Browersville. Arctic Research is operated by the military. They picked us up with a vehicle that had skis on the front and a rubber assembly cat track on the back. A quonset hut had been made into a theater for the film showing. While there, we tried to reach home by radio. A friend of mine, Bart Rypstra, was an amateur radio operator near my home in Michigan. We couldn't make connections due to weather conditions. After Fred finished showing his films, we took advantage of their recreational facilities. There were pool tables and ping pong. It was a real nice evening.

During our stay in Barrow, I taped interviews with several of the Eskimos. One, Ned Nusinguia, lived across the street from the hotel and we became well acquainted with him. Ned was an old timer, probably in his late seventies. At his home, Ned regaled us with stories of his adventures in that rugged climate. During the winter, he and his wife had often taken a dog sled to go out trapping and hunting, for arctic fox and wolves, camping out in a tent for weeks at a time. Only rugged individuals endure that cold climate. Once, Ned froze his fingers in fifty degree below zero temperatures.

Ned was a beautiful craftsman. He showed us the new dog sled he was making, built with wood. He was in the process of weaving sinew or gut, from a seal. This was used to hold the sled together in place of screws or bolts. Fred was really impressed with his workmanship. While interviewing him, I asked Ned how many children he had, and he said to his wife, "Mama, how many do we have? Ten, eleven maybe?" We never established just how many children he had, but perhaps that prompted him to count them at a later date.

Ned interpreted the Minister's English sermon into the native tongue at church services. Fred and I attended several of these services, and Fred accused Ned of ad libbing too much of the minister's sermon—he did not take a lot more time on each sentence than the minister did to deliver the sermon.

We were invited to a native dance one evening which was held at the theater building. The Eskimos wore their native fur parkas and as the room warmed, the parkas gave off a pungent odor because the hides are tanned using human urine. The natives took turns performing dances, simulating the hunting of a seal, walrus or polar bear. Several Eskimos had round drums, about two feet across, three inches thick, and covered with the skin of ugruk seal. They looked like large tambourines. They beat on these drums and chanted, making music for the dance.

When one performer finished, there would be a slight pause. Then one or two others would go up on stage. One Eskimo crawled around on the stage floor, moving his arms like flippers on a seal. Another took the part of a hunter, stalking the "seal" and killing him with a spear.

As we left the theater, a fight broke out behind us. One guy took a swipe at another fellow with a whiskey bottle. Just at that moment his girlfriend lifted her head and he hit her between the eyes. The bottle broke on impact, cutting a six-inch gash on her forehead. There was blood all over the place, and Fred and I decided this was a good time to make a quick exit. We got the hell out of there and walked across the street. Even at that late hour—12 o'clock midnight—it was still light enough to read a newspaper.

One Eskimo had driven his snowmobile up in front of the theater, and was fortunate enough to have three girl-friends who wanted to ride home with him. He killed a whale that day and was the village hero. They all got on the machine, he gave it full throttle, and they hung onto him and each other. Everything left except two purses. I don't know whether that group ever returned for them or not. About this time we decided we'd better get to the hotel and hit the hay.

Mary Klineburger wanted to shoot a polar bear and George asked Fred to ride along to get a preview, and to be the cameraman. His story of their hunt was amazing. Mary shot a big bear and everyone toasted her with a drink. We took pictures of the bear hide and she treated us to a rein-deer steak dinner at Al's Café. When Fred and I returned to our room he told me a very interesting part of the hunt that hadn't come to light so far.

In a laughing mood, but acting almost embarrassed, Fred reached the good part of the story. As George started to skin the bear, Mary said she wanted the bone in his penis for a swizzle stick. This is a common use for the bone that is in the penis! George handed Mary his hunting knife and she promptly cut the penis off and put it in her purse. I asked Fred if he got a picture of this event. He sheepishly said no. I couldn't imagine Fred so shook that he forgot all about taking pictures.

The next day, a guide took his nine-year-old son polar bear hunting and damned if the kid didn't come back with a bear. I told Fred we'd better give up our hunt when the women and kids start beating us.

Instead, we headed out of Barrow the following morn-ing, starting the many sorties that would follow the next ten days.

As always, George called the tower as we flew out of Barrow, telling them the direction we were going and how long we would be gone. Later we were able to call the tower, to get our vector to lead us back to Barrow.

We picked up a good track about 40 miles out. For sev-eral miles we followed until we saw the bear. He looked pretty good when George flew over him, so we landed to give him a go. A strong wind was coming out of the northwest. It was so cold when we got out of the plane and started after the bear, that Fred and I had to back into the wind. George wore a wolf parka with a wolverine ruff, and could peer through the fur protecting his face. But I'm sure Fred and I would have frozen our faces if we had walked very far with our faces to the wind.

The bear passed us at seventy-five yards, moving along at a pretty good gait, so Fred didn't take a shot at him. We then followed him by plane for several miles. When it looked like he was going to go down a rough lead, similar to a fence row only made of huge blocks of ice, we landed about half a mile ahead of him and set up an ambush. Apparently he saw the airplane, and the wind was blowing in the wrong direction. He passed us nearly a hundred yards away, again too far away for a good shot.

So we started back towards the airplane. Suddenly George held up his arms signaling us to stop. We thought he spotted another bear, but he took his rifle butt, slamming it through the ice in front of him. I don't know how he determined the thickness of the ice with two inches of snow on it, but if Fred and I had been alone and kept walking, we would have gone through the thin ice and into the water. The bear continued on down the pressure ridge. We landed four more times trying to get into position to get a shot. Each time the bear avoided us, and finally we gave up on him.

The next day, two hunters from Europe came in— Willie Bogner, a famous hunter and ski garment manufacturer from Munich, Germany, and his hunting companion, Maurice Erikson from Norway. His brother is the famous skier, Stein Erikson, here in the States. Bogner hunted all over the world, including Nepal, Africa and Alaska, but he had never hunted polar bear. Another hunter, Ed Shuman from Hawaii, also appeared on the scene. He was married to Miss Hawaii. George and Pete had arranged to take Willie and Maurice out, so Fred and I rested for several days while they hunted. In just one day, the two Europeans got their bears. As I had indicated earlier, shooting a polar bear with a gun is not too difficult, but with a bow and arrow, it's a different ball game.

Fred and I took off the following day, again heading in a northerly direction. Coming into a real thick mess of jumbled ice, George picked up a track. He twisted and turned and followed it for a long way, and we finally came upon the bear. The ice was so rough that we couldn't land the plane within three miles of the bear. George made several low passes at him, trying to get the bear to run toward the smooth ice. However, he was not in any mood to move, and stood on his hind legs, acting real mad when we flew by.

George thought if we fired a shot close to him, he might move, so I took his 300 and slid the window open. We made another low pass at about one hundred feet and I took a shot near the bear, being careful not to hit him. The shooter must concentrate on not shooting the prop wash or shooting off the wing strut. The bear was in a large bowl-like area resembling a huge football stadium with ice all around, probably two hundred yards from one end to the other. We took one more low-level pass to give us a real close look. When George cut the air speed down, the engine sputtered. Quickly righting the plane George said, "By damn, something's wrong!" He slammed the throttle forward quickly.

We headed directly toward a huge chunk of ice at the end of the ravine. It was about fifty feet high, and just before we reached it, George pulled back on the stick and we slid up over the ice. This was the closest we ever came to crashing. We patted George on the back, gave a sigh of relief, and decided to give up on that bear. The rest of the day we only saw two sows and a cub, and so returned back to the landing strip at Barrow.

When we got out of the plane, we noticed the hindquarters of the bears the Europeans had brought in were lying nearby. Fred asked if they were good to eat. George said, "Well, ya, they're okay." The dogs around the landing strip hadn't touched them; that should have told us something. Anyway, we thought we'd like to try them. We took one on a sled, dropped it off at Al's Restaurant and he prepared polar bear steaks for us that night.

The polar bear feeds on seals, which in turn feed on fish, so the bear meat has a fishy taste. The color of the meat is similar to liver, but almost purple, very dark, very tough and stringy. The flavor is strong and oily like a seal. Outside of that, I guess it's okay, but Fred and I ended up eating bacon and eggs.

We were amused at the way the Europeans described their hunt that day. They had seen a walrus, which they called "whale ross," and Willie Bogner told of his experience in shooting moose. Their European language sounded much different than the regular talk we heard from the natives here.

The next two days, the weather was referred to as a "whiteout" condition. The wind didn't blow, there was some fog and overcast skies. You couldn't tell the horizon from the sky or the ice, so we were not able to fly.

On Thursday, Ed Shuman went out with Jules Thibidue, who was referred to as "Walking Jules" because he had walked home from several plane crashes. Ed was successful in getting a large bear that day. A year later, Walking Jules' luck ran out. George found his remains in a crashed plane that had hit a mountain top. He was flying a load of Coca Cola in his 180 from Fairbanks to Barrow when he hit the last mountain in the Brooks Range, just south of Umiat. There were only a few bones left when George found his remains, as the bears had gotten to him.

The cold weather caused a problem with my prostate, and Pete had to land several times during our flight to let me relieve myself. He suggested I take a coffee can with me the next trip out, which I did. It's difficult to empty a coffee can from the window of a plane going a hundred miles an hour, without spilling the contents inside and outside of the plane. When we landed back at Barrow, George walked over and noticed a strip of ice about a quarter inch thick, spread along the side of Pete's airplane for about six feet. Several Eskimo kids were standing around waiting our return. George asked Pete, "How come you let Munger throw that coke out the window?" With this remark one of the kids stuck his fingers in his mouth, licked them, rubbed them on the ice, and then put his fingers in his mouth again. George asked him, with a smile, if it tasted like coke. The kid grinned and took off.

We were weathered in with another whiteout over the ice pack. So George flew back to the Brooks Range to check on grizzly bears. He returned late that afternoon with a huge grizzly that he had shot. This really interested me, and I wanted to book a hunt right then to get one of these beautiful pelts. The hair is much longer than on the Alaskan Brown bear and has a beautiful rich brown color. I later succeeded in doing that trick with George and my bow.

The next morning, we left in search of our elusive polar bears, picking up a track about eighty miles out. Following it for a while, we came upon a large boar shuffling along a large pressure ridge. He looked like a good-sized bear, so we plotted our ambush.

There is more to this than one might think. It's important that everyone be in the proper position so that no one blocks another's view and so nobody's hurt if the bear comes from the wrong side, or crosses over the pressure ridge and comes up directly behind you. This creates lots of excitement, as well as causing a very dangerous situation.

We landed well ahead of the bear, and walked about half a mile down the pressure ridge so it would not see the plane. George picked out a spot in the pressure ridge where there were some huge twenty-foot boulders of ice. He placed us in position, planning that the bear would continue on the same side of the ridge and come from our right. If it changed course, there would have to be a quick shuffle, and probably no pictures. If the bear came up behind us, he would probably be about twenty feet away, and at that close range no one knew what might happen. I said a prayer wishing that he'd come by on our right side as planned. It's hard to look two ways at once, and a polar bear makes no noise as he shuffles along in the snow.

Fred and I sat looking at each other for fifteen minutes. No words were spoken, no one smiled. Then we saw George raise his rifle. Fred and I readied ourselves, about thirty yards to our right came the huge white beast we were waiting for. He was shuffling along quite fast, and it appeared that he might pass twenty-five yards in front of us.

I had him in the camera lens, and Fred was slowly pulling back his bow. At this moment, the bear turned his head and looked at us. I think he spotted George's dark colored fur parka. He didn't lessen his gait, and Fred judged that this was as close as he was going to get. He released the arrow, it buried deep in front of the bear's hindquarters. Whirling with a quick motion, the bear came for us in bounding leaps like a huge cat. Somewhere around fifteen yards, George's 300 broke the silence. The bear collapsed instantly and slid to a halt, laying on his right side. George apologized saying, "Sorry Fred, I had to do it."

Fred nodded in silent agreement. We approached the bear, it showed no sign of life. Since I couldn't see any blood I asked George where he'd hit him. He answered, "In the chest." George leaned his rifle against a block of ice twelve feet from the stretched-out bear. This almost proved to be fatal.

By this time I had removed the camera sling and unzipped my parka. I approached the head of the bear, knelt down, and put my hand on his chest, checking for blood. There was none. Fred put his foot on the bear's hindquarters and started to pull out his arrow. To our amazement, the bear raised his head. Right in my face. His head looked as big as a bushel basket. I quickly raised to my knees, as it looked like he was about to get up. George had no time to get his gun. I grabbed my 44 magnum revolver from my shoulder holster, flipped it to George and lunged backwards to get out of George's way. George shot him behind the front shoulder, the bear dropped his head and lay still.

After catching our breath, we checked and found that the rifle bullet had gone in the bear's right eye and out through his skull. He was laying on his right side, so we couldn't see any blood. We concluded his movements were merely reflex actions. But at the time I was patting him on his chest and he raised his head, I was scared to hell. Again, Fred looked very dejected, and I sure felt for him. Nothing much was said as we skinned the pelt and took one of the hindquarters. My feeling was that it was a damn good thing that George put one of his lights out when he made that charge.

We skinned him and loaded everything into the plane and headed back to Barrow. The hindquarters along with the skull and hide filled the plane. It was a sad ending for Fred—to be foiled again at taking a bear without a bullet in him. Fred could have used my license, but he didn't feel it would be proper. That evening, I suggested that we make a trip out to a whaling camp the next day, hoping this would get the bear hunt off Fred's mind.

In May each year, the bowhead whales migrate from the Bering Sea into the Beaufort Sea, and groups of Eskimos band together to form hunting parties. Fred wanted to film the harpooning of a whale and George arranged to have us go out with an Eskimo friend of his who had a dog team and sled.

We arrived at the man's home about 8:30 the next morning. The scheduled time to leave was 9:00 a.m. However, we found him still in bed, so we went back to the hotel and waited another hour. On our return, he was finally up and harnessing the dogs. There were seven dogs on the sled, the lead dog at the head and the others following in pairs. The sled was an antiquated thing, made from two by fours and two by sixes, and rather heavy. The dogs were neither friendly nor vicious, paying little attention to people. If you attempted to call one over to pet it, it would not respond.

We started through the village, passing by and in

between the houses, then finally across the fresh water lake towards Browersville. It wasn't long before I discovered that a dog sled ride was not the greatest sport I had ever encountered. The dogs, having been inactive for awhile, frequently had to relieve themselves, and tried to do this in the process of trotting. As they tried to brace their legs, the other dogs would jerk them. This became a smelly, messy, hazardous deal, because what they left behind was thrown up in our faces. Never volunteer for the front seat on an open sled without a windshield!

The snow had drifted quite deep along the open lake and out beyond Browersville, to the point where we would strike out for the whaling camp. Point Barrow, named after this famous point, is a spot where the natives shoot thousands of eider ducks in their migration, while they fly across this narrow piece of land every fall.

We headed directly north after reaching the point, and traveled several miles. The dogs seemed to be gradually slowing down, and finally came to a screeching halt. They all laid down and stretched out on the ice. After a brief rest, the Eskimo got them up and we started on again. He generally trotted along ahead of the dogs.

Fred was on the sled, and I sensed he didn't feel well. I was standing on the rear of the runners behind Fred. Sometimes I would jog alongside when the dogs weren't running too fast. It took us two hours to get out to the first rough ice. We stopped to rest the dogs and the Eskimo scaled a chunk of ice fifty feet high and surveyed the area. I climbed up there with him and asked, "What are you looking for?" He said, "I look for whaling camp."

I was startled, George had told us his friend had been out there the day before. So I said, "I thought you were out here yesterday." "Oh," he said, "I was, but I didn't find it." By this time we were far enough away that we couldn't see Barrow on the horizon. Our destiny lay in the hands of our friend and his dogs as to whether we might make it to the camp, and hopefully, back in the same day.

We continued on through the rough ice and came to a spot with a tremendous crack—a large three-foot wide crevice. We judged that it went down at least forty feet. The Eskimo jumped the crevice, the first five dogs also jumped across. The last two dogs, however, slipped and fell into the crack, hanging four feet down by their harness. I guess each one thought the other had pushed him as they were engaged in a real donnybrook down in the crevice, chewing each other. The five other dogs were pulling to keep from sliding backwards into the crevice. They dug their toenails in the ice, and we were fearful that they all might go in. The dog sled was moving towards the huge crack, so I grabbed it and held it back to prevent it from going down into the crevice. The Eskimo grabbed the leashes and harnesses fastened to the dogs, and finally, with the help of Fred and myself, pulled the fighting critters out. We were a bit reluctant about giving assistance because we didn't know what they might do with their snapping teeth when they got back on the ice, but they were just glad to be on solid footing again and posed no danger. We pulled the sled across the chasm and worked our way through the rough ice ahead of us.

At last we heard the barking of dogs, and soon came upon the spot where the whale hunters had tied them. Surprisingly, a huge bowhead whale is very sensitive to noise, sight and smell, so the dogs were tethered about half a mile from the lead. The Eskimos also set their tent camp far enough back so they can't be seen, heard or scented by the whale.

As we approached the camp, we saw four Eskimos sitting near a little canvas tent. Their hunting gear was all laid out on the ice in preparation for the hunt. There were whaling guns, hand harpoon spears on a long handle, skin boats with ropes and buoys made from seal skins. The whaling gun is a heavy brass weapon that fires a spear with the thrust provided by a ten gauge shotgun shell. The harpoon carries a dynamite charge. The skin buoys are used to keep the whale afloat after the Eskimos harpoon it. They also had rifles for shooting seals and a number of seals lay on the ice around the tent.

The Eskimos were cooking seal meat, and offered us

some for lunch. The smell just about knocked us out. We hated to decline their hospitality, but from the smell we couldn't bring ourselves to eat the meat.

This day turned very cold, and the open leads froze with a thin layer of scum ice over the water. The thick ice was in the form of fingers that protruded out into the open lead. One peculiar thing we noticed about the ice was that, due to the tide and the pressure, we could see and hear it shifting. I could check my watch by the noise it made. Every twenty seconds or so it would shift several inches, making hissing noises as it moved. Then it would be silent for twenty seconds and shift again. This went on all the time we were there.

The method the Eskimos used to hunt was to crawl out onto one of the ice peninsulas and wait for the whale to swim under it. They would either shoot it with a harpoon gun or harpoon it by hand. Both of these weapons were equipped with a dynamite charge approximately an inch in diameter and a foot long. They would try to place this charge in the head of the whale, between the eyes.

They explained to us that there is a large opening in the skull of the whale, about two feet in diameter. The explosive dynamite has a delayed action which allows the spearman eight seconds to get out of the area. They all make a run for it before the charge goes off. This dynamite charge kills the whale by shattering its brain and the whale floats to the surface. The Eskimos take their skin boat, go out with a rope which they secure around the tail, and fasten the end to a big block of ice so it won't get away. After this, they chisel a ramp on which they slide the whale out, tail first.

The Eskimos claim that the heads of some of these whales can weigh up to eight tons. In 1962, a whale's blubber oil and the mucktuc, which is the skin, was worth around ten thousand dollars to the natives. Mucktuc is about an inch and a half thick, and about the color of a tire. Fred and I tried some of it, and we both thought that it tasted a little like a tire too, and just as tough. The Eskimos leave a little of the blubber on the mucktuc. They cut off a large chunk, put it in their mouth, and cut off a bite-size portion with a knife. The blubber adds a little grease to flavor the meat. They, of course, eat it raw, though Fred and I tried it cooked. We both agreed it would never replace a sirloin steak.

I took twenty pounds of the mucktuc home with me, as well as the hindquarter of a polar bear. I threw a party in my basement and served both mucktuc and polar bear. The stench filled the house—basement, the first and second floors. After having several stiff drinks, some of the fellows said that they liked the bear and seal meat, but most of them admitted that they didn't particularly care much for it.

The Eskimos told us that when they harpoon a whale, they go back to the village to get a hundred or more villagers to help them with the meat. The man who actually kills the whale has first choice of the meat, then the rest of the party take their share. The remainder is divided up among friends and relatives.

Even in those days, mucktuc brought a dollar a pound and was considered a real delicacy. Sometimes the natives go through the whole hunting season without killing a whale. Other seasons they may harpoon as many as fifteen. The tradition of whaling has been practiced for centuries yet now whales are considered subsistence food.

We started back, hopefully, to find the village of Barrow, retracking our steps. Fred was not feeling any better, and when we broke out on the open flat ice, he stayed on the sled. Trotting alongside one of these dog sleds gives a person a lot of exercise. They don't go real fast, but you have to maintain a pace similar to jogging. We returned to Barrow about seven o'clock that night, tired, cold and hungry. It was disappointing that we couldn't film the actual kill, or have a chance to film some whales, but just the same it was a worthwhile experience.

That night we got our gear together and packed it in preparation for our flight scheduled the next morning to Fairbanks. From there we boarded a flight to Anchorage. We left Fred's polar bear at Jonas Brothers. Bert

Klineburger showed us a fine collection of snow leopard pelts he had in his office. I have kicked myself many times for not latching onto one of these for my trophy room. Fred wanted to stay at the Westward Hotel, but there was a convention going on there and every room had been taken. Fred knew the manager, who treated Fred like a long lost buddy. He looked through the reservations list and said, "Well Fred, we have only one space that isn't occupied. Normally we never rent it, but you can have it for one night in this emergency." He said with a smile, "It's the Presidential Suite." Fred mustered the courage to ask how much it would cost. The manager gave him a special emergency rate, so we took it. We felt pretty damn important, too!

The elevator took us to the top floor. As we stepped out we saw the coat of arms emblem—golden eagle on the red, white and blue shield—on the door. This suite occupied the whole top floor, and it was gorgeous. There were huge chandeliers in the dining room, one about the size of a Volkswagon; a large dining table; three bedrooms; a bar and kitchen; plus a breathtaking view overlooking Cook Inlet. Mt. McKinley was visable in the distance, one hundred miles to the north, and the view of the mountain range, to the east of Anchorage, was awesome.

We didn't lose any time asking some of our friends to stop by for a visit so they could share this wonderful view with us. Bert Klineburger had just returned from a hunt in Nepal. We invited him over for a drink, not telling him we were in the Presidential Suite. He was really amazed when he saw the layout. That evening, when we went out to dinner, Fred kept remarking that he couldn't wait to get back so he could sleep in the same bed that Ladybird Johnson and Jackie Kennedy had slept in. The stay in the presidential suite helped ease the disappointment of our hunt. In the morning I called a buddy of mine, Bill Gamel, and his wife, Beth. He was a contractor and developer in Anchorage. We invited them down to the hotel to have breakfast with us. I suggested that they meet us in our room. They, too, were pretty impressed when they found us camped in the Presidential Suite.

Fred was still thinking about the hunt. He felt that he could salvage the unsuccessful filming of the polar bear hunt if we went on another brown bear hunt on Kodiak Island. We called Ed Bilderback and told him we were on our way.

Reflections

Many times since our polar bear jaunts I have thanked God and would be willing to kiss our pilots for safely returning us back to our main camp at Barrow. According to my field notes, we logged 23 days flying out of Barrow in the two years of hunting.

I don't know how many landings we made during our twenty-three flying days, but it must have been a hundred plus. Many days we made six to eight landings or more, during the two years that we used planes. When you realize that each landing is the first time that a plane has tested the ice at that particular spot, you wonder what your percentages are. The pack ice is made up of all sorts of unknown thicknesses.

The other day I stood watching a crop duster slide between trees and under the light wires risking his neck. I guess I didn't associate our flying experiences at the time as being on the brink of something, but as I think back on some of our close calls, it scares the hell out of me and I'm darn glad it's behind us.

A normal polar bear hunt with a rifle, often times, requires just one landing on the ice. The shooting range of a gun affords a real advantage as one can drop his bear from a distance of 200 yards or more.

In bow hunting, one has to get within 50 yards or closer. This creates a problem. Also adding the third man with the camera coverage tends to gum up the situation. It's a lot easier for one man to sneak up on any animal, but when you add the back-up man plus a cameraman it gets real tough. I kept no record of how many landings we made during our 23 flying days, but it must have been nearly a hundred plus. I know that many days we made six to eight landings or perhaps more, during the two years that we used planes. When you realize that each landing is the first time that a plane has tested the ice at that particular spot, it prompts you to wonder what your percentages are. The pack ice is made up of all sorts of unknown thicknesses.

How thick is the ice? When we punched the rifle butt through the ice to test its safeness ahead of us and hit water, I wonder what the hell might have happened each time we touched down with the plane.

George Theile has the reputation of being one of the best trackers in the business. When the wind blows strong, the bear tracks are quickly obliterated as the snow is blown off the smooth ice. In order to see a track under these conditions, George would sometimes fly less than one hundred feet off the ice. This isn't too bad as long as you go in a straight line. But when you lose the track and have to twist and turn in order to back track, trying to pick up the trail, it gets quite exciting. I was surprised that Fred and I didn't get sick. Could be that the twenty degree below temperature had something to do with it, or maybe we were too scared to get sick. After you log enough hours doing this, I guess you get calloused to the situation. It's colder than hell sitting in the back seat and after a time you become numb and sleepy. Peering out of the window, you get a little dizzy watching the ice formations zip by. It felt like we must have been hunting on the surface of the moon. Landings are treacherous because of the gusting winds.

V

Brownie: The Big Kodiak 1962

For the second time, we returned from Barrow and our polar bear hunt with a let-down feeling. It hardly seemed fair after days of logging many hours flying and making many hazardous landings that we had to pick out another bear with the same nasty temper as we had two years ago. Fred and I were disgusted about the way the hunt had turned out again.

It seemed like the only thing left for us to do was to go back to Kodiak Island and take our spite out on one of the brown bears.

We took off the next day for Cordova, where Ed lives— a short flight down the Prince William Sound. After checking into our hotel, we looked up Ed Bilderback. Two years ago Fred had told Ed that we would be back for another hunt with him. We found Ed working on a boat, busily getting ready for his spring seal hunt. He collected a $300 bounty for each one and he also sold the hides. In addition to seal hunting, Ed also was a commercial fisherman and a top-notch brown bear guide as we found out on our previous hunt.

When they made the mold for Ed, they used it once and threw it away. He is quite a character, and a real "going institution." Ed told us that marine regulations required that he paint the bottom of the boat if he was taking someone on a charter trip. Fred asked him, "How can you do that when the boat is in the water?" Ed replied, "You come down about four o'clock in the morning, and I'll show you how it's done."

Fred and I arrived at the appointed time. Ed and Harley King, the first mate, were busily engaged in rolling on the paint with huge sixteen-inch rollers. They wallowed around in the mud in their hip boots. Ed had secured the *Valiant Maid*, the fifty-seven-foot purse seiner, to the dock pilings at high tide the night before. He also sunk some weighted blocks that he now slid under the boat. At that time of year there was about a fifteen-foot tide, and when it went out the boat was left high and dry.

Fred ventured to inquire, "Ed, don't you have to let that boat dry for the paint to stick?" and Ed replied, "Well, there's nothing in the regulations that says it has to stick—it just says you have to paint it."

Well, it took us another day to get things organized. Ed rushed around with all kinds of last minute preparations. He bought a new motor and had to try it out. It takes a lot of groceries and supplies to go on a trip like this. Ed planned to be gone for two months, leaving us off at Kodiak Island after our bear hunt, and continuing on with his seal hunt. This gave Fred and me a little time to look around town, and between the two of us, we came up with what we thought would be an amusing trick to play on Ed.

We put an ad in the local paper, saying "Sea otter pelts and eagle feathers for sale. See Ed Bilderback." We paid for a good-sized ad and told the paper to run it about eight weeks later. That would be the time Ed planned to return from his seal hunt. We later discovered that, upon his return, he was met by the Fish and Wildlife, who had flown a man down from Anchorage and had turned Ed's house and garage inside out, looking for the illegal sea otter pelts and eagle feathers. It would burn this paper if I disclosed what Ed said to us about this dastardly deed.

Several years later while sheep hunting with Ed in Hawaii, he got even with me for my sea otter-eagle feather escapade. He knew a game warden there and planted the warden in the bushes after copping my hunting license from my wallet. The warden had me convinced that I was going to spend the night in jail until Ed belted me and said, "Now we're even, the game warden is my good friend and neighbor." My wife helped Ed pull the trick by removing the license from my wallet.

We chugged out of the harbor on the 27th of April, and it sure was good to be back on the *Valiant Maid* again. Ed hired a friend of his, Dan Korea, to go along as cook. That day we went as far as Sheep Bay, where we tied up for the night. Ed, Fred and I went ashore to target in my back-up 375 browning rifle. Fred worked the tape recorder and described what I was trying to do. The first time I fired it, the rifle just made a little click! I had forgotten to put the shell in. This raised many laughs, much to my embarrassment. I finally got the thing properly loaded while Fred gave me the business about not having my gun ready, and asked if this was his back-up gun?

There was a heavy snow fall that spring, much more than usual, and we were concerned whether or not the bears had come out of hibernation. While cruising along the shore on the Keni peninsula, Fred spotted some black bears on the beach. We anchored the *Valiant Maid*, took the skiff and went around a long point of land. Getting on the back side of this would put us in the proper wind direction. The bears were feeding on kelp in the sunshine on the south side of the beach, and we now had a good spot to pull a sneak on them.

Fred took the camera from Harley and suggested that I take the first chance. I sneaked up within fifty yards of the bears and took a shot at one of them. The arrow slid over its back. The second arrow I shot threw sand in the bear's face, hitting low. The two bears spooked then and ran past us into heavy timber and brush. They neither saw nor smelled us. I guess it was the noise of the arrow that scared them.

Harley took Fred's camera and Fred and I started out to pull another sneak on the bears. They were just leisurely ambling along ahead of us, as we came to a real thick spot where both of the bears went to the right of us. The thick brush was located near the edge of a frozen pond. I elected to go to the left and stay on land, while Fred started walking slowly across the pond ice. He hadn't gone very far before he came upon the bears some thirty yards ahead of him. He shot one in the midsection and they both took off.

Then there was one hell of a crash followed by a splashing sound. Fred had broken through the ice and was up to his belt in water, making a tremendous noise. I ran to the other edge of the brush to intercept the bears. Rounding the brush I met a bear headed in my direction. He stopped and I let go with an arrow, hitting him just ahead of the hindquarters. Surprisingly, he scurried up the first tree he came to.

There was a lot of action for a while. Fred was floundering around in the ice up to his hips, and my bear was climbing up the tree. Fred finally got out of his predicament, took his boots and pants off, dried himself the best he could, and proceeded to track the bear that he had shot. In the meantime, Harley stood guard beneath the tree that my bear had climbed.

After tracking his bear about two hundred yards, we found him dead on the edge of the beach. We hurried back to the bear I shot, which had climbed about a hundred feet up a huge Douglas Fir. Ed offered to climb the tree next to the one the bear was in and scare him down. I shot several arrows, but missed. They all went out of the timber and came down on the rocky beach. We were using fiberglass arrows that year, and when they hit the rocks they would break. I wound up with only two arrows, one of mine and one of Fred's. Fred patched the two together. He took a stick and made a plug to put inside the hollow arrows, then taped it shut with electrician's tape. The front half was his arrow and the back half was mine. I shot it completely through the bear, and he came plopping down out of the tree. Fred stood by with a club just in case he might come after us. What a bear hunt!

That night we tied up to an abandoned cannery in Graham Bay. Fred and I had a big time scrounging around inside the cannery, picking up a few pieces of furniture for the boat. There were a couple of overstuffed chairs that we borrowed to put on the back deck. This provided us with all the solid comforts of home. The cannery had been abandoned for a long time.

The next morning, we spotted a bear up on the side of the mountain. Ed said, "You guys have been havin' too much fun. I think it's about time I had a little fun and shoot myself a bear." He grabbed his bow and jumped in the skiff. Harley started to get in too and Ed said, "Where in hell do your think you're going?" "Well," he said, "I was going to go along and back you up." Ed retorted, "I don't need any back up like those dudes. It's man against beast, and either I'm going to get him or he's going to get me." He took off in the roar of the forty horsepower motor.

Fred and I sat in the overstuffed chairs watching with binoculars as Ed slowly made his ascent up the mountain after the bear. It looked like a black bear, but we couldn't tell for sure at that distance. We followed the bear with the glasses until Ed got within forty yards of him. The bear apparently sniffed Ed and looked at him, as Ed shot an arrow over his back. Ed returned disgusted. Our critical comment didn't help the situation either.

That afternoon, we went on a hunt down the east end of the bay. After three or four hours, we had still not seen any bears, and returned to *Valiant Maid*. To our shocking surprise, the *Valiant Maid* was lying practically on its side. The tide was at low ebb, and the boat lay on the bottom of the bay. The bay near the dock had filled in over the years since the big boats discontinued coming into the cannery, Ed had assumed the water was a lot deeper when he tied up the boat.

Ed ran down to check the engine room, and found boxes and crates floating in four feet of water. The rope he had secured the boat with broke one of the huge pilings. It snapped under the weight of the boat, and the stern and bow lines were holding the *Valiant Maid* from rolling completely on her side.

We sat there for a couple hours, waiting for the tide to come in, the boat slowly righting itself. Ed was able to start the pumps, and fortunately there was no damage to the engine.

While Ed was working below, Fred and I sat on the back deck in our overstuffed chairs having a beer. We noticed a small skiff coming across the bay. This was the first human life we had seen in two weeks. As he approached, we saw that he was a wild-looking, pirate type of character. He wore a red bandana over his head, and had a lot of tattoos on his arms. In one ear he wore a large gold ring. Fred threw him a line, we secured it to the boat, and he climbed aboard. He took one look at Fred and said, "You're Harry Bear, aren't you?" Fred said, "Yes," with a hint of a smile on his face, as he winked at me. Ever since then I've referred to Fred as Harry—that was his Dad's name.

We invited the fellow to join us for a beer, and the three of us sat chatting and sipping our drinks. Ed had heard the motor of the skiff and came out of the hold to see what was going on. He took one look at our visitor, then reached up on the rack for his 30 caliber Carbine rifle. Without sparing any words, Ed screamed out, "You get the hell out of here! I've got no damn use for you! Get going, and quick!" —the four letter words were more descriptive. Ed slammed a bullet into the chamber to convince the guy he meant business. The guy scrambled over the side into his skiff without a word.

Fred and I sat, with our mouths open, confused and dumbfounded. We had finally found a friend to talk to, we thought, and Ed promptly had kicked his butt out. Our parting friend took off at full throttle. Ed hollered after him, "Don't plan to anchor in this bay tonight, or you might have to dodge some skipping bullets!" He disappeared around the point, and we never saw him again. Ed then explained, the guy had shot and killed his best friend several years before, and had served two years for the crime.

We waited two days for the weather to calm down before we made our run to the Barren Islands some seventy miles away. The trip was rough. Fred and I are opposites when seafaring. He can't stay topside in the wheel house without getting squeamish. He'd go down in the stinking noisy engine room and lay on a bunk. I couldn't stand it down there, so I'd stand up alongside Ed. We both took our dramamine when Captain Ed told us in advance that the sea was going to be rough. I also found that a small bourbon snack helped my tummy, or so I thought.

I have been with Fred many times when he was asked, "If you had one more hunt to take in your lifetime, regardless of the cost, what would you choose?" His answer was always, "A brown bear in Alaska by boat, with Ed Builderback." I'd have to agree with him. It's a breathtaking, fun experience even if you don't see a bear. To cruise the remote shore lines without seeing any evidence of human life gives one an undescribable degree of personal satisfaction. You are constantly kept entertained by seeing a variety of sea life.

Each day we saw hundreds of hair seals and sea lions. Sea otters played along the rocky shores. Whales spouted and sounded within one hundred yards of the boat. The bird life was fantastic. Some small islands looked as if they were snow covered, with thousands of terns and gulls. Ducks and geese filled the air at the horizon. The scenery was breathtaking: rocky cliffs, alder-covered mountains with snow down to about the one-thousand foot line, streams cataracting out of the valleys and spilling into the sea. Rainbow trout, Dolly Varden and salmon were abundant for the taking. The shallow bays were filled with halibut, Dungeness and King crabs and small shrimp. When the tide was out, we gathered buckets of razor and butter clams. All in all, a trip like this is an adventure in good eating. Who needs a bear?

It's hard to spend a couple of weeks here without seeing several dozen brownies. During the two hunts Fred and I made we saw over eighty bears. Lots of eagles perch on and sail around the rocky ledges. Dozens of foxes cruise the shoreline at low tide in search of goodies. Beach crows caw constantly.

It took six hours to run to the Barren Islands. Fred and I remained dormant during the trip.

Whoever named these the Barren Islands sure hit on an appropriate description. I've never seen such a bleak, barren area. There are several small islands situated halfway between the tip of the Kenai Peninsula and Kodiak Island. The largest of the islands is about one mile long. There are no trees and very little low brush. This is uninhabited except for the thousands of birds and seals. Ed threw the anchor out in the shelter of three small islands. He was chomping at the seals, wanting to see if this was a good place to hit next month. He suggested that we go along as we might be able to film some sea otters. The next morning we took off in the skiff. We left Dan aboard the *Valiant Maid* to take care of things.

We went to the island about a mile east of us. The wind was blowing twenty knots. As we approached the western shoreline, we could see hundreds of seals sunning on the rocky beach. Ed headed the skiff around the north end of the island. We landed in a rocky cove about nine o'clock and left the skiff. The four of us topped the one-hundred foot high rocky ledge, and Ed started counting the seals.

Fred and I went up the rough shoreline in search of sea otters. We filmed them lying on their backs in the water, breaking clams with rocks. When we returned we didn't find Ed, Harley or the skiff. It was around noon when we sat down to wait for Ed and Harley to return. We waited about two hours. Then Fred suggested that we check to see if they had gone down the rocky shore at the other side of the island. We topped the high rocky ridge and scanned the shoreline. There was still no sign of the skiff, Ed or Harley. The wind was blowing strong off shore out to sea.

It was a perplexing situation. Finally we concluded that they had started back around the north tip of the island and had some kind of trouble. If they had engine trouble, the wind might blow them out to sea. This was not a very pleasant thought. Fred asked me if I had any matches. I fumbled through all my pockets and found none. He said he didn't have any either, and I almost wished that I hadn't quit smoking. This wiped out any plan for a smoke signal. Fred then said, "I wonder if there's any fresh water on the island." This posed another problem for our future existence. We spread apart and walked about a half mile to the other end of the island. We then turned back and returned to the spot where Ed had left us. No fresh water. We sat down to discuss our miserable situation. Immediately, we both wanted a drink of water.

We had no fresh water, no food, and no matches. This represented three large strikes against us. Off in the distance, we could see the *Valiant Maid* lying at anchor in the cove. It was useless to expect any help from Dan. Even if we could signal him, he didn't know how to start the engine or work the radio gear. Also, this area was not on line with any routine commercial flights. Likewise, no one knew where we had gone, nor was anyone expecting us at any given time. Ed had told them in Cordova, "I'll see you in two months." Chances were that no search party would be looking for us. I think that Fred and I each had a large lump in our throats.

We couldn't swim in that cold water, especially with the fast running tides. We were dressed in our thin camouflage clothing, and knew how cold it got at night this time of the year. I don't know whether Fred will admit it, but about this time I figured that this was the end. It occurred to me that it might be a long time before someone stumbled across a pile of bones on this God forsaken island. Fred and I stared at each other, with panic expressions on our faces. We both knew what the consequences might be, and wondered how long we could survive.

Someone once said, "It's always darkest just before the dawn." Well, to our delight dawn came disguised as the sweet hum of an outboard motor. We jumped to our feet and saw the skiff with Ed and Harley breaking around the north point of the island. We could hardly believe our eyes. It was four and a half hours since they had disappeared. I think I had the privilege of seeing Fred's happiest smile.

The boys beached the skiff and briefed us on what had happened. It seems that Harley tied the skiff up under some overhanging rocks, which blocked Fred's and my view. By the time Harley got back, the tide had started out and left the skiff high and dry on the rocks. Harley, knowing he couldn't move it himself, decided to take a nap. When Ed went back and found the skiff stranded, he too decided to take a nap and wait for the tide to come in. The tides sure made a thrilling experience for Fred and me. It took several hours for the tide to pick up the skiff so they could return to pick us up.

We jumped in the skiff and started for the *Valiant Maid*. The sea was rough and at times water splashed over the sides. What a wild ride!

As we neared the *Valiant Maid*, Ed exclaimed, "What the hell's the matter!" Looking closer we could see the boom swing back and forth, loose from its tie down. White dish towels were flying from the mast, Dan stood waving his arms like a scarecrow. Dan hollered, "By God, boy, don't you ever leave me alone on this boat again!"

It seems that in Ed's haste to leave he had neglected to turn off the diesel engine. Unbeknownst to Dan, a bell alarm system triggers itself after the engine runs for ten minutes. When this happened, Dan panicked. He went down in the engine room and started ripping off wires to silence the bell and hopefully keep the engine from blowing up. After he succeeded in this task, he thought he should cut the ropes on the boom in hopes that we would see it swinging, know that something was wrong and return to the *Valiant Maid*.

After the experience that Fred and I just had, I couldn't help but let out a little chuckle and wink at Fred. Ed looked at me with a disgusted glare, and said, "I wouldn't laugh too hard just yet. If I can't patch this, we might be here for a month!" We both shut our big mouths. Well, with Ed's resourcefulness, he was able to get things back together.

Fred and I often talk of that day on the Barren Islands when we were staring death in the face and time stood still for us.

We headed for Aflognak Island the next morning, cruising the eastern shoreline. The first game we saw was a herd of elk. These elk, which have a fall hunting season, have been planted on the island. We anchored near the mouth of a small stream. I asked Ed if there might be any fish in it. He said it probably had some Dolly Varden and rainbow trout. I suggested to Fred that he and I go ashore and see if we couldn't flip out some for supper. Sure enough, there were many twelve-inch rainbows by the mouth of the creek. We walked to a waterfall that we could hear as it tumbled out of a small lake.

Fred excitedly pointed to the tail assembly of an airplane sticking out in the brush. We climbed up to the lake shore and discovered the wreckage of a small plane. It appeared that it had happened some time ago. We later found out that two hunters were killed when they attempted a take off on the lake with an overload of elk meat.

During the course of the next three days, we saw eight bear, but most of them too high up the mountain. The evening of the third day, we spotted two bears headed our way through the sparse brush on the beach. They spotted us when about forty yards away, and spooked. Another almost, but that's the way hunting is.

We found a large sea lion, approximately six-hundred pounds, dead on the beach and wired it to a twenty-inch thick and twelve-foot long log, with some number nine wire. Fred built a blind on a rock ledge nearby. We went back the next morning to check it out and see if we had any action. Sometime during the night a huge bear had dragged sea lion, log and all, up the mountain side. Ed decided we should run in to Port Williams on Shuyak Island pick up supplies at the cannery, then come back and try to sneak up on the bear that stole our sea lion.

We tied up at the dock and were surprised to learn that the cannery manager was a former Michigander. It was not in operation at that time of the year, and they had just a skeleton crew around. The manager invited Ed and Fred to go on a tour, so they took off into the cannery.

I stayed on the boat and fleshed out the bear hides. A weather-beaten fisherman came along and started a conversation. He was known as "Big Bay Ben," and was part Aleut Indian. He noticed the bear hides stretched out on the back deck and said, "Oh, you like to shoot um bear?" and I said, "Yah." He then said, "You wanta shoot um big bear?" and I said, "Sure do." He said, "You come with me."

I followed him back down the wharf where he had a small boat with a cabin on it and we went aboard. He went up to the bow and reached down underneath the table and came up with a stick. The stick was eighteen inches long. The fisherman said, "That's his track, he's got long track!"

Well, I couldn't wait for Fred to get back to show him this bear track stick. Big Bay Ben said, "I know where the bear lives. He lives near my cabin. Every time I go back there, the bear walks by the cabin." He said, "I shoot over his head with my gun and scare him away, cause I don't like to have bears around. I let him know somebody's on the island besides him."

Fred thought this sounded like a likely spot, and we summoned Ben for a conference. Ed got his charts out and Ben showed us how to get into this bay. Ben said it is a tricky maneuver, even with his small eighteen-foot boat. Ed figured, to get the fifty-seven-foot *Valiant Maid* in there, it would have to be done at high tide. There was a narrow neck of land on the west side of the island, and with a heavy sea rolling out of the west, one slip and we'd be on the rocks. The marine charts only show up to two-hundred yards from shore, and there are lots of submerged rocks. But Ben said that it was deep enough at high tide for Ed's boat, and showed him just exactly where the shallow spots and rocks were. Ed said, "Let's give her a go."

We picked up the supplies we needed and took off in wild anticipation. We waited two hours for high tide. We ran out into the open sea, headed up the west coast line, and then towards a small channel. Shown on Ben's chart, it was about five miles from the cannery in a remote area in the northwest corner of Shuyak Island.

We all held our breath as Ed brought the *Valiant Maid* very slowly through the jagged wall of rocks projecting on both sides. We could almost touch them. I don't think the channel was over seventy-five feet wide. We slid in following Big Bay Ben's sketch, turned to our left, going to the end of the bay about half a mile from the channel entrance, and threw out the anchor. We were practically back out to the beach. There was a rocky bluff to the west that separated us from the open sea. The anchorage there was really well sheltered. After securing the ship Fred thought that we should go shore. It was about five o'clock in the evening.

Fred said that I didn't need to bring the camera because the light was going to get bad. The three of us hit the beach and secured the skiff. There was a small, sloping, sandy grade that formed a saddle between the little bay we were in and the actual coast line. The three of us approached together. There was sand on the east side, the beach side was covered with rocks and huge logs and there was also a good supply of kelp.

Ed was looking south to his left, and Fred was looking to the right. I happened to be the only one looking straight ahead. Directly in front of us, not over forty yards, stood a huge brown bear feeding on kelp. He had not seen or heard us. A fifty knot wind was blowing on the shore, and the surf was pounding. The bear had his head down and was busy pawing the kelp.

I grabbed Fred's arm. He jumped as I pointed to the bear, fumbling to get an arrow on the string. The bear turned around, looking our way. Instead of running he stood up on his hind legs. This was a real thrilling sight, for a camera. Fred had never before had a standing shot like this of a large brown bear.

The strong wind was blowing from the south and Fred had a cross-wind shot. The bear stood with his front legs hanging down. Where I was standing, I could look down the arrow as Fred drew back to shoot. When he released his arrow, it looked as if it was headed directly toward the center of the bear's chest, but the stiff wind caught it and blew it off course. It slid to the right and passed between his front leg and his chest. A clean miss.

The bear, frightened by the arrow, dropped to all fours and ran seventy yards then stopped broadside to look at us. Fred took another shot and slid an arrow just over his back. He whirled and ran up the beach. Fred and I made a big circle in hopes that we could cut him off, as we knew he had to be on this little peninsula. Fred felt he had a pretty good chance of getting another whack at him. But the bear disappeared in the heavy brush before we could out-flank him.

In disgust, we headed back to the skiff. When we got back to the *Valiant Maid*, Dan Korea, the cook, was again in a state of shock. The *Valiant Maid* was anchored a hundred feet from shore. The bear had come trotting down the beach near the boat. Dan thought he was going to swim out and get him. He was all excited about the whole thing.

The following day, we went to shore for a scouting trip. Fred wanted to take the camera and photograph an eagle's nest he had spotted, high on a rocky ledge. He and Harley took off and Ed and I continued down the shore line.

We came into an area where the brush was very thick. Bear trails and tracks were going down through this brush toward the beach. The branches extended over our heads. We almost walked on our hands and knees in order to get through the brush. It gave us an eerie feeling. If we met a bear in there it would have to be a real quick and close shot for Ed. We walked in the huge bear tracks on the trail they had traveled for many years.

We went about a half a mile through the thick brush and as we rounded a little peninsula and looked off to our left, here were two huge brownies: one of them eating kelp, the other taking a nap on the sandy beach. The wind was coming out of the southwest and blowing on the beach at about fifty knots. Ed exclaimed "What a set up!" We hurried back and tried to locate Fred.

After searching and shouting for half an hour, we gave up and went back to see if the bears were still there. They were. Ed said, "Well, it would be a shame to pass up a chance like this. Do you want to shoot one of them?" Ed thought if we waited for Fred, the bears will be gone, as one had already started to move toward the brush. I debated just what I should do. This was a tough decision for me.

I was convinced that Ed was right, that Fred wasn't going to have a chance at them, so I said okay, that I would shoot one. I wished I had my bow but it was back on the boat. Ed handed me his 300.

We started our sneak around to the edge of the bay. They were a quarter of a mile away from us at that point. We went back in the thick brush and got downwind, then crept out to the high grass that bordered the sandy beach. We were fifty yards from the bear, crawling on our hands and knees, when Ed hit me with his foot. Here was one of the bears walking past us about thirty yards away, heading for the brush. He hadn't seen nor smelled us, so we lay down and kept very still until he passed out of sight.

Ed gave me the signal to shoot the other one. This bear was standing broadside at forty yards, looking the other way. I fired, hitting the bear directly in the front shoulder, and he collapsed in his tracks. Ed ran over and kicked the bear right in the rear with his hip boots and said, "There, you old bugger! Serves you right for getting out in the daylight on the beach like this! You should know better than that!"

In another twenty minutes we saw Fred and Harley coming. They had heard the shot. We were perched on a log admiring the huge bear as they approached. After Fred congratulated me, he and Ed struck out after the other bear, knowing he was still on this little peninsula. They thought maybe they could circle around and intercept him, but the wind was bad and the bear was spooked. Fred didn't get a shot.

They went back to the boat for more camera gear and brought Dan Korea back with them. It took the five of us to roll the bear over and put it into position where it was possible to take a respectable picture. It seemed simple with a rifle, after having chased these brownies around with a bow for so many days, Yet, I was grateful to be able to take this bear with a gun. Ed figured it weighed twelve-hundred pounds. He said that if I had shot the bear in the fall, it would have weighted three-hundred pounds more after feeding on salmon all summer.

When bears come out of hibernation in the spring, they haven't eaten in a long time and they're quite skinny. We cut the bear's stomach open and found little sand fleas and a couple of rocks, the size of a golf ball, that he screened out when he was licking up on the sand fleas. Fred and I went on a picture-taking spree.

When we finished skinning the bear Ed brought the skiff down as close as he could to help transport the hide. The hide weighed one hundred and seventy eight pounds. The bear squared a good ten foot. I had him mounted in a standing position for display in my sporting goods store. His skull measured 28 7/16 in *Boone and Crockett*.

We left the area the next day. There were huge rocks, the size of automobiles, all around us projecting out of the water at low tide. Only one little channel would lead us back out into open sea. We waited for high tide to ease our way out and headed south.

As we cruised along the east side of Afognak Island we spotted a bear next to the brush on the beach and decided to give him a go. Harley stayed with the skiff, and Ed, Fred and I went up the side of the slope to try to get close to the bear. There was a high ridge that we had to top over and there was some low brush but not many trees.

Just as we topped the ridge, we met the bear head on, coming up the other side of the slope. It saw us and immediately came bouncing toward us in a full charge. At the same instant we saw another bear coming. Ed knew we had bumped into a sow with her cub. From the *Valiant Maid* we had not been able to tell the size of the bear. The bear came right at Ed, woofing and knashing it's teeth. She stopped twenty feet from him as Ed hollered, "If you take one more step, you've had it!" The noise of Ed's voice drew another woof out of the bear, then both of them scampered off into the brush. I'm glad she understood Ed's language.

It was an exciting moment even though Fred didn't get a shot. We caught our breath and decided to climb to the top of the mountain where we could look over the valley. From here we could look sixty miles across the Shelikoff Straits and also see the snow capped mountains of Kodiak Island that lay to the south of us. This is truly a beautiful area. It's a real privilege and pleasure to have the opportunity to see this country. We dropped anchor in a coastal spot about two hundred yards from the beach, because we had no harbor.

That evening we had the usual seafood platter with seal livers and king crab. We all went to bed early, but about four o'clock in the morning I woke up. The boat was heaving back and forth and rocking around. Ed was also awake and hollered, "Everybody up! We've got to make a run for it, and get out of here!"

The wind had changed during the night. It had swung around and now was blowing us toward shore. We hurried, got the anchor up and started toward Kodiak Island. We had to go out around a rocky peninsula of land in order to head south and to a protected harbor. I had never before been in a storm at sea like this. The waves were at least thirty feet tall and every sixth one, which Ed called "comers," was ten feet taller.

Ed headed the bow into the wind. All of us had to hang on for dear life and I thought it was absolutely the end. If we'd capsized, the rapid current would have crashed the *Valiant Maid* onto the rocks.

The wind was blowing so hard it blew the white caps of the waves right off. This blinded our vision. Ed did an excellent job fighting the wheel. When we'd crest the waves he'd steer the boat to the right, slide on an angle down into the trough of the waves, and when he started up he'd head it back into the wind. He was fighting that wheel for about half an hour, and I thought it was curtains for all of us. That's no place for a fifty-seven-foot boat in a sea like that.

Thank God, we made it down around the peninsula and finally slipped into a calm little harbor which looked like paradise to me. Ed admitted that was a pretty good sea rolling out there. We asked him if he'd ever been in anything worse than that. He claimed that he had. He ran the mail route out of Cordova in the Prince William Sound for several years, and said that in the winter time the winds sometimes reached ninety miles an hour.

Evidence of running in the high seas was marked by the big ten-foot patch on the side of the bow of the *Valiant Maid*. Ed told us about his experience when he and his wife were running in the dark and they hit a submerged iceberg. It tore a huge hole in the starboard side of the *Valiant Maid* near the water line of the hull. With his quick thinking and seamanship, Ed ran down in the hold with his flashlight. He took a mattress off a bunk and stuffed it in the hole, where the water was coming in. He then went topside to a skiff that was hanging in a sling fastened to the boom. He used the power winch to lift the skiff overboard and dropped it sideways in the water, then righted it, full of water. He winched it up and swung it out overboard on the port side. This weight raised the starboard side with the hole in it out of the water. He then was able to slowly creep back to port. This ingenious feat was a pretty fancy maneuver indeed.

I told Fred I had better head for home soon. At four the next morning, we set out for Kodiak so I could catch a flight to Anchorage. Fred decided he'd stay on with Ed. I kissed 'em all and took off.

I took the evening flight to Seattle and boarded the plane about nine o'clock that evening. It was dark as we taxied out to start our take off. I was visiting with the fellow sitting next to me, who seemed jovial and willing to listen to my conversation.

After a brief stop to make the final engine checks, the pilot turned the plane around and poured the power to the engines. The jet surged ahead on its takeoff run. We got about two-thirds down the runway, when all of a sudden he cut the engines and applied the brakes. We came to a screeching halt, near the end of the runway. Naturally, we all wondered what was going on. Word came over the intercom that everybody should keep their seats; we were returning to the terminal to deplane. The pilot said he had just been informed that we might have a bomb aboard the aircraft. This was just what I needed!

All conversation ceased. Everyone acted as if the guy next to him was the culprit who planted the bomb. We returned to the terminal with screaming sirens of fire trucks, police cars, and ambulances.

The guy ahead of me made a run for the terminal. After he got to the building he turned around and hollered back, "Blow up, you bastard!" It was quite a spectacle with fire trucks, police cars, sirens, and red flashing lights. A loud speaker directed us to go to a designated spot, and we all clamored for the exit. They herded us into an enclosure like a flock of sheep. The plane taxied away from the terminal. One at a time, they called us for interrogation. We were told to go in the baggage room and point out our luggage. It took an hour to get the luggage off the plane and spread out in a huge room. State Police, local security guards, the military and the FBI were there. I got to thinking that I could be in trouble because I had my 44 magnum revolver in my suitcase.

Two officers went with me as I identified my luggage. They asked me to open it, which I did, and the policeman said, "Well, what's this?" referring to my revolver. I had the 44 in the holster, and wasn't totally sure whether it was loaded or not. I always kept it loaded on the trip, and couldn't remember if I had taken the cartridges out.

Fortunately, I had. When he said, "What's this?" I said, "It's a revolver," and he said, "I know it's a revolver, why do you have it?" I told him that I'd been hunting, with bow and arrow, with Fred Bear, and we used this as back up. He acted as if he felt it wasn't a very likely story, but after showing him a picture he accepted it. Fortunately, he didn't ask me for a permit. I had a permit to carry it in Michigan, but not in the state of Alaska.

Then he saw my tape recorder, which was a reel type—one of the old fashioned varieties. That was a conspicuous looking gadget to have in your suitcase, and he wanted to know what it was. I told him that I recorded the events of the trip. He took me into a room where a very stern looking man was sitting behind a desk. He had a length of credentials that stretched four feet across the desk. He introduced himself as agent so and so from the FBI, and questioned me as to who I called or talked with, or visited in Anchorage while I was there. He wanted a complete run down as to why I was there and who I was. For half an hour I answered his questions.

When I got back to the terminal it was about one o'clock in the morning. I figured that inasmuch as I got up at four o'clock that morning and was pretty well whipped, I'd cancel my flight and go the next day. I went to the airlines and told them that I'd like to stay in Anchorage that night and would like to have my luggage. "Well," said the attendant, "your luggage is back on the airplane now." When they told the police that I'd requested my luggage, I was again a prime suspect. The questioning started all over again, and they wanted to know why I didn't want to continue on with that flight. I got the whole thing straightened out finally and checked into the Westward about 3:30 a.m.

The next day, I caught a flight out and came back home to Michigan. What an exciting wind-up to another exciting hunt. I was pleased to hear later that Fred had been successful in getting some real footage on bears and had shot a good-sized brownie. Harley King took over my job with the camera and was able to film the whole sequence. You may have seen this on film in "Kodiak Country" by Bear Archery.

One sad note, 12 years later Harley was shot and killed, while riding his snowmobile, by some guy who had gone nuts. Fred and I thought a lot of him.

Fred's third attempt at a polar bear on A.B.C. Television hunt, Barrow, Alaska, 1966.

Playing cards with Cliff Robertson.

Fred shooting a polar bear.

Taking a shot at a polar bear ice sculpture.

Bob Munger practicing his photography.

Fred and his polar bear.

Harry Holcomb's caribou.

Bob White's moose.

Bob Munger and his caribou.

Fred and an Alaskan brown bear.

The grizzly had our lunch.

Old mossy antlers.

Fred, Bob, and Fred's bear.

VI

Brush with a Grizzly
1962

During the summer of 1962, Fred called and asked if I would like to go with him on a grizzly bear hunt on the Kispiox River in British Columbia. This was Fred's favorite hunt; he had made three previous trips out there. Fess Parker joined him on one hunt, and ABC made a movie of it for TV. Fred also invited Chuck Kroll and Dick Mauch to go along, and he was taking a cameraman for the State of Michigan.

I had managed to become a casualty at a party where I received a bad cut in my thigh. I told Fred that I doubted whether I could make the hunt as infection had set in and I was laid up for about two weeks. The closer the departure came, the better my thigh felt. I decided to call Fred and tell him that I would meet him in Seattle.

When the plane rolled to a stop and the steward opened the door, a red skycap appeared with a wheel chair and the steward paged for Bob Munger. I had my bow with me in its case. The skycap put me in the wheel chair and wheeled me down the ramp. Here was Fred and the gang waiting for me. One of them held my hand as Fred wheeled me on a fast ride through the Seattle terminal and out to the luggage claims. One guy went ahead and removed everybody from the road shouting, "We have an emergency here!" People looked at me and shied away as if I had the plague.

The next day, we were checked through customs at Vancouver on our way to Smithers. We were the last members on the plane to exit. We had lots of gear and customs checked everybody else through first. Fred was the last one in our group to be checked. Customs asked if he had any firearms with him. Fred said, "Yes, I've got a 44 revolver." Well, it's illegal to carry a revolver in any province of Canada. Even the guides couldn't get a permit to carry one at that time.

All eyebrows raised when Fred said he had a permit to carry it. He reached into his briefcase, pulled out the permit and handed it to the customs officer. The customs officer said that in all his years, he'd never seen one. He called in the head honcho. He also shook his head and said that he'd never seen one either. But it was an official document from the Canadian government allowing Fred, while he was hunting with a bow and arrow, to carry this weapon for safety precautions. Fred had secured the permit years before when the laws were different. The officials finally let him keep the gun and we passed through customs.

The next day, we flew into Smithers and were picked up by Bill Love, one of our outfitters, who took us back to the cabin where he and his partner, Jack Lee, lived. We spent a day there grooming up our equipment and getting ready to take off for their Swan Lake Hunting Camp.

We flew to Swan Lake the day after to start our hunt. Fred suggested that we take a horseback ride down to the river to see if there was any sign of fresh bear. With my hunting knife I whittled a hip pad from a piece of cedar and taped it on my thigh. If the horse decided to rub up next to a tree it wouldn't open up the wound.

We started around Swan Lake to the area where they

wanted to camp by a little creek. This was Fred's favorite spot as the grizzlies came down to feed on the salmon in the creek. We were halfway up the mountain when Jack Lee stopped the pack train. He came back and asked us if anybody would like to shoot a grouse. Of course we all said we would.

Fred, Chuck Crowell and I grabbed our bows and followed Jack. He pointed to several Franklin grouse sitting in the trees. Chuck took a shot at one. His arrow passed over one bird's back. Fred took a shot and he missed, too. I had a flu flu arrow that I had brought along for just this type of occasion. Much to my surprise I centered the grouse on the first shot and down he came, flopping to the ground.

Jack discovered another grouse sitting a little further up the branch. We repeated the same procedure. Chuck was the first to shoot, and missed. Fred then shot and missed. And again I staggered one in there and down the second bird came. We looked up into the top of the tree and spotted another one. Again we repeated this performance. Chuck and Fred both missed. I was the third to shoot and I downed the bird. This was the first time and the only time in my life that I ever outshot Fred Bear!

The little stream that connected Stevens Lake and Swan Lake was filled with thousands of salmon at this time of year. At the mouth there were schools of Rainbows and Dolly Vardens that were very receptive to our spinners. The salmon in the lake were jumping out of the water. Sometimes there would be a hundred salmon leaping in the air. They seemed to swim around in circles until the time came for them to make their run up stream. Generally, if you catch them in the lake, they will be a silverish color, but as they move into the stream their bodies turn a brilliant red and their heads are green.

The bear trails were padded down like a sidewalk along the stream that stretched between the two lakes. Fred had taken several grizzlies in this area in the past, and we were wild with the anticipation of seeing our first grizzly. I'd never seen a grizzly before.

We soon realized that Fred had been overly generous with his invitations. Either he had invited too many guys, or there weren't enough bears to go around. We wound up having to flip a coin to see whose turn it was to take the shot. Even the cameraman turned out to be a bow hunter.

Well, as I said, we had to flip a coin to see who was going to shoot first or second. Dick Mauch won the flip and got the first shot. Bill Love went with us. We hadn't gone up the stream very far when we heard splashing noises ahead of us. Bill alerted us and said, "That's a grizzly fishing for salmon."

We sneaked through the brush. The wind fortunately was in our favor. We got within forty yards of the bear. He was coming downstream toward us, picking up salmon with his mouth. He would take them up on the bank and put his paw on the head, eat the meat off one side of the body, then flip it over and eat the other side. When he finished you could pick up the head with all the bones and the tail intact.

Dick took a shot at the bear and put the arrow over his head. The bear lunged out of the creek with a big splash.

The following day we took the horses around the lake to another small stream. My guide had a high spirited horse. We saddled up and I mounted my steed with my bow and my back quiver full of arrows. Fred stood nearby watching and bidding us farewell, good luck, and all that stuff. All of a sudden the guide's horse started to buck a little bit. My horse observed this and concluded that this looked like a lot of fun and thought he'd try it, too.

I'm not a horse lover in any sense. I figured that all horses don't like me and they also know that I don't like them. Well, he proceeded to put on a rodeo act, bucking up and down. After a half a dozen bucks, I caught him when he was coming up as I was going down. We met halfway and he flipped me out of the saddle in a somersault. I think I made a complete loop.

After I left the saddle I wound up kerplunk, on the ground, with my bow and my arrows flying all over. The damn horse took off on a dead run. I started feeling myself to determine if I had any broken bones. I saw Fred laying on the ground laughing his fool head off. He thought this was a great sport. Fred couldn't talk for about five minutes. I didn't think it was that hilarious. I'd have shot the damn hayburner if he hadn't run off.

We got the horses under control and took off across the stream. We spent the day in a biological desert—saw nothing!

Fred suggested that he and I take the motor boat down to the mouth of a stream. We took Bill Love and a big, strapping Canadian by the name of Rob Roy, who was sort of a roustabout helper in the camp. We tied the bow of the boat to the shore and got out. Rob Roy was to stay in the boat. Fred thought it would be wise to make a circle around the mouth downwind of the creek and hit the creek about a quarter of a mile up so that we wouldn't spook any bears.

This we did. Apparently, in the process the wind shifted and a bear caught our scent, and headed down the bank of the creek toward the boat. Rob Roy was really afraid of bears. The grizzly came out practically at the bow of the boat. Rob jumped in the boat and tried to push it off the shore, but he forgot that he had tied it up. The bear let out a "woof" and took off.

We didn't see any bears so we went back to the boat. Rob was out to the middle of the lake in the boat. We hollered at him to come in. He said, "If you guys want me to crap myself to death, just send me another one of those damn grizzlies down here!" He told us the story and Fred and I got a big kick out of it.

The next day I went with Fred up to the same area. We hadn't gone two-hundred yards when we could hear the splashing of a bear feeding on salmon around the next bend. We sneaked up, while the bear was looking for salmon in the middle of the shallow stream. Fred was about to release his arrow when he winded us. He started running up the creek, making lots of splashes and scattering the salmon.

Fred took a shot at him on the run. The arrow hit the bear between the eye and the ear on the right side of the skull. He was using a 72 pound bow, and the arrow penetrated the skull bone. The bear traveled about seventy-five yards and dropped on the edge of the stream.

Fred decided we had better wait awhile before approaching the grizzly so we walked back to the lake and sat in the boat. Fred remarked that a head shot is usually fatal. This was the best shot I'd ever seen—on the run at full speed. We returned in a half hour and skinned the grizzly for a life size mount.

Dick Mauch, Jack Lee, and I went up the creek the next day. It was Dick's turn for first shot, again. I was glad that I wasn't in Vegas. We ran into a big grizzly walking along the opposite bank of the creek—he was about a forty-yard shot. Dick shot at the bear first, I shot shortly afterwards, we both thought we'd hit the bear. We went across the creek and found Dick's arrow, showing no sign of blood. We then found a pool of blood where my arrow had hit the bear, but no arrow.

We trailed him through the thick brush. I wasn't too confident about the back-up equipment. Jack had a 97 Winchester shotgun, loaded with double "o" buckshot for the first shot. He then had a rifle slug and followed it with another double "o" buck. He claimed that was the best back-up gun there was. It might be, but I didn't like the way he carried it. He had a habit of carrying it by the barrel with the stalk of it in the air over his shoulder.

We trailed a good blood trail for a quarter of a mile. I thought that this was one time that we were really taking a chance. Had the bear jumped us in the brush, we'd have had a bad back-up situation. I found the arrow I'd lost earlier, one hundred yards down the trail and covered with blood. It started to get dark on us so we had to give it up for the day.

The next day, Bill and Jack announced that our supplies were getting very low and that the horses had eaten all the grass in the pasture. They suggested we go back to their house. I would have to give up on my grizzly. Dick, Bill and myself decided to take the canoe down the Kispiox

River and meet the boys who had gone by horseback the day before.

As we were floating down the river, we came to a big bend where a huge grizzly was standing in the middle of the stream. He was looking in the opposite direction. We picked up our bows. Dick was in front and I was in the middle. Bill tried to control the canoe in a real quiet fashion. We slid up to within twenty-five feet of the grizzly. Just then the grizzly turned and saw us and made a plunge for the shore. Dick and I both threw an arrow at him. I was in a bad position as the canoe turned and could not get full draw. The bear jumped in the brush and took off.

We met the guys that evening. They had already got the camp set up. In the morning we went back to the main camp at Stevens Lake. There was a good chance to pick up the grizzly that I hit, so we discussed going back to find my bear. We had scheduled a flight to pick us up from Smithers, but instead we had him fly us back to Swan Lake where we set up a new tent camp on the shore, not far from where I'd shot the bear.

We found a cache of five fifty-five-gallon drums of gas which came in real handy. Gas was a quick method for starting a fire in wet weather. We set up our tent on the edge of the lake, it was very cold and rainy. Fred had a little pup tent that he used to sleep in.

The next day when Fred, Jack and Bill went to pick up our boat, Dick Mauch and I amused ourselves by rigging up a television antenna. We fashioned a TV set out of an old crate. We got a kick out of Fred after dinner when he excused himself and said, "I'm going to the tent and watch TV for awhile before I go to sleep."

The following morning the weather cleared. Bill Love and I spent the whole day trying to find my wounded grizzly. So much rain had fallen that it was impossible to find a blood trail. It's a sickening feeling to have a lose trophy like this. Bill was sure the bear had died, but we couldn't find him.

We took the boats across the lake the next day. Bill, Dick, Chuck and myself were in one boat and Jack and

Fred in the other. Fred and Jack wanted to go down to the south end, so we went north to the opposite end. A good breeze was blowing, and we fashioned a sail out of a plastic drop cloth. It was tough rowing in the high waves and the sail helped us quite a bit. We didn't have a motor and this was a big lake, about four miles long.

We got halfway up the lake when we heard two shots. This was highly irregular. Fred, we figured, would never fire a shot with his 44 unless it was an emergency; so we turned the boat around and went back, quite concerned. The rubber raft was on an island just off the shore of the lake.

Somehow they had punctured a hole in it with a snag and it had started to sink. They were able to reach shore but thought they might need our help to give them transportation. We patched up the boat and continued on our way. They looked like they were standing in a large paper bag.

Fred, Dick, Jack and I decided to run up the creek late in the afternoon. We hadn't gone very far before we heard the familiar splashing sound of a grizzly catching salmon. We all crouched down as the noise became louder. Again it was Dick's turn to shoot.

A huge log about thirty inches wide lay across the stream. The six-foot root end was on our side of the stream making a perfect blind for Dick. Fred, Jack and I sat back to watch the show. Jack covered Dick with the shotgun and Fred with his camera. We watched the bear for fifteen minutes, catching and eating salmon. All of a sudden he jumped up the log and started across to our side.

Dick had to keep his head down, and in doing so he couldn't see the bear. The bear walked about half the length of the log and stopped, looking into the stream. He then continued on his way toward us. If he kept coming he would be nose-to-nose with Dick.

Nobody knew exactly what to do. It started out to be funny, but Fred sensed the danger that could develop in this situation. Fred flicked a stick, hitting Dick on the back. Dick slowly turned his head toward Fred, Jack and me. We were sitting on another log ten feet behind him.

Fred nodded, and Dick read the signal. He slowly raised up and saw the grizzly fifteen feet from him on the log broadside, looking down at the salmon. Just as he released the arrow, the bear saw him and plunged four feet down into the stream. Dick's arrow slid off his back. The bear ran into the brush and we all breathed a sigh of relief.

Dick, Bill and I took the boat up the lake to the creek mouth the next morning, and started up the creek. We didn't spot anything, so we decided to cut over a ridge and hit the lake shore. Bill thought there might be some bears in that area. About noon we reached the shoreline of a lake and decided to have lunch. I went east along the shoreline with my spinning rod and caught a few Dolly Varden trout. We fried the fish for lunch, took a little rest and headed back east toward our boat. We'd gone as far as the spot where I'd been fishing, when we came to thick brush that made it impossible to stay along the lakeshore, so we cut up over the top of the ridge and hit the creek again.

Bill was leading. He had a pack over his back containing our cooking equipment and his 270 rifle on a sling hanging across his shoulder. This territory is covered with thick moss, and it's very difficult to walk. There are rocks and logs and these are all covered with thick moss, also lots of devil's club, a real thorny, prickly type bush about five feet high.

It was a quiet afternoon, suddenly I heard a loud woofing noise behind me. I turned around to see a grizzly coming directly at us full bore. I made a giant step and hollered, "Watch it, Bill!" Bill didn't understand what I said. I got behind him. Bill still didn't understand what was going on, because he was looking up in the air. Dick jumped to the other side of him. Dick had a sixty-pound bow which he had quite a bit difficulty pulling back, but during the excitement, he managed to get arrow on the string and pulled it back so far that he pulled the string completely off the bow.

I hollered to Bill again. This time he saw the grizzly

coming. He whirled around, dropped into a sitting position and spun the rifle off his shoulder. By this time there were three bears coming. This was a sow strolling along the shoreline with her two cubs. Thank goodness we didn't intercept her down in the brush. She had apparently come out of the thick brush, looked up and either heard us or saw us on the side of the ridge. She made a whoop for her cubs, and when she didn't get an answer, she charged us.

Bill shot her at twenty feet, coming full bore. Her mouth was open, she was snarling and huffing. This had to be one of the most exciting times I ever spent in the woods, with a grizzly and two cubs bearing down on us like that. Thank God for Bill.

Fortunately for us, she had to come uphill to get us. She couldn't come as fast uphill as if she had been on ground level. She was tearing huge plate-size chunks of moss out with her paws as she dodged through the brush charging us. Bill had to dodge back and forth between the trees in order to get a clean shot. As he fired, the bear dropped and slid about ten feet from us. Both of the cubs kept on coming, knashing their teeth, like Mama. I had a full draw on one of them. At six feet, I thought he was ready to climb my frame. They were probably two-hundred pound, year-old bears. I was puzzled when Bill hollered, "Don't shoot!" The bears heard him shout they whirled and took off. Thank God!

The sow tried to get up and Bill shot her again. Needless to say, we were all panting to catch our breath and ready to clean out our drawers. In a apologetic soft voice Bill said, "I really don't think she would have stopped." Dick and I could have kissed him. We skinned the bear for a rug mount for Bill to show our appreciation because he saved our lives. Since this harrowing experience, I no longer believe in the story *Goldilocks and the Three Bears.*

Fred and Jack had heard the shots and returned to see what was wrong. Fred was quite shaken by the bear story about our life or death experience.

The next day, I decided to do something a little less

exciting, like fishing. I went up the Kispiox River to a deep hole. I had a deep sea fishing rod with a twenty-pound test monofilament line on it. I hung into a huge fish, right on the bend, and fought him for a half an hour. He made runs down towards a big log jam, but I was able to turn him around. He made several leaps. I thought it was a big king salmon.

They catch kings here up to a hundred pounds in nets. Indians at Smithers trapped some eighty to ninty pounders this fall. I was surprised to see, when I got him in shallow water, that it was a steelhead. I didn't have a landing net and had to spend time wearing him out. I had slid him up the beach. He weighed twenty-eight pounds, six ounces and was forty-one inches long.

We went back to Vancouver the following day, where I managed to lose all my fishing tackle at the airport. Fred, remembering that I had done this same trick on one of our polar bear hunts, cautioned me to never get my gear mixed in with his because he figured it would be a goner for sure.

This had been a hair-raising hunt. Dick and I were very fortunate to have had a very competent guide who was cool enough to handle a situation like this. Thank God for Bill.

VII

Ontario Black Bear Hunt 1963

In the spring of 1963 I told Fred about my bear hunting trip in Ontario, Canada. He seemed quite interested as I explained the layout to him. I showed him a map of the area, now known as Lakehead, which lies twenty some miles east of Fort William at the west end of Lake Superior. My hunting spot is a peninsula that juts out into Lake Superior from the north, and was, at that time, loaded with black bears. The previous year I had seen a number of large black bears and was fortunate to take one with my bow. My son Rick had also taken one that year with his rifle. I knew that Fred wanted to get a large black bear for his museum, so it didn't take much persuasion on my part to convince Fred that we should organize a hunt up there in the spring.

Fred invited Knick Knickerbacher from Crozet, Virginia, a previous hunting companion of his, and Dick Mauch, a salesman and stockholder in Fred's company, from Bassett, Nebraska.

I arranged to pick Fred up at Grayling, and arrived

there about 4:00 A.M. I had left my home in Charlotte about midnight. Knick had flown in from Virginia, and they were waiting for me. We headed for the airport at the Canadian Soo to catch a flight across Lake Superior to Port Arthur. Just at the break of dawn, near Vanderbilt, we spotted a small herd of elk along the side of the highway. These animals had only recently been introduced into Michigan.

We left the car at Sault St. Marie and caught our flight to Port Arthur. There we rented a car and found a motel, we made our headquarters and waited for Dick Mauch, who was supposed to fly in with his own plane the next day. However, the weather the next two days was so foggy and rainy that he gave up on flying. During the time we were waiting for him, we snooped around the town and checked out the sporting goods stores, got our licenses, and made preparations to leave as soon as Dick joined us. We also did a little fishing in the creeks that dumped in nearby Fort William and caught a few rainbows. Dick arrived the next day.

At last the weather improved. We chartered a couple of float planes and flew to the little peninsula where we planned to do our bear hunting. The terrain was rocky with lots of undergrowth, there were many open, grassy spots on the tops of the ridges. Trees were sparse, but altogether it made an ideal area in which to sneak hunt. Ridges in the area rose three to four hundred feet above the water. During my previous hunt there I had seen six black bears, at the same time, feeding on grass within half a mile of me. For some reason the bears took a liking to the tender shoots of the first grass of spring. Fred and Dick took off first.

Knick and I took the second flight out. As we landed and taxied the plane up to shore, the pilot found that he was not able to get close enough without stepping out in the shallow water. Knick made a fuss with me for not telling him to bring a pair of boots.

Somehow we got the gear unloaded, but Knick got his feet wet which he blamed on me. He started off mumbling with Fred around the south end of the point as Fred's plane took off for Fort William.

My pilot taxied Dick and I up to a sandbar on a little

island in a narrow neck of the bay and let us off. It was the only sandy place that he could slide the floats on. We had to shed our clothes and wade to an island in the cold water holding all the gear above our heads as we crossed a stretch of deep water chest high. Lake Superior is cool this time of year.

After drying off, we put our clothes back on, and proceeded to sneak up on a rocky ridge where we spotted a nice black bear after about a half hour hunt. Dick pulled a sneak on him, but he spooked. We spent several hours giving the peninsula a complete go over with no success. At five o'clock we returned to the sandbar and waited for our pilot to pick us up.

We taxied over to the place where we had left Knick and Fred. They were sitting huddled beside a campfire. They had both seen bears but were unable to get a shot at them. Fred was real excited about our hunting spot, and wanted to make camp and spend the night there. The pilot had a pup tent in the plane which we tossed out for him, along with a sleeping bag. He had no food, but was well supplied with water. We gave him what heavy clothes we had, wished him well and took off for Fort William, planning to return for him the next morning.

Knick, Dick and I took in a movie that evening to help pass some time. Dick and I bought a box of popcorn, when we started chomping on it, Knick got up and moved to the other side of the theater in complete disgust.

The next morning the weather didn't look too promising, and Knick decided to stay at the motel. Dick and I went down to the plane where our pilot was waiting for us. We took off in very low cloud cover and headed out over the lake.

As we approached the peninsula, we saw a huge puff of white smoke streaking up in the sky. I pointed it out to the pilot and said, "Hey! There's Fred's camp." We made a low pass over the campfire and spotted Fred standing near it trying to keep warm. A respectable sized bear hide was stretched on a rack nearby. We landed and taxied up to the shore.

Fred was real pleased with his take. He told us it was quite exciting, he was a little concerned when he shot the bear. He had come upon him unexpectedly and was closer than he really wanted to be. The bear was looking at him when Fred shot him, he let out a loud, snarling growl. With no backup, Fred said this was a tense situation. Fortunately the bear whirled and ran into the brush. Fred found him dead at one hundred yards, just before dark.

Fred flew back to Fort William with his bear. Dick and I planned to spend the day on the peninsula, having arranged for the pilot to pick us up shortly before dark. It was an exciting hunt, sneaking around on the rocks and ledges, looking for bears. About 2 P.M., Dick got within thirty yards of a good sized bear and scored a hit. We had tracked him for two hundred yards when the blood trail dried up. It was just a flesh wound, we never saw the bear again. During the afternoon, we sighted four more bears, but couldn't get close enough for a shot.

The pilot picked us up about 7 P.M. and took us back to Fort William. While we were having our sundowners in Knick's room, Fred brought in the bear hide from the car to show to Knick. He stretched it out on the floor and was petting it when Knick began to give Fred the business.

He started with, "Fred, why in hell did you stay out there and leave the rest of us here? I thought we came up here to have a good time hunting together, then you stay out on that island and leave the rest of us to entertain our-selves!"

With this blast of hostility, Fred scooped up his bear hide and with flushed face, left the room without a word. A cool hush hung in the air.

I went back to Fred's room. The first thing Fred said was, "Bob, would you run me out to the airport at 8 A.M. tomorrow morning?" He followed this with, "I don't care if I ever see Knick again." He left the next day without good-byes to Knick.

In all my experience with Fred this was the first time I had ever seen him mad. I felt real bad about the "blowup" and thought I should try to patch things up, if at all possible.

Fred arranged to have the annual stockholders meeting upon our return to Grayling at the plant. Knick was the guy who put up the money for Fred's factory in Grayling in the early 40s. Knick has told Fred that if he'd move out of Detroit and go upstate somewhere, he would stake him. Knick was the largest shareholder in the company next to Fred. Both Knick and I were on the Board of Directors, and Knick had been friends with Fred for many years. I thought that if I could talk Knick into going fishing with me for a few days, maybe it would smooth things out a little and he might go back with me to the stockholders meeting. Knick is an avid fisherman, fortunately he took me up on my offer.

We chartered a 180 on floats to take us to the Albany River, which is about two hundred and fifty miles north of Fort William. We went down to the plane at the agreed time and started to load the gear. Knick was eyeballing the airplane and asked the pilot if he had topped the tanks, the pilot assured him that he did. Then Knick quizzed him about the oil, but the pilot hadn't gotten around to that yet. This disturbed Knick a bit. Knick has had a long background of flying experience himself. He used to fly the mail from Denver to San Francisco across the Rocky Mountains back in the 20s. He told me he had walked away from two airplane crashes in the past. I guess he had a good right to be a little jumpy, and he didn't quite trust anybody else at the stick.

Knick got in front with the pilot, I sat in back with the gear. All seemed well as we taxied down the river to get enough run for our take-off, the current was strong. The pilot gunned the throttle in an attempt to spin the plane around quickly to head into the wind. The current proved to be too swift, we slid across the stream toward a huge growth of alder brush. Before the pilot could cut the engine, the prop chewed up the brush like a buzz saw, pieces of leaves and sticks flew all over, landing on the windshield, floats, and tangled in the struts. This just about did Knick in.

The pilot killed the engine, but the prop was still fanning as we slid to a stop. The current was gyrating the plane around in a circular motion down the stream. We were heading towards a huge log jam. Getting the floats stuck in that would be disastrous!

Quick to size up the situation, the pilot started the engine, opened the throttle and spun the plane around, heading it up the river. We thought he would stop to take the brush off, but he gave it full throttle, and we roared up the river, lifted off the water, shedding leaves, sticks and brush as we became airborne. Knick was white and speechless, so was I.

About halfway to our destination we ran into a blinding blizzard. This was very unusual for the month of June. Knick uttered, "Why in hell am I up here in this God forsaken place?" As we progressed further, the ground became covered with snow, we could see many moose tracks. By this time Knick was a nervous wreck. Ten miles before reaching our destination, we flew out of the storm, it was clear when we landed on the Albany River at the commercial fishing camp operated by Superior Airways.

There were several cabins and a large log lodge. Brian Maxwell had managed this camp for many years. He had a supply shop in an old log shed in back that served as a store where he traded with the Indians. They would come in, pick up their supplies for the fall season, and he would charge them to their accounts. Later that fall they would come back with their furs and balance their accounts.

There was an abundance of walleyes, northern pike, speckled trout and some sturgeon in the area. I was looking forward to some good brook trout fishing.

We taxied into camp and noticed a number of plastic jugs floating in the lake, they were set lines for sturgeon. Early the next morning I tagged along with an Indian who was going out to lift his lines, as I wanted to take some pictures. We chased jugs for half an hour, he brought in four sturgeon that were anywhere from forty to seventy pounds each. He shipped the fish and caviar to New York.

We decided to take a trip over to a favorite spot of mine

where I had taken some sizeable speckled trout over the past few years. We lashed a huge, freighter type canoe onto the floats of the plane. This gave Knick some more shakes. We arrived at the lake, taxied to our destination at the mouth of a small river that flowed into it, and started fishing. About the third cast, Knick tied into a good speckle trout. After a ten minute struggle, he netted a beautiful four and a half pound brookie. This settled his nerves a little bit. I thought he should be a bit more excited than he was, but he's used to battling Atlantic salmon in Scotland and bill fishing in Nassau and didn't get too turned on with his big brook trout.

We fished the better part of the day, catching several speckled trout and northerns. The pilot picked us up about 6 P.M. and took us back to the lodge. After dinner we went fishing on the lake and must have caught over fifty walleyes.

Then the rain set in. It rained for two days and the size of the cabin got smaller and smaller. I was locked in with a very unhappy Knick, listening to his complaints and sputters. His favorite pastime was peeking out the windows and saying, "This f——ing weather!" We did, however, have some super meals of fried fish, etc., at the lodge, and thank God the Scotch supply held out. The weather broke the next day and Knick ordered the pilot to get us the hell out of there.

From Fort Williams we took Air Canada back to the Soo where I had left my car. I talked Knick into going to the meeting, hoping that when we all got together in Grayling things would simmer down. It was a cool meeting. It took a couple of years to smooth over our bear hunt. Several years later they patched things up and Fred asked Knick to go to Africa with us.

A few years after this hunt, Fred sold out the business to Victor Comptometer, a larger company. Knick was not in favor of the sale and I'm sure will always condemn Fred for it. I was on Fred's side. The sale turned out to be the kiss of Death! Brief details about the sale are in chapter 19.

VIII

Michigan Whitetails, Geese and Bears 1963

In 1963 I received an invitation to go to the upper peninsula of Michigan to Blaney Hunting Lodge and be part of Fred's Chowder and Marching Society, as they were known. This was a select group of a dozen fellows who met over a number of years at this spot to hunt deer. All were bow hunters.

Michigan takes on its golden hue in October. It's a beautiful time; the colors of the upper peninsula's maples and aspens are gorgeous. The other fellows arrived a day ahead of me.

Blaney is a large piece of real estate. It covers twenty-two thousand acres, located seventy-five miles west of the Mackinac Bridge. Blaney operated as a hardwood lumbering complex for many years. It was owned by Stuart Earl and his brother who ran it as a recreational facility. For twenty-five years I took my family there during the sum-

123

mertime for a week's vacation. It was an ideal spot to take children, as they had poolside supervision and horseback riding. Mom and Dad could play golf and go fishing. They had a huge dining room and recreation building for parties, bingo, and dances. It had the reputation of being the best place to eat in the Upper Peninsula. There was a great bar and daily smorgasbords. Blaney has an air strip, and about fifteen houses on the main road as well as a hotel, swimming pool, tennis courts, golf course and many trails throughout the wooded area. A real fun place.

Blaney was also a famous deer hunting spot. This was also where Fred met his wife, Henrietta, some twenty years earlier, when she was a receptionist.

At their other complex, twenty miles east of Blaney, there were eleven-thousand acres known as Simmons Woods, where you could catch your limit of large brook trout on every trip. Blaney guests were given permission to fish at Simmons Woods.

I arrived at Blaney just in time for cocktails. The party was gathering steam in one of the large houses on the west side of the road. The hunters stayed in the houses located on the main highway, but we ate at the large lodge across the road. Stuart's son Bill was our host and hunt supervisor. The group was made up of fellows from various parts of the United States and all walks of life. One fellow was a professional football player, another one was a doctor, and one was a disc jockey from Detroit. He knew every story that was ever told in the Detroit area on the night club circuit, and kept us highly entertained.

We had one fellow who couldn't stand the mirth and wet his pants during one of these fun sessions. After the cocktail party, we adjourned to the huge lodge for dinner. The table was set near the fireplace at the end of the lodge. A big fire roared and snapped to add to the warmth of the occasion.

The first order of business was to drink a toast of sparkling champagne which was served in beautiful glass goblets. Our leader then turned and threw his glass against the fireplace, breaking it into thousands of pieces. At this moment, the manager walked in and made a bee-line for our table. Her name was Miss Webber. She was built like Paul Bunyan and could have whipped any man in our group. Also, we would have been fighting out of our weight class. We didn't know whether to stay or run at this point. The leader offered to pay for the glass, and this smoothed things over.

After a feast of venison, provided by one of the hunters, they had a fun fest. Fred made my formal introduction as I was new to the group. Of course I had to make an acceptance speech of some sort. Having known Fred for many years, I was aware how he enjoyed putting me on the spot. I had given this considerable thought on the trip up, and felt that I had come up with a pretty good way to defend myself.

I had purchased a scarlet satin vest, like the rifle hunters wear. My wife sewed silver bells on the bottom of it, to make it the noisiest thing a person could possibly wear.

I addressed the group, telling them I felt that as we were amateurs competing with a professional that there should be some sort of a handicap system devised to make the odds even. I presented the vest to Fred which he accepted graciously. I suggested that he wear it while hunting. The group heartily agreed. Fred said he would do so, and added that he would also like to bet me $20 that he would bring in a deer the next day. Well, I couldn't wait to get my $20 out. We placed the money on the fireplace mantle. This, I thought, was a lead-pipe-cinch bet if he had to wear that ridiculous thing.

The next morning we got up before daylight and made hurried preparations so we could head to our special spots. Fred suggested that I go along with him. At daylight he looked for signs around the ground near his blind. Much to my surprise, he found a blood trail. I soon discovered that I had been suckered into the bet. When he made the bet he had neglected to mention the fact that he had hit a deer just before dark. It looked like a cinch for him to win the bet.

We followed the blood trail, and I tried to make him believe I was trying hard to locate the blood trail. We trailed it for about two hundred yards and found to our surprise that someone had dressed the deer and taken it. We never learned who it was.

That evening Fred took Knickerbocker and me to a spot where Bill Earl had placed some bear bait. Fred left us and drove to his blind. I left Knick and went up the trail about a quarter of a mile, each of us sitting there till dark. Finally, I saw the headlights of Fred's car. He picked me up, then we went down to Knick. Knick was boiling mad because Fred was a little late, he chewed Fred out for not getting there earlier. But Knick had seen two bears and that took a little tension off the situation. He didn't get any shots, however, as they were too far away.

Again that evening we had our regular cocktail program at the house and then adjourned across the road for our dinner. Before we sat down, Fred rang a bell and said that he had a little presentation to make. I knew that Fred was going to come up with something for losing the bet.

Fred called for the chef. The chef made his entrance carrying a large serving tray. On it he had twenty crisp, one dollar bills, all crunched up like lettuce, in a huge salad bowl with mayonnaise, pineapple and all kinds of fancy fixings. Fred said, "Here, you won the damn bet, now let's see you eat it!"

The next day I went hunting with Nels Grumley, who was Fred's leading bowyer back in the days when they actually whittled bows from a stick of osage orange yew or hickory. Nels had the reputation of being quite a bow hunter, and I welcomed the opportunity to go with him. We drove down to the shore of Lake Michigan and decided to sneak hunt in the sand dunes and stay together along the beach. There were a series of rolling sand dunes built up from the surf over the years. They were covered with spruce and pines. We had been told that this was an excellent area to hunt because in the evening the deer come down to the water to drink.

The east wind was blowing fairly strong so we walked

directly into it. This was an ideal spot for sneak hunting. I took the shoreline route closest to the lake and Nels was about fifty yards to my left, back in the spruce trees. We moved slowly and kept each other in sight so that we could sneak on a deer if we saw one.

I went about a third of a mile in this fashion—walking a little bit, then stopping, walking and stopping—up and down over the sand dunes, some of which were thirty feet high. As I topped one of them I looked down into the bottom of the dune, thunderstruck to see a nice six-point buck standing with its head down, broadside, feeding. He couldn't have been over twenty yards from me.

Luckily it hadn't winded me or seen me. However, as I drew my sixty-pound bow back to take a shot, the buck raised up and looked me straight in the eye. He had detected a movement out of the corner of his eye. His eyes looked as large as golf balls. This prompted a hurried shot which resulted in the arrow sliding just over the top of his back. He whirled and ran in a flash. I looked to my left and saw Nels standing there watching the while thing with a grin on his face.

The buck, apparently not having winded me, was not totally spooked and he stopped about seventy-five yards away and looked back my way. I crouched down and remained motionless, so I don't think he saw me. Nels began making a bleating noise like a young doe. I didn't know exactly what was going on at the moment and I guess the buck didn't either, because he started walking back in our direction.

I remained in a crouched position and watched as the buck worked his way towards Nels' calls. Nels actually called the buck to within good shooting distance. When the buck was thirty yards away, he turned and gave Nels a good side exposure. Nels was known as a snap shooter. When he shot an arrow off a bow, he pulled it back quickly and as soon as his hand hit his cheeks the arrow was gone.

Nels took his snap shot at the buck and missed, the same as I did. I went over and congratulated him on his deer calling, and we congratulated each other on our good

shooting. That's really the best part of bow hunting anyway, regardless of whether or not you get the deer. It gives
you a good feeling to outsmart the critter in his own environment.

We went back to the lodge and had our evening cocktail party, along with wild tales of the day's hunt. Knick got
to talking about the fact that we ought to have better bear
bait. Fred said that the next day we'd go to Manistique, a
town twenty-five miles to the west, and buy some goodies
for the bears.

We took Knick's car the next morning and drove into
town. As we approached the outskirts of the town we
noticed a deer walking across the pavement in front of us.
We slowed down and saw that it was a huge buck, with
either an eight or ten point spread. We also noticed something that looked like blood, coming down the side of the
deer's neck. It turned out to be a red ribbon with a bell on
it, and we later learned the deer was the town's pet. To keep
hunters from shooting it, the townspeople tied the ribbon
and bell on him. They pen this deer up each year during
the rifle season so that he doesn't get shot. Later that fall
I read that some characters broke into the fenced area and
shot it.

Knick bought all kinds of goodies for bear feed—
sweets, molasses, brown sugar, marshmallows, Karo
syrup, you name it! Anything that sounded good to the
guy's sweet tooth went in the box. Knick spent about $25
for the bait. Fred and I took a stroll down the street while
he finished his shopping.

That fall was an election year. One of the old store
buildings near where we parked was the democratic headquarters. Fred and I thought we'd have a little fun with
Knick—Knick is a staunch Republican. We went in and
picked up a bumper sticker. When Knick wasn't watching,
we put it on the back bumper of his car. He saw this when
we got back to Blaney, raised holy hell and gave Fred and
me a good chewing.

We set out the bait for Knick's bear. He spent two

nights waiting, but apparently the bears didn't have a sweet tooth or had left for the winter.

The next afternoon, Bill Earl volunteered to take Fred and me out with him and place us in our blinds for the evening hunt. He said he knew a couple of good spots. We hopped in his car and headed for the hot buck area. About a half mile north of the main camp there is a little lake on the left hand side of the road. As we passed this lake I noticed a flock of Canada geese swimming out in the middle. I remarked to Bill that I'd rather shoot one of those than a deer. I had never been too successful in shooting Canada geese. So he spun the car around in the road, we went back to the lodge and got a shotgun for me. Bill dropped me off near the edge of the lake and I proceeded to stalk geese.

I got pretty wet going through the swampy area. I crawled on my hands and knees, fearful of frightening the flock. I waited there for twenty minutes, hoping they would come closer, but they never did. About the time I was ready to leave, the geese picked up, flew across the lake and landed on the air strip which was right in back of the lodge. I took off around the west side of the lake in hopes of sneaking up on them. This time I was able to get closer, but there was no place for me to hide, only the high grade at the end of the runway where it had been bulldozed. I carefully peeked over and could see the geese some seventy-five yards away.

Pondering the situation I concluded that the only chance I had was to jump up and run at them as fast as I could, hoping to get close enough for a shot. This I did, and gave them three of my best shots as they burst into the air. One of them dropped. I don't know if it was the one I was aiming at or not, but anyway, I got a nice fat gander.

I took it back to the camp and when the boys came in from hunting, I was proudly plucking my goose. When Bill asked how close I got to the geese, I told him I'd made a beautiful stalk through the swamp. He laughed, and said, "Well, Bob, I hate to tell you this, but those are Dr. Christopherson's pet geese."

Dr. Christopherson, a naturalist, was an interesting, elderly gentleman in his 80s and keeper of the ducks and geese at T Lake, about three miles off the main road. He lived in a cabin and watched over the wildlife—a real outdoor person. Then Bill said, "If you had just stood up and said, 'Wa, Wa, Wa Wa,' these geese would have swum right up to you. That's how Dr. Christopherson feeds them. He calls them by saying 'Wa Wa'." This is the Indian name for goose. The geese come right up to him and he feeds them corn out of his hands.

This goose hunt was now a problem for me. Fred thought that, in fairness to Dr. Christopherson who loathed anyone who would ever shoot one of his birds, he should be invited over for the goose dinner. Fred would have invited him over just to see me squirm. I lived in constant fear the next day, wondering whether Fred was going to bring the good doctor for dinner. I was quite relieved when he finally backed down.

That evening, during the cocktail hour, Fred told a story about Dr. Christopherson and himself that he claimed was true. It seems that workers at one of the lodges would pick Dr. Christopherson up, and bring him over to the lodge for dinner. Dr. Christopherson was a dignified, somewhat serious and handsome man, with a full snow white beard. He looked something like Santa Claus. He always dressed for dinner in a dapper suit, white shirt and tie.

One evening the doctor came over to Fred's table and told him that a squirrel had been bothering his song birds. He didn't know what he was going to do about the situation. Fred said, "Do you have a live trap? You could trap the squirrel without harming him." The doctor said, "Yes, I do." "Well," said Fred, "You trap him, and I'll come over tomorrow morning and pick him up. I've got to go several miles north of here, and I'll take the squirrel with me and turn him loose there."

That pleased the doctor very much, so Fred went over the next morning and sure enough, the squirrel had managed to eat his way into the trap. Fred took the trap and headed for town. He took the squirrel about halfway to the gate, which is a mile, and let him out of the cage.

In the evening the doctor came in at the regular time for his dinner, Fred was sitting at his favorite table. Dr. Christopherson came over and said, "Fred, where did you take that squirrel?" Fred responded, "I took him about halfway to Germfask." This is a small town about ten miles from Blaney. "Well," said the doctor, "Would you believe it, that squirrel's back?" Fred said, "No, that can't be the same squirrel! You must have another squirrel." "No," the doctor said, "I'm sure it's the same squirrel. It's got a white mark on his left ear." Fred said, "I can't believe that! But I'm going in to Manistique tomorrow. If you catch him again, I'll swing by and take him there. That'll get rid of him for sure." After dinner, Fred drove the doctor back to his cabin at T Lake.

The next morning Fred went to check on the squirrel. Sure enough, the doctor had caught it again. This time Fred took him all the way to the gate and let him out. At dinner the same conversation occurred. The doctor came over to Fred's table and asked, "Fred, where'd you take that squirrel?" Fred said, "Why, I took him about halfway to Manistique!" And the doctor replied, "Would you believe that squirrel is back again?"

Fred said it was all he could do to contain himself, but in a serious vein he said, "I can't believe that! This has got to be another squirrel." But Dr. Christopherson said, "No, it's the same squirrel, he's got a white spot on the left ear!" "Listen Doctor," Fred said, "You catch him one more time and I guarantee you'll never see that squirrel again." Fred promised he would take the squirrel to Manistique the next day and get rid of him for good. "Well," said the doctor, "We'll give it one more try." The squirrel was in the trap the next morning and Fred loaded him in the trunk. This time he took the squirrel just a little bit further, outside the gate, and again the squirrel scampered home to the good doctor.

That evening at dinner, Dr. Christopherson came up to Fred's table and said in a rather stern voice, "Fred, I don't care where you took that squirrel, but he's back, and I think he likes me, and I'm going to keep him."

We vowed the next evening, before we left camp, that we'd all return the next year, the same time, the same place. I don't know what happened but the group never got back to "good old" Blaney again. This was a sad ending for a bunch of fellows who came from all over the United States to spend a few days together, swapping yarns, jokes, and hunting together.

Fred did quite a bit of hunting at Blaney prior to the group going up there. He took several nice bucks back in the 30s while hunting with Jack Van Couvering, then the outdoor editor of the *Detroit Free Press*.

Two years later, Charlie Berthune, manager of the resort complex told me that there were lots of bear around that summer. I mentioned this to my good friend, Jerry Anderson, from Grand Ledge, who owns the Anderson Archery business in the central part of the lower peninsula. He wanted to make a film with "Michigan Outdoors," a popular sports TV program featuring hunting and fishing throughout the state. At that time it was hosted by Mort Neff. Jerry convinced Mort to send his cameraman, Gene Little, with Jerry to make a movie for the television show, showing the shooting of a black bear with a bow and arrow.

Jerry spent two or three days up north and was successful in killing a nice bear. The film was shown on the TV show several times. During the course of this hunt he saw a huge bear, much larger than the one that he got, but he wasn't able to get a shot at it. He told me about this, and I related it to Fred, asking him if he would be interested in going up and trying for this monster. Charlie Berthune thought the bear probably could go in the five hundred pound class.

On display at Fred's museum in Grayling, were a life-sized polar bear, grizzly and an Alaskan Brown bear. But, he didn't have a large black bear. So Fred was really enthused about trying for this big bear. He would have it mounted life-size and put in his museum with the others.

I drove to Grayling and picked up Fred one afternoon

and we continued on to Blaney. The lodge was closed so we stayed with Charlie, at his house. Charlie told us of many bouts he had had with bears during the summer.

Blaney is a very popular place for rifle hunting in November. Local guides take you hunting for a fee. The guide takes you out, places you in one of the blinds, picks you up for lunch, and takes you back for the evening hunt. If you shot a deer they would dress it out and drag it in for you.

Fred, Charlie, and I went out the next morning and scouted the area to find out if we could locate the tracks of this huge bear. Charlie baited a spot near a swamp some two miles north where the bear had been seen and we combed the area. We built a small blind out of brush near a spot where the bear had been clawing the wild cherry trees. We spent that evening, sitting, killing mosquitoes and saw absolutely nothing.

Fred wasn't really satisfied with the blind, and felt he could improve on it. He asked Charlie if he had any boards and nails. Charlie fixed us up with all the essentials the next morning. Fred and I went back and cased the area where he wanted to build the blind. I was the carpenter's helper and stayed on the ground, passing boards to Fred, cutting them off at the proper length.

Satisfied with his carpentry job—there was a little perch on a fallen limb—we went back to the lodge for lunch. We came out much earlier that afternoon, about 3:30, hoping we'd get there in plenty of time and carefully walked in so we wouldn't disturb the bear. Fred wanted to get a movie of him shooting it, so I took his camera. He selected the only tree in the area that I could climb that would be high enough to have a good view of the action and avoid giving off any scent.

It was a beautiful sunny afternoon, warm for that time of the year. We had sat there for probably an hour. The ground was covered with dry, brown ferns, two to three feet high. They were so thick that when you were up in the tree you could hardly see the ground.

I was sitting, looking to my left, when I heard an awful

crash to my right. I turned and looked, but not quick enough to catch the action. I looked at the fallen tree where Fred was supposed to be, but there was nothing there. No Fred, and no platform. All I could see were the ferns quivering down at the base of the fallen tree limbs.

I scurried down from my perch as fast as I could and ran over, thinking that I might find Fred in a painful condition with broken bones.

Fred was sprawled out with boards laying across him. I asked if he was hurt. He rubbed himself and said, "Gosh, I don't know." I picked the boards off him, he sat up and felt himself in several spots. The spill could have been serious as hell but we both burst out laughing. I told him it was an honor to hunt with the world's best bow hunter, as well as the world's worst carpenter.

We nixed the idea of rebuilding the blind and picked out a different spot and sat there till dark. Just before dark a small bear came along but Fred wouldn't shoot it because he wanted the big one.

That evening Fred got a call from home, saying he should get back to the factory on some urgent business. So the next morning we took off for Grayling. As things turned out, I guess it was just as well. Fred and I had pledged to stay there for a week or two to get that big bear, but we later learned from Charlie that the big bear was never seen again that fall.

IX

African Bow Safari 1965

In 1965 I joined Fred on a bow hunting trip to Mozambique, Africa. A trip of this magnitude involves a little more than a visit to your local banker, and I was indeed fortunate to have a coach like Fred, who had learned how to sift through all the red tape on his previous hunt there the year before.

Fred gave me all the information I needed in order to apply for my passport and visa and to meet medical requirements. He also made arrangements for tickets and reservations for all the members of the group. Even so, it still took nearly a year to make all the trip arrangements. It takes time to get passports and visas in order, and to get the required shots to guard against some African disease. If it had not been for Fred's assistance with the details, I might have given up the trip and stayed home.

The members of this hunting expedition included Bob Halmi, film director; Zoli Vidor, photographer; Jim Crow, writer and Outdoor Editor of *The Detroit News*; Knick

Knickerback from Virginia; Bill Wright from San Francisco; and Dick Mauch from Nebraska.

Fred suggested that everyone purchase a Browning 375 magnum rifle with the same type of peep sight. This was a smart idea as we might be changing hunting partners and vehicles. Regardless of which Toyota we were in, and if we grabbed the wrong gun, the gun would be the same and so would the ammunition. After all, our wives did expect us to return, this would be good insurance and was practical.

On Fred's previous hunt, they filmed the hunting of different African animal species starring Fred and his friend, Arthur Godfrey, in the film. But he had wanted to get a Cape buffalo, which he was unable to do. So this trip he wanted to make a movie of his attempt to hunt Cape buffalo.

In June we all met in New York the day before the flight of the first leg of our journey. Here I met Bill Wright for the first time. Bill was my roommate for the night. His desire for the hunt was to shoot an elephant with a bow. Bill, I would say, was about 5 foot 8 inches tall, but very muscular and stocky. He had worked out with weights the preceding year, to build himself up in preparation for using the one hundred and twenty-pound bow that Fred made for him.

Bill was curious to see what I was using for the shoot, so I took one of my bows out of its case and strung it up. It was a sixty-pound Bear super magnum. He pulled the string with the greatest of ease and jokingly remarked, "Do you think you can kill anything with this little bow?" Then he said, "Let me see your other bow." So we strung that one up too, and darned if he didn't take both bows and pull them back together to full draw. I have difficulty just getting the sixty pounder back. He was a Paul Bunyan of a man!

Bob Halmi, our director and camera man, arranged a dinner party for us at Barbara and Spearo Scourses' apartment on Fifth Avenue. They were strongly involved with 20th Century Fox movies in Hollywood. They were going on a safari at the same time we were and were going to hunt out of the same camp. This was my first chance to peak over the velvet curtain of New York's Fifth Avenue society. It was gorgeous, gracious and exciting.

The next day we limoed to the LaGuardia Airport and were ushered into the VIP suite by the Chief Director of Alitalia Airlines.

We took off at 7:00 p.m. in a plane so loaded it used practically all the runway to get off the ground. Fred and I sat together during the flight to Rome. It was an indescribable feeling to fly above the clouds over the ocean, sitting next to the world's greatest bow hunter, on my way to a thirty-day safari. Plus, Fred planned a trip around the world on return. How fortunate I was to have such an experience. Many hunters would give anything to take my place.

We arrived in Rome and were met by the manager of Alitalia Airlines. He hustled us through customs ahead of the other passengers, vouching for us and assuring us he would take care of the luggage. A limousine was waiting to take us to the hotel where Halmi had arranged for a suite of rooms. Bob had been there a dozen times before and he said, it seemed that everywhere he went—in hotels or shopping—everyone knew him. He seemed to be right at home. The hotel manager met him with open arms and personally escorted us to our rooms, a plush suite overlooking the street. Little sidewalk cafés lined the street below. The balcony offered a beautiful view of the city. Large baskets of flowers and huge bowls of fruit had been placed in the rooms in anticipation of our arrival.

The next morning Fred, Halmi and I went for an early walk before breakfast. We bumped into a movie set in operation and watched for awhile as they did their filming. After breakfast we went shopping with Bob. Again, he was met with a jovial welcome at every shop where we stopped. He made arrangements for us to make a little tour of Rome, but cautioned us that we should not get out of the car as we didn't have enough time.

Bill Wright, Dick Mauch and I took advantage of the tour. A big Cadillac limo picked us up and drove us around Rome for a couple of hours so we could see the sights.

This, of course, is not really enough time, but we took pictures so we could enjoy a more leisurely tour upon our return home. I think we set a record by taking in most of the sights of Rome in two hours.

We checked out of the hotel that evening, and were waiting for the limousines to pick us up when Fred was presented with the bill. We thought he was going to fall over when he looked at it, the bill was over $750. A little discussion followed. Fred learned that Halmi requested all the special favors. Fred was more than a little irritated that the bill was so high.

We arrived in Athens about midnight, and wanted to stretch our legs after the long flight, so we went into the terminal. Returning to the plane, Fred, Knick and I sat down in the seats reserved for us, side-by-side.

Two ladies got on and sat down in the last seats available in the front of the plane. Shortly thereafter, two men got on and found the ladies in their seats. They informed the ladies, in a courteous manner, that the seats belonged to them, but the ladies wouldn't budge. There were still two seats in the rear but they did not want to sit in those. Quite a disturbance ensued. Passengers who had been dozing were awakened. The talk got louder and louder, until the steward finally told the ladies that if they didn't take the rear seats he would call the captain, which he finally did. The captain told them they would have to take the rear seats or leave the plane.

This disturbed the ladies greatly, they jumped up and stomped to the back of the plane. As they passed us, Knick broke the silence by shouting out, "You ugly Americans, if you don't like this, why don't you buy your own dammed airplane?" Fred and I slid down in our seats so, hopefully, we wouldn't be identified as the culprit who made that remark. However, a round of applause followed Knick's comment.

We landed in Nairobi to refuel, then continued on to Salisbury, Rhodesia. The flight took us in a direct line over Mt. Kilamanjaro. The pilot announced over the intercom that we were approaching the beautiful, dormant, volcanic mountain peak that was over twenty-thousand feet tall. He also announced that if we would care to take a picture of it, he would circle it once. It was the first time that I had ever been on a commercial flight where they included some tourism.

We circled the mountain at about twenty-five thousand feet and everybody used up a bit of film. You could see the crater, which was completely filled with snow. The top one- to two-thousand feet of the mountain was also snow covered. It reminded me of Mt. Fuji in Japan.

We landed in Salisbury and were again met by the head man from Alitalia Airlines. He took us through customs and accompanied us to our hotel. I believe that of all the cities I've ever seen in my travels throughout the world, Salisbury must be one of the most beautiful. It is a relatively new city, and has many boulevards with flowers growing alongside of the road, and was very clean. Many of the road signs advertised American products, such as Coca Cola and Ford. From our hotel room, we could also see advertisements for many American made products. There was American music on the radio, and had I not known better, I would have thought I was back in the U.S.A. I went with Fred to the Post Office in Salisbury where he made arrangements to mail seven-hundred cards, one to each of his dealers and friends. He hired someone to put the stamps on, the total bill was $560.

The morning after our arrival in Salisbury we took a prop jet to Bira, a rather dingy and dirty seaport town on the Indian Ocean. We stayed there one night and flew out the next morning on two small, twin engine planes, which took us to our camp. The pilots wore sharp looking uniforms, with gold braid on their caps, just as the larger airline captains did.

Knick rode up in front with the pilot, and Fred, Dick Mauch and I rode in the back of the plane. As we swung out on the ramp, the pilot gunned the motor and started down the runway. Knick thought he was going to take off, and said to the pilot, "You'll never get this thing in the air taking off downwind."

The pilot kept up that speed until we reached the end of the runway, then he stopped the plane with a jolt. He turned it around, looked at Knick and said, "You're right," he said, "It won't fly." Of course, he had only been taxiing at high speed to the other end of the runway for the take off *into* the wind.

We flew low enroute to camp, about an hour away. From the windows we could see all kinds of animals in the tropical vegetation. We landed at Safarilandia, which is the concession that organized Fred's hunting expedition the previous year. Safarilandia is a hunting complex two hundred miles wide and three hundred miles long. One hundred hunters are allowed within the area during a season, therefore you don't have much competition for the game.

We passed over the Sauve River just before we landed. Fred noticed it was down quite a bit from the previous year. We later found out that the river, which flows out of the mountains of Rhodeais, was exceptionally low, and therefore hunting was much better as the animals had to seek out water holes.

We were met at the plane by Warner Von Elvinslaben and our white hunters. They were all dressed in safari clothes and loaded us into their Toyotas and took us to Camp Rourke, the main camp. It had been named after Robert Rourke, the famous writer, who had made a safari there.

The lodge was similar to a hotel. It was made of a material that looked like cement and was painted white and had a thatched roof. The rest of the buildings were placed in a circular fashion and had been constructed the same way. The dirt grounds were swept clean—it was a very neat camp.

Fred had said at the onset, when he invited me on this trip, that I could do whatever I wanted. If I chose to go with him on the buffalo hunt I could. Or, if I wanted to hunt by myself, that would also be O.K., as on this particular occasion he had two photographers. I had given this a great deal of thought on the way over, and had come to the conclusion that this would probably be the only time I would ever be in Africa. I'd better take advantage of the opportunity to do some hunting myself.

We were all assigned a white hunter. George Dedick would be my guide for the month. He arranged to take me north about fifty miles to a tent camp. George took me to the commissary where we shopped for supplies that I liked and stocked up for a month. George assured me that he would do everything in his power, to see that I would have a pleasant stay, and all whims would be taken care of. I wasn't used to this treatment.

After sorting over the thirty-eight pieces of hunting gear the group had, I found that some of my things were not there. Incidentally, the equipment we had weighed eleven-hundred pounds. Halmi said the transportation cost on this weight would be equal to three extra tourist fares, for the twelve-thousand-miles trip. I found that it's a helluva long ways to Africa, even by jet.

The hunting group met at the main lodge to say good-byes, as we all prepared to leave in different directions. We planned to return on a Sunday for a get together two weeks later.

Fred suggested that I keep field notes and a record of all the animals I took with my bow. We were testing some of Fred's new bows. I had two super magnum forty-eight inch gold bows.

These are the field notes that Fred suggested I write.

Field Notes

Next day at 1:00 p.m. they threw me and what little gear I had in a Toyota. First time I'd ever had four black chauffeurs (trackers). George was at the wheel of the Toyota.

First obstacle was to ford the Sauve River. The air is let out of tires and fan belt removed. The water is about three feet deep and two hundred yards wide, with a sandy bottom, crystal clear and cold. Upon reaching the other shore, tires must be inflated, the fan belt replaced, and then we are on our way. Weather seventy-five degrees in daytime.

Fifty degrees at night. Hadn't gone but half a mile before we started seeing all kinds of game. Reed buck, impala, nyala, sable antelope, wildebeest, hartibeest. Many others I'm not familiar with. Took a shot at an impala but shot over. I have never shot in public. I'm wondering how this is going to work, to have field judges sitting there watching every shot. Just another mental hazard. June here is like our autumn in Michigan. Trees colored much the same. Air crisp when the sun goes down. The Bush country in this area is flat, mostly small trees something like our northern Michigan oaks. Lots of small tufts of palmetto shrubs the size of a lilac bush. Back at camp, I explained to George, that I wished to use a bow and arrow. He had never taken a bow hunter out before this. Twice he reached for my gun, once on a beautiful sable antelope and once a large kudu.

At campfire he said, "You were very lucky. Some hunters stay four weeks and never see these 'extremely exceptional trophies'." I think he's a little disgusted with me. "George," I said, "How many animals did we see this afternoon?" "Oh, maybe five hundred." Let me add that, the guy who says the Michigan whitetail is the wariest game, I don't believe has checked all the animals in Africa.

Camp is real nice—straw building, thatched roof and side wall—including shower room and john. Sleep in tents. Separate dining area for two with linen table cloth, candle-light, dressed waiter. The works. This is reported to be the most "crude" camp in the concession.

After a lousy night, looking at the top of the tent and listening to the leopards yowl, the cook brought my coffee at 6:00 a.m.

During this first day we saw many more of same type of game plus about one thousand baboons. They are extreme-ly fast and stick to the ground. I caused one a bit of worry when I stuck an arrow next to him. He acted like he had a notion to go over and get it and bust the darn thing. Sur-prisingly enough, most all game is very shy and spooky, making it difficult to get within bow range. With a rifle, a hunter could have his pick. I'm afraid I strained my bow several times reaching for those long ones. The game is in such enormous herds. Not uncommon to see two hundred in a bunch. This gives them about one hundred and ninty-nine "lookouts." Doesn't add to the success of your stalk.

I took many shots. All clean misses. Warthogs are quite plentiful. They should be warned about flying arrows in the next three weeks.

George presented the camp with fresh impala for himself and me, and wildebeest for the natives. Have about fifteen natives working in this camp. Try to sneak in a little practice on trees around camp. Haven't shot much since last fall. Hit very few trees.

This morning I saw many warthogs, baboons, hartebeests, impala, etc. Saw two fine herds of sable antelope. They are black and look somewhat like a small horse, but with long graceful horns curling back. Maybe three feet long. Very wary. One shot at one-hundred yards. Shot over. I find that these African animals have learned how to "jump the string." Consequently, what few good shots I have had have missed their mark. Saw a lone wildebeest about noon. Tried to get close but not too much cooperation. Came to small patch of brush where he disappeared. On the other side he had stopped to take a peek at me. He stood facing me. My best chance yet, about thirty yards. Have perfect line. However, was three feet to right.

Grabbed another arrow just as he started to run. He ran broadside. I shut my eyes and let fly. The arrow passed completely through him just behind the rib cage. This brought the audience to their feet. I was given a standing ovation in Swahili. The wildebeest disappeared in the brush.

The trackers are like a bunch of hounds that have been cooped up in the trunk. Really wild to get into the act. We took the trail. No leaves. Mostly very hard sandy ground. We went through a wooded area. Trackers yelping like a pack of beagles on a hot rabbit track. Suddenly they pointed up ahead. There lay the animal dead. It traveled two hundred and seventy-five yards. Took some pictures. Came back to camp for a bite. Went out this afternoon. Saw where poachers had killed some game. A zebra was lying unused on the ground. Came upon smashed brush and tree branches. Fresh elephant sign. This is when you take out the soft nose bullets and replace them with hard jacket type. Followed trail for half an hour. Did not see them. Saw twenty some zebra. George tells me if I want one, I'll have to use a gun. They are very shy. George always carries a stick in his mouth, like a cigarette. Three days now he has not changed sticks. A cheap habit!

June 3, 1965

Sunrises are gorgeous.

Left for place where we would see water buck. Ran into the usual zebra, kudu, impala, etc. Boys pointed out an animal in brush on left trail. As we approached thicket I heard leaves rustle at my right. All signs pointing to left. But something said look right. Behind a clump of brush framed by the fork of a huge tree, stood a large animal with big horns. I took a fast fling. Heard a sound that told me my arrow had scored. I told George that I thought I had a hit. At that instant, from behind the brush ran a large nyala buck with my arrow buried deep in his back. Waited twenty minutes. Found him dead at one hundred and twenty-five yards. Beautiful trophy. George says some hunters come here for this trophy alone. The nyala is found only in this area of Africa.

Pretty damn lucky if you ask me—to spear a nice trophy with one shot. George says his horns will go twenty-eight inches.

Took him back to camp. Missed a thirty-yard shot—standing—at big Water Buck. Another watched me at twenty yards unnoticed until after I shot. I really got buck fever on this, I think. Missed him a mile. They are a big animals—six to seven hundred pounds. Big as an elk, with slightly curved horns. Got my mind set on one of these.

Started back to main camp for supplies. Saw all kinds of beautiful trophies.

Got another close chance at wildebeest. Hit him just behind shoulder. Found him dead at two hundred yards, too dark for pictures. Will take in a.m.

Met Fred and Halmi on the trail while returning to camp. They are doing the Buffalo film. They had a brush with one. The guide did all of the shooting with his 458. They found that this buffalo had been in a poacher's snare and developed a poor disposition with a sore leg.

June 4, 1965

Started at 7:30 a.m. Cool. A bit windy. Saw several hartibeest. Got one shot. It went directly over his back. Came upon large group of impala. Several nice bucks off to side. Made a lucky shot through the neck. The buck traveled less than one hundred and fifty yards in open and dropped. Took pictures.

While going back to camp with impala, we met Knick with his crew. We arranged to have lunch together at our camp. During the next half hour we spotted four eland. Worked up near them. They bolted. Had another running shot (this you probably won't believe), but as luck would have it, the arrow disappeared just behind the ribs. We trailed it for half a mile. I was able to finally get close enough to get another shot. This did it. Have good pictures. George estimated it to weigh approximately twelve hundred pounds. Eland are the largest of antelope family, some weigh two-thousand pounds. With use of block and tackle we were able to bring it into camp without cutting it up. I wanted Knick to see it. A native came from nowhere out of brush. He wore only skin shorts. Armed with hatchet, he helped us. We rewarded him with stomach lining for his lunch.

Knick pulled into camp for lunch with beautiful Sable antelope. Over forty-inch horns. He took this with his 375. They are very difficult to get close to. I took shot with bow at ninty yards the other day. George said that is as close as I probably will ever get.

I am keeping all of these field notes reports brief for the reason that we are constantly on the go and I'm pooped at night. I think these will bring to mind all of the vivid details of the stalk and kills to make an exciting story later by referring to this material.

Left camp late at 3:30. Shot at two hartibeests. Clear miss again—over. Went to area for water buck. Saw four Kudu. One large bull. Tried to get in range. Took eight-five yard shot. He jumped the string. The bull would be fifty-five to sixty inches. Had a sixty yard shot. Strummed the bow in my excitement.

When we next saw them, they had added another bull. They ran into a thicket. All standing in the thick brush. All at once both bulls moved out. The largest one stood broadside at sixty-five paces. I let fly. Couldn't have done much better with a rifle and scope. Right behind front shoulder. Disappeared in tall six-foot grass. Went over to the direction where he disappeared. Found him dead at fifty paces. Beautiful spiral horns nearly five feet. A tremendous trophy. Probably eight to nine-hundred pounds. Took many pictures. George said he should be in the *Rowland Ward Trophy Book*. George congratulates me with warm handshake after each trophy and a toast of gin and tonic. "What bloody luck you have." Boy, an eland and a kudu in the same day. As we loaded it into truck, with power hoist, a "go-away" bird sat in a nearby tree and said "Go Away." We went. I am amazed at the large size of many of these animals.

I am taking pictures only of the freshly killed trophy. My extra film is still in Bira. Expected daily. The "Mallet-heads." But if these pictures don't get lost en route home, I will have enough for a fair bow safari. Have five species now. One extra wildebeest. Three weeks to go. I can't believe it. This is not like North America.

Went east of camp at daylight. Had coffee. Checked on buffalo prospects. Hence, north twenty-five miles. Scrub palm country. Picked up local native. Another help you can't count on in North America. He will know which tree the buffalo will be standing behind on his back forty. And he did.

We hadn't gone far. Fresh tracks were seen. Tick birds flutter up behind some palms. This with a small cloud of dust told us exactly where to look for buffalo. We approached a thick patch of scrub palms about ten feet tall where the tick birds had last been seen. As we worked around the edge of thicket there stood about a dozen large, black and very impressive cape buffalo. One large one stood a little to the right. About forty yards. My intentions were to try for a chest shot. This didn't seem too difficult as it was about the size of the three bales of straw I've been shooting at in my back yard. I was a bit flustered at the sudden sight of these huge beasts. Shot about three feet to the left of the rib cage.

Normally this kind of a shot doesn't score well. In this case the buffalo's neck happened to be in the same area.

The arrow severed the jugular vein. He traveled less than one hundred feet.

The natives went wild. It took the promise of a keg of wine this evening to calm them down.

Many pictures were taken. George and I were both very pleased.

We can hear lions and leopards every night. Loud growls.

Today was my best luck bow hunting *ever!*

From 6:00 a.m. to sundown makes for tired lids at night. I hate to take time from hunting to write. The sun here at noon passes to the north.

These native trackers would renew your faith in Santa Claus. They are terrific. I can't say enough for them. I've seen some fancy tracking in my time. Nothing like this. They are all thrilled with me using the bow and arrow. This, along with the spear, is their weapon too! All natives we meet have them. I let the trackers use my bow at lunch time.

Came back and showered. Sat around campfire for our sundowner (drinks). Listened to George tell his experiences. Quiet and peaceful. Heard from natives that buffalo had charged Fred's Toyota. They had to shoot him. Not too dependable source.

June 8, 1965

Most of these notes are written early in morning when I wake up, from four to six in a.m. Or, nine to eleven at night by candlelight in tent. No time during day. I'm on the hunt from daylight until dusk.

Met natives on trail this a.m. Reported a small herd of Cape buffalo had just gone through. We made stalk, but no good. No sight of them. The buffalo like tall, grassy country—grass six feet high and bushy, thick, lots of tufts of scrub palmetto. This makes them hard to locate. Came into fairly open country. Spotted three warthogs. These beasts have given us the slip many times. I have shot at them probably a dozen times. They manage to keep well ahead. Just out of range. They also jump the string.

Warthogs run with their tails straight up. About a foot and a half long with little tassels on end. Looks real funny. Finally got to within thirty yards. These running shots would allow little time for the shooter to adjust his bow sight for the proper yardage. One of them made the wrong turn. My arrow passed through him just behind front shoulder and out of chest. This speeded up his gait considerably. After about five-hundred yards he ran out of gas. Keeled over. We took pictures. This makes second day in row that I have taken three trophies.

The ground is so hard and sandy. With no sod it's practically impossible to lose any arrow. But of course there are always five pair of eyes watching and helping. If I just can't find the arrow, all three of the trackers start a search. It doesn't take them long to find it. Have not lost one yet.

The hunter has several important advantages here in Africa that you do not find in North America, which makes for a more successful and easier hunt. To begin with, you have the professional white hunter, or guide who is second to none. You have transportation available. This enables you to look over more area daily. Game is abundant. Not uncommon to see five-hundred to fifteen-hundred animals in a day. This in itself raises your chances for success. Another assist in hunting here that you do not have in North America are the native trackers. They are incredible. I never cease to be amazed at how accurate they are. I honestly have never hunted with any dogs that could do as good a job.

Another advantage in the hunter's favor is the tick bird that rides on the backs of most of the game. When the animal runs, the tick bird flies above it, giving the hunter a clue to the animal's whereabouts. When the bird hovers down and disappears you know he is sitting on the animal's back. If all this fails, you always have air cover. An animal when wounded, even if slightly, will by nature lie down. Somehow by a sixth sense the vultures detect this and start their methodical circling. This gives you the clue and a surrounding attack is started. Consequently, if you can score a hit, you have all of these things working for you. Very little game will ever get away or be wasted. We found my hartibeest by observing vultures. By the time we reached the spot, over a hundred vultures had gathered, eating the kill. I can't understand it. You can search the clear blue sky silly and you can't see any of the bloody things. But within a half hour after you have hit an animal, they arrive.

I have the three native trackers and a boy to carry my bow and jackets to and from the Toyota. We have two cooks and a waiter in full dress—with freshly cleaned and pressed uniform. All of this service comes with bows. "Yes sir, boss." "Thank you, boss." Etc. I am awakened by the waiter with piping hot coffee at my tent. One house boy cleans my tent. Dirty clothes are thrown on floor. When you return that evening, they are all neatly washed, pressed and folded. One boy sweeps the camp clean of leaves. He also takes care of shower and toilet. Another fellow takes charge of the Toyota. It is washed free of blood and dirt each time we come back to camp.

All animals are brought in whole. Not field dressed. Have two boys who process the meat, prepare horns, capes and skulls. They boil the skulls in water. Come out bone dry and white—no smell.

Going to main camp today. George is worried. No one has come up with my hunting license yet. I purchased this in February. But like other things here nobody knows where it is. Regulations are that white hunters must carry license and report trophies on same day they are taken.

June 8, 1965

Went back to main camp—two and three-quarter hour trip—to pick up my license. Have to record kills, dates, etc. White hunters worried game warden might make it difficult for them. Saw pack of fourteen Cape wild dogs. These beasts look like wolf with hyena-shaped ears. They are black and white spotted. I shot one with 375 at one-hundred and twenty yards. The rest vanished in brush. It is impossible to ever get close enough for bow shot. These are Africa's worst predators. Everyone hates them. Unlike leopard and lion who kill and eat the game, these monsters make a game of running in and just taking a mouthful at a time out of the live, running, helpless prey.

Mocambique (they spell it with "c") has no bounty system. Came upon tremendous-sized porcupine. George says natives regard them as one of their favorite meats. Shot it with bow at their request. Quills over twenty inches long. Guessed him at over fifty pounds. George says these are what makes lions and leopards ugly. He claims most of them taken have evidence of quills.

As we approached the porcupine, two others scurried from the tall grass. One between one of the tracker's legs. The other between mine. While doing a toe dance to avoid things on the ground, my neck became tangled with a thorn tree. I promptly had sharp quills at both ends. George got out his first aid kit. Patched me up.

Sat by water hole for one hour before dark. Lots of noises but nothing showed. Drove twenty-five miles home in rain. Got soaked. Knick and Rui in camp, when we arrived, to spend a few days with us. Knick disgusted with Camp Ruark, especially the women in camp. Had our "Sundowner." African term for "Happy Hour" cocktails.

Rui started to main camp at 1:00 a.m. Came back shortly with report of seeing buffalo. Knick grabbed his gun and they took off. Saw him running but Knick wouldn't settle for a running shot. Rui left for main camp for repairs on Toyota. Knick stayed with me.

Saw nyala, kudu, impala, wildebeest, and hartibeest. Shot warthog at thirty-five paces. Sent arrow through his chest. He took off. Native trackers proved themselves again. They found where he had turned off. He lay dead at one-hundred and fifty yards. Took pictures. Saw a few hartibeest but no shots. Saw another really large warthog. Big tusks. Gave him a go. I slid an arrow in his chest at forty yards. Lucked out again. He took off. Natives trailed him six hundred yards into thick elephant brush. Found him dead. Saw large sable.

Back to camp for lunch. Game warden came. Signed licenses. Went out at 3:00. Saw spot where lion made a kill. It's been another successful and lucky day. Tomorrow I'll try for water buck. Returning after dark we could smell the odors of cooking at the camp. Or so I thought. When remarking to George we must be near camp, he said that smell came from a certain kind of tree. Thought he was pulling my leg. But he was right.

Rui back from main camp. Says Bill and Dick got a seventy-five pound tusk elephant with gun. They got water buck with bow today also.

On 12th, George and I went after water buck about thirty miles from here, no shots. Shot a bush pig at twenty-five yards. Going to concentrate on sable, water buck and zebra now.

Sunday June 13, 1965

Still forty miles away from main camp and regular mail pickups. Having a ball. Everything going well, aside from the trots and the regular problems with spicy food.

New entertainment every day. Lots of game. All kinds. Having to bang this off in hurry. One of fellows is going to make a run to the main camp. Want to catch the outgoing mail.

My shooting is still fairly satisfying. I missed a big sable antelope several times a couple of days ago. No one has one of these, except one Knick got with a gun.

Yesterday shot eight times at water buck. Nearly as large as an elk. Also some reed bucks that are like deer.

Lots of game, ninety to a hundred twenty yards. Just luck if you get close to them. Concentrating on sable, reed buck, water buck and zebra. All tough. Saw some ostriches yesterday.

Can't make it seem possible that I'm here when I wake up each morning.

Knick provided us with dove and guinea fowl dinner with his shot gun. I have used the gun on three occasions, securing camp meat for the natives.

Plan to stay here for few more days. Then move back to main camp with the gang. Haven't heard from them in a week. Knick says there is much more game in this area. He's in bad mood today. "Out of Scotch." They made a mistake and brought gin.

Took pictures of Strophantus tree and pods. This is
how the native gets the poison for his arrow. Seeds when
dry are pounded into pulp-like flour. Water is added to
make paste. The stuff is placed on arrow points. Generally
not too effective on large game. The wire snare is more
productive. See abandoned poachers' camps daily. Campfire ashes and bones.

June 14, 1965

Air filled with weird noises at night. All kinds of birds
and beasts. Can hear the brush crashing. We hear lions
roar every night. Rui says you can hear them for two
miles. If your head is in the direction of the roar you can
generally spot them at daylight. He says you go a ways,
then wait for another roar. They make this roaring noise
when they have made a kill. I suppose to tell all of the animals about the kill. Lounged in camp Sunday a.m. Slept
and took shower.

Knick went out and shot a tremendous eland. Rui
claimed it would go nearly two-thousand pounds. Knick
used my 375 with 300 gr. silver tip points. It took five of
these to bring him down. Have quoted George before.
African game is "easy to hit but hard to kill."

Knick took the afternoon off. George went to main
camp for supplies. Rui asked me if I would like to go out
with him. He is a dashing, good-looking, twenty-seven year
old Portuguese. Does not smoke or drink. Told of shooting
a crocodile seventeen-feet long last week. Cut him open
and found silver bracelet in stomach, also native boy's pair
of shorts. He says they kill many natives who get too close
to the water. They lay motionless and wait near shore.
When the women come to wash clothes, the crocodile
strikes them with it's huge tail, throwing the native into
the water. Then make short order of ripping her apart.
Says they get many animals when they come to drink too.

Last evening while spinning yarns at campfire, just
after sundown, heard native drums in distance. Very plain.
When asked if these were restless or unfriendly natives,

the white hunters laughed and said no, they are probably having a dance.

Our Natives start mumbling and talking about 4:30 a.m. Woke me up. Had a terrific time with Rui. Came upon large bush pig. Missed first shot. Arrow hit brush. He ran about one hundred yards. Stopped. He let us sneak within twenty-five yards—thinking that he was hidden in the bushes. I slid an arrow completely through him in the liver area. He ran thirty yards at top speed. Then tumbled end-over-end like a running rabbit hit with scatter gun. He was dead on our arrival. Rui said that he would place among the top five of record book (*Rowland Ward*). The tusks are the determining factor of record. Looks like he would weigh about one hundred pounds. Took pictures. Rui real pleased. Wanted to have me take his picture with pig. Spotted eight bull sable. Maneuvered into shooting position. Gave them five of my best arrows. Not good enough.

The animals frequent bushy areas much like alders bordering Michigan streams. You just are not able to get close to them.

Saw another herd of forty sable. Two bulls. Gave them two more of my poorer shots. Knick insisted that I shoot one with gun. He feels it is the most prized and wanted trophy in Africa.

Schanotsi trees with black and orange beans. Mopani, thick brush where buffalo live. Marabo stork. Usually second bird to spot kill. Large bird with eight foot wing span. First to kill is the Bateleur Eagle. He takes the eyes. Saddlebill stork—black, white, red. Saw water crane—rare.

Went east about twenty-five miles for sable. Saw all varieties of game but only one spooky sable. We thought Knick and Rui went north. At 11:00 a.m. we sighted exceptional warthog with tusks that looked like a fork horn white tail buck. He hid behind the thick brush about forty yards. Had to hit him three times to stop him. First shot hit his hard skill. Bent the broad head completely double. Did not even draw blood.

George says no one in our party will get one as large. His upper tusks must be close to one foot long. I've taken several deer with shorter horns. Grotesque looking beast. I think I'll have his head mounted. Saw vultures hovering in distance. See this practically every day. Always suspect lion and pull sneak with 375. George advises against stirring up a mean lion with an arrow in this tall grass. Found dead hartibeest. Upon examining it, we found it still limp with signs that death was only in past few minutes. Looked closer. Found a small cross-cut hole that passed through right hip and into stomach. This had to be a result of Knick's arrow. Backtracked it. Found nothing. Brought the animal in with us.

Here in this vast area, where we both covered over twenty-five miles in different areas, our paths had nearly crossed. At this very point Knick took his only shot of the day. Hit and lost the animal. I think the reason they lost track of that animal was that he was with a herd. Lots of bloodless tracks. And he apparently didn't lie down.

Of all my hunting experiences, this is the most unusual happening—tops—finding the proverbial needle in the hay stack.

Saw herds of zebras. In attempt to circle around them, contracted our third flat—no zebra. Shot an African hare for natives to eat. Mostly because of their wager that he couldn't be hit. They look like our rabbits only larger and longer ears. Don't see them very often. Picked up nice set of shed sable horns. Now all I need is the other end.

June 16, 1965

Went to Camp Ruark for supplies and to visit gang. I went with Rui while Knick and George went to another camp for gas. Rui missed two baboons with rifle. He shot a beautiful bird that he will skin for me. He does this for museums. He is filled with wild tales of the bush. He is champion skeet, trap and live bird shooting of Mocambique, so he says. His shooting however with gun was no better than mine with bow today.

While he only missed one bird in air, his average dropped when he missed a quail on the ground. We saw over one-hundred and fifty water bucks. I shot many from long distances. The climax came late in the day, just at dusk. A large bull obliged, by standing only ten yards from me. I rattled the arrow off his thirty inch horns.

Fred has completed buffalo film. Got good pictures of his shooting two nice buffalo. Mauch and Wright are pleased with their large elephants. Bill hit his with arrow at thirty yards. The bull immediately charged him. Wally Johnson shot him with 458. Dick took movies of charge. I am satisfied merely to hear the story rather than to have been an eyewitness. I think trying to shoot an elephant with a bow is a bit too much.

Bill had hit a warthog this a.m. and they were unable to find it. On our return home the vultures led us to where it had died. We will make Bill a present of the hog tomorrow when they come to our camp. We agreed yesterday that we all meet back at main camp Sunday for lunch to decide what plans are to be made for our last week. We probably will swap camps. Some of the game that I have been lucky to take does not live in the area where Dick and Bill are hunting.

Hear no news of outside world. Once every other day we hear plane in distance. Knick is registering a major complaint against my snoring. He may move. With my three weeks growth of beard, Halmi is calling me Hemingway. Saw eight hippos yesterday in river. River filled with fish. Can see hundreds of them swimming about. These are tiger fish, talapia, bream and catfish.

Took my first drink from a watervine. This is a large vine, about one to two inches in diameter, growing on a tree. When cut, the water runs out like a slow faucet. Tastes good.

While presenting Wally Johnson with a baby baboon, Rui got his finger too close to the baby's mouth. As a result he has bandaged fingers.

Starting out again for water buck. My fifty day. I'm getting real disgusted. May give up on them and go after something else. Knick orders me to cut off my whiskers every day. I tell him I will tomorrow.

June 17, 1965

Rui and I started back to our favorite water buck spot to waste some more arrows.

Knick suggests that we change white hunters. George is more his age and drives slower. On way we broke the universal joint on rear drive. Had to go to main camp. Could not cross river without the four wheel drive factor so took off our clothes and swam it. The Sava River is about two hundred yards across at this point. Got part we needed. Picked up mail. All postmarked June 3rd. So you can see how current all correspondence is.

Met Dick and Bill at main camp. Invited them to our camp for lunch. They are changing camps today and will be about ten miles from us. Expect to see more of them and hunt some together. Knick's latest gripe is "no pajamas" and "can't sleep with Bob's snoring." Brought his pajamas from main camp and another tent. Now he is happy! Had lunch with guys at our camp. Rui shot a huge baboon, on the run, with his rifle. He is making a cap for me out of the fur.

Went out at 4:00 p.m. for scouting trip for zebra. Hunted near camp in Chinatisi brush. Heavy cover and high grass. Rui is constantly setting fire to the tall grass. Large areas are burning continually. This makes it better to tour country and not hit things or ruts with Toyota. Also makes it easier to see game. Got several glances at half a mile away. This is about par as, I have been told by all white hunters, they are the spookiest of all game. I would be real lucky to get one with gun. They tell me that in the big plain country up north you can get closer to them than here. The places they inhabit here are thick patches of cover, much like alder brush in Michigan. Knick has been pursuing them daily with his gun. He missed two long shots running through Chinatisi brush yesterday.

As we came out in a small clearing, three zebras left the herd and stood at edge of brush, watching us. Rui's reflexes are like lightning. He sped around a patch of brush where he thought they might run. His calculation was perfect. He gave me a running shot at thirty yards. After many clear misses at water bucks in the past two days I redeemed myself with a most spectacular shot. I just can't have any more lucky shots left. Hit him about four inches behind front leg. Arrow penetrated deep into chest or lung area. He ran at top speed for about seventy-five yards. Then toppled end-over-end. It was again unbe-

lievable. Don't wake me up. As my old Alaskan guide Ed
Bilderback says, "How come I keep doing it?"

Again the trackers went wild. Rui gave me one of his
strongest hand shakes. "Bob, you've got your zebra. Wait
till Knick hears about this!" Took pictures as sun was setting. Hope for enough light. These are beautiful and graceful animals. Now I have my shopping out of the way for
Nancy, my young daughter. This is what she said she wanted me to bring her from Africa. A zebra skin rug. I am real
happy to be able to get it in this fashion. The skinners are
fixing the whole hide, head and hoofs. You can't imagine
the look on Knick's and George's faces when we returned to
camp. Had quite a time convincing them that I took it with
an arrow. We are invited to other camp for dinner tomorrow
evening. Can't wait to do a little bragging to Dick and Bill.
They told me later that I should not have swum the Sauve
River for fear of getting bahriza, an infection caused by
microscopic snails. I had to sneak another dozen arrows
out of Fred's private stock at main camp. This makes my
fifth big game trophy. Plan to keep after much wanted sable.
Rui says with my luck he thinks we'll do it. I doubt it.

Went out this afternoon with Dick. I will take movies
while Dick hunts. Spotted some eland off in thicket to left
of trail. We started over in their direction. I was getting
camera set to take picture of one of those monstrous antelope. I was monkeying with camera and had let go of one-
inch bar that natives in rear hang on to. Just at this
moment the two front wheels dropped into a hole about
two feet deep. Fortunately we were not moving very fast.
Just the same it made for one hell of a sudden halt. I went
sailing forward. Before I had time to make any recovery,
my throat met the bar. I'd swear by the feel that I had put a
bend in it. After I tried to remove the milky way from my
eyes, I tried to talk. The only thing still working were my
lips. I spent the next two days in a state of uncomfortable
silence, with a trophy sore throat. My only concern was if I
would ever be able to get my voice box bumped out. I lost a
good deal of my desire to hunt, eat or drink. Word came
that a doctor had arrived in the main camp. I needed little
encouragement, when Knick insisted that I go in and have
him check me over. I will always recall that long cold dark
forty-mile ride. My attitude went up fifty points when he

told me it would be O.K. It never pays to be a worry wart I guess, but it seemed to be the thing to do at that time.

The doctor told me not to try to talk for a few days. Good thing I'm not a woman. Got quite a kick out of Fred and Halmi. When I whispered to Fred he would whisper back. Guess he thought I was telling him some secret. Halmi treated me in reverse. As if I were deaf and talked unusually loud.

The natives are most interesting to observe. Most of them carry bows and arrows, a big machetti and an old broken knife. They sharpen these by putting a little dirt on a stick and using it as we do emery dust. They are dressed in the shabby discarded clothing from hunting clients of several past years. Tattered and torn.

Went from Alveslema Camp to our tent camp with Walter Johnson Jr. and Bill Wright. Decided to run back in to main camp with George. Took all of my gear. I plan to be in Camp Ruark with Fred and camera crew for the balance of the hunt.

Just before dusk a leopard ran in front of Toyota. They are very fast and quick. He stopped for a glance at one hundred yards. I jumped out and took a kneeling shot. Leopard flipped sideways then disappeared. George felt it best to return in the morning saying a wounded leopard is nothing to fool with. Out of the one-hundred clients on safari last year only two leopards were taken. They are quite rare in this particular area. Hope was high that we find him in the morning. Also pondered the fact that hyena or lion might eat him for a midnight snack. I was very lucky to find him in perfect shape, only seventy-five yards from where he was hit. A 375 bullet passed through the back end of lung. Just missed spine. Beautiful animal. Sleek with delicate brown shades and mottled with black spots. Hardly enough for a coat however. Halmi tells me for only another $3,000 I can buy enough pelts for a coat for my wife.

Many pictures taken as all gang arrives to make plans for final week. Plane came in to pick up Jim Crowe. Camera crew did movie and sound tape, staging Fred's arrival for movie. Took an hour and a half. Sequence of Apache trailer was shot. Two more hours. Took my picture sitting on top of trailer with my leopard. Halmi said he'd try to make a commercial out of it.

June 18, 1965

Out with Rui at 7:00 a.m. Saw huge warthog. First arrow hit his right tusk. Chipped off a piece of ivory. About four inches. Second arrow hit just in front of hip. He flipped over in one hundred yards. Rui talked me into shooting him, for the ivory, for him. He makes knife handles, etc. Saw bull sable. Got a shot at thirty yards after several attempts. Hit him in front of rear leg. Arrow went toward chest area. Got second arrow into hip. Traveled three hundred yards. This is most beautiful trophy yet. A tremendous climax to the already successful hunt. Horns over thirty inches. Their hair is black with streaks of white on head, and is similar to a horses' hair.

Had lunch with Dick and Bill. They got a warthog, wildebeest, and a hartibeest this a.m. Went with Dick in morning and took pictures. Dick shot warthog. Home at dark. Bill Wright had hit large bull buffalo.

Saturday a.m.

Knick shot good bull buffalo with gun. I went with Bill Wright after a buffalo. Exciting hunt. Blood trail followed. Trailed it for half a mile on foot through thick scrub palms. Rather scary with Walter Johnson parting brush with his 408. Found buffalo dead. Bill very pleased. Quite a job to get it in Toyota even with chain hoist. Bill shot a big warthog on way back to lunch. Plan to run to main camp either this afternoon or tomorrow.

After we found the buffalo we tried to find the Toyota. Couldn't find it. Wandered around for an hour and finally located it. Quite relieved.

Had conference to decide who would go where and what we should tip white hunters. Bill and Dick are going to finish out at Alveslema. Knick back to our tent camp. Fred and movie set at Camp Ruark, and I'm tenting out on an elephant hunt with Rui.

Had big gang at lunch. Eighteen in all. Many stories.

For days Knick has stressed that he wanted a leopard. He did not know that I shot one. I figured if he knew I had it, he would be harder to live with. We staged a little skit. Led him into conversation on leopards. After he was given enough rope to hang himself, a native entered at the precise time with my leopard skin. Asked me if the skinning job was ok. All seventeen were in on the gag. Knick called me unnice names. Gave me hell in general.

Lots of stories swapped.

Fred asked me if I'd like to spend a day with him on a lion hunt. We took his white hunter and crew. Spent a long day searching for lions. At lunch time we stopped by a big water hole. We saw eight different species come and go as we sat eating our sandwiches.

After lunch Fred suggested that we do a little target practice. Me shooting with Fred is like a Sunday duffer playing with the top pro golfer.

Fred spotted a square object that proved to be over a hundred paces. It was a honey bee trap that the natives put up in trees to attract a swarm of bees. They get the honey out by smoking out the bees. It's made out of a bark much like birch bark. This one had been cut down and discarded as it was partially burned. Fred said let's shoot at that bee trap. Fred's always generous. Suggested that I shoot first. I didn't come very close. Fred drew down and released his arrow. There was a "kerwhack" sound as his arrow passed through the trap. I never cease to be amazed at the way he shoots. I've been very fortunate to have had the opportunity to see him perform many of these unbelievable shots. It's hard to believe the accuracy he has. Even a moving target doesn't seem to give him too much trouble.

Rod Lee came in today. This is his third month on safari, having been to Kenya and Ugandi collecting material for stories and pictures. Said he had taken sixty-thousand feet of film so far. Sounds like a lot of film . . . or you know what.

Fred has located a lion that lives in palm brewery, an area where natives have cut off palms to make their beer and wine. He hopes to try the lion from a blind. That could be a long wait, and many beers. This beer isn't too bad after you pick out the bugs. If left for several days it turns into a potent wine. The natives get a lot of mileage out of this.

Dick shot warthog on way into camp. A rifle hunter brought in à giant kudu with nearly sixty-inch horns.

I am using George's 458 on elephant, or my 375. *NO BOW.* George says the reason he shoots a 458 is because they don't make a 700.

June 21, 1965

Sleeping on canvas on ground next to native hut. Weather cool. Have quilties on. Rui all bundled up. Have tarp thrown over us to keep dry from heavy dew that will soak everything by morning. We were awakened by shots. We are only ones hunting for miles. I awakened Rui. Shots continued twenty-three times. Seemed to be well spaced about every thirty seconds. Rui thought it might be the Scourses at first. Then he thought it might be crocodile hunters. Shots sounded about three quarters of a mile away. Rui awoke native. He said it was natives scaring elephants out of their gardens near huts by banging on a stretched hide. I felt relieved as it sounded like a gun distress signal.

Had one of most thrilling experiences in all my hunting days today. Loaded all gear in Toyota for camp-out on elephant hunt. Left main camp at 12:00 noon. Drove about forty miles through bush road. Came to native hut. Rui checked native out on elephant prospect. He said that in view of dry country many elephants were coming each night to a lake about four miles from here. Elephants from all around were using this lake for their water supply. Rui said the dry season had forced them to come from the Rhodesian border.

We threw out our gear and Rui said he'd check out the situation. We took a local native with us as well as Rui's three trackers. Walked about two hours. Came to small clearing and heard the blowing and trumpeting of elephants in the distance. My vision of elephant hunting has changed more in the past few hours than I thought possible. Country is brushy. Much like the hunting area for brown bear in Alaska, only the country is flat. The elephant spends the daytime feeding in the heavy, thick brush. As result, if you wish to meet up with one, you have to sneak through the heavy cover to get up to him. Sometimes it's impossible to see one at fifty yards.

We listened a few minutes while the native tracker determined if they were moving. Rui started checking the wind. Hadn't gone but a quarter of a mile when we heard brush crashing. I can't over-emphasize the noise of snapping brush and small trees. We checked the wind. Determined it was necessary to slip around to the right. When we hit his track Rui said it was a lone bull. Looked very impressive to me. Hadn't gone but two-hundred yards when we heard the brush really crash. A slight breeze on the back of our necks told us that he had got our wind. We circled more to the right. Traveled about a half mile. Stopped to listen. Again heard grunts, groans and trumpeting in distance. Worked in that direction. Hadn't gone but four-hundred yards when heard the crashing of brush again. Kept going slowly. Checking the wind every twenty feet. They kick the dusty dry ground to see which direction the dust cloud floats and respond accordingly, sometimes changing direction of stalk. The bushes are very similar to alder brush. Very thick.

We narrowed gap in ten minutes. They sounded like large caterpillar tractors pushing over trees ahead of them. We were all going tippie-toe and shushing each other. You can see a little better if you bend over slightly.

Then I saw my first elephant at about forty yards. Then another, then another, and so on. Rui whispered in disgust that we had worked our way into the herd. Rui kept motioning for me to get close to him. By this time we were with fully loaded guns. Magazine and barrel. Rui had briefed me earlier to shoot between the eyes if facing us and a side shot either just behind front leg for heart shot or a described line running vertical on middle of ear for a brain shot. I had determined that I would not attempt to take one with my bow. However, we were close enough to do so.

Perhaps Bill Wright's experience had helped me to come to this decision. As I have said, he had hit a large bull at twenty-five yards with a one-hundred and twenty pound bow in the right spot and immediately got charged by all five tons at full speed. Wally Johnson Jr. handled the situation with two shots in the brain at fifteen yards. They were lucky to drop him. One has a different perspective of an elephant here in this situation, than when they are parading in the circus with their trunks and tails hitched.

A bad condition had developed as we had about one hundred of the beasts within two hundred yards and in three directions all at one. This, Rui whispered, was bad. The females have their young with them. And like all animals will take quick action to protect them. By now we could see huge masses of them on practically all sides at forty yards or less. One of our trackers left us. It seemed that it would be inevitable that one of them soon would get our scent or work on the other side of us and stampede. I didn't care for this "penned-in" feeling.

At this moment Rui came up with a very serious remark that I didn't recall reading in the brochure. He called me close to him and said if they charge us, or if they stampede in our direction, "run like hell." I didn't dare ask which direction or how fast. I could see myself, running through that thick tangled brush. Easy interpret the run bit. But what do you do next? Trees too young to climb. No holes to duck into.

There were horrifying groans, belly grunts, blowing, trumpeting and various other monster noises. Rui is on all fours. Trying to peek through the herd and spot a big bull. He continually picks up handfuls of dust or grass and lets it filter to ground to recheck the wind. See if we are still winning. It was quickly proven to me that the elephant has very poor eyesight. We were sneaking parallel to the whole herd, at thirty to forty yards. I'm sure I could have slid an arrow in one if the urge had touched me. I never realized how big those bruisers looked before. They paid no attention to us.

Many times I have had a rather helpless feeling come over me when I was toting a bow while stalking a bear. I now had the same helpless feeling with this puny 375. I really had not thought of elephant hunting as being much of a challenge or thrill. I have a very definite different impression now. These monsters mean business and play for keeps. I was hoping to hear Rui say "Let's work our way back out of here" to avoid a charge or stampede. Contrary, he motioned me to follow closely to him, in sneaking position.

They all passed us except a few cows and calves. These were the ones that worried Rui and me. This is where he put me on the spot. He whispered "How do you like this?" I didn't answer at first for lack of words. He said, "There's a pretty good bull in this herd but he is leading the bunch. Do you want to go after him?" I don't know why but I said, "Whatever you think." However, I quickly whispered, "Do you think it's advisable to mingle in such a large herd." He shrugged his shoulders and said, "That's the chance we've got to take if we get a shot at him." After my rather unenthusiastic "Yes" we continued. This led us into a slightly more open area. We could see a little better what we were up against. We were within one hundred yards of at least seventy-five of the herd. A very impressive sight. I think the only reason I said yes is that I sure would hate to quit and have to come back and repeat this tomorrow. I felt that we were close to a chance and let's get this damn thing over. I have felt this sometimes when I was climbing mountains for goats and sheep in Alaska. Let's get it over with today. That, I believe, was the only thing that spurred on my enthusiasm. For the next half hour it was touch and go as far as I was concerned. We were running in a crouched position as best we could. The amazing thing to me was that here was the whole herd only seventy-five yards away. It was difficult to catch up with the leader of the herd. He was always either too far ahead or was facing away from us.

It's difficult to pick out the right one in a large herd like this. They all looked so big to me. The cows have tusks too. Finally—it seemed like an hour—we maneuvered into a position by running ahead of the herd. Just at the moment I was getting ready to give it to him, he turned and looked at us, flapped his ears, and whirled to run. Rui still didn't loose confidence. At this point I actually felt that he was continuing the chase just to make me feel like it was a good try but that our chances of getting a shot had gone forever.

By now Rui was pulling me by my hand. I was exhausted and ready to give up. It seemed like I had no breath left.

After another four-hundred yards of sneak running, we closed the gap to about fifty yards. He stopped. Rui summoned me to his side. Natives all running. One with my camera, another with bow. "Now!" Rui said, "Give him a heart shot!" I didn't need any more encouragement. However, I wondered if I should shoot with the large herd so close to us. We could get trampled to death by them trying to escape. No time to debate. I leveled off with the feeling that this one better be good. I hardly felt the gun go off, or heard it. He shrugged forward then, to my delight, bolted the other way with the whole herd. I gave him another shot on the other side as he turned. Everything disappeared in a tremendous crashing of the bush and a cloud of dust. Rui took off in hot pursuit. He hadn't gone far, maybe fifty yards, when he hollered back and said "He's down!" This I think was one of my life's greatest reliefs. As I approached he made a movement to get up. I gave him another in heart area. This did him in. Rui and all the natives slapped me and shook my hand. We took a few pictures with fading light. Guessed the tusks to be five feet long. Not the biggest, but I'm real pleased. The ivory, Rui said, would go over fifty pounds each. I didn't have much time to spend searching a real big one because I had spent all my time hunting with bow for the past three weeks. We cut off the beast's tail. Rui will make bracelets from hair taken from it.

Long, hard trip back to Toyota, after dark. Heard elephants crashing brush. All natives real pleased. Rui gave local native $3.00 and priority on the meat.

Ate dinner and took flash pictures of the native's eighteen kids. Gave them oranges and apples. Girls all bowed down on their knees to accept the gifts. Dressed in rags. Probably this is the biggest thing that ever happened to them. All stood about and watched us eat by lights of Toyota.

Expect a big day of surprises tomorrow. Natives coming from throughout area for the meat. Expect to do some big picture taking. Word goes out, by signal given with tom tom drums, when they hear a shot in the elephant hunting area. Some come from twenty miles with baskets on their heads for meat.

Quite an experience seeing the natives operate on the elephant. News spread throughout the area of the kill. We took seven natives with us and went in at 7:00 a.m. Took pictures from all angles. One from top side, up in tree, showing how he sprawled out and with the ten-inch tree he took down as he fell. Took three and a half hours to remove tusks with axe. Rough measure is over five feet with approximately six inches diameter base. Nerves inside tusks removed, nearly three feet long. Cut off the ears. I hope to have coffee table made from skin of the ear. Took the two front legs for waste basket and stool. Also took the trunk for meat for natives. It took three natives to load trunk in Toyota. Tusk imbedded in solid bone skull. Has to be removed with an axe. Tried to take a tooth but broke axe. Rui said that when the natives—mostly women— arrive, the carcus will be completely cut up within an hour or so. They take everything except some of the larger bones. This is moving meat faster than a supermarket giving triple green stamps. Rui estimated the weight of the elephant to be over five tons. All natives for miles alerted by sound of shot, then by native drums.

Note: Native scrape mud from elephant gums next to tusks to sell to the medicine man for his kush kush. A magic cure in native witchcraft. All natives go for this in a big way.

On return to camp ran into huge bull Cape buffalo. We were able to maneuver into a good shooting position. I was carrying 375 with all intentions of using it. Rui whispered to me so softly I couldn't hear what he said. However, I got the general idea when he took the bow from tracker and handed it to me and in same pass took my 375. Had I had more time to rationalize this fast shuffle, I'm sure that I would have felt that it was not a fair exchange.

Anyhow, here stood Mr. Buffalo, forty-five paces broadside viewing this transaction. I guess that when one is excited it doesn't take much to make snap judgements. I let fly. The arrow went low in chest area. Penetrated about twelve inches. He ran off in a charging fashion but in the opposite direction. Trailed him six-hundred yards after waiting a spell. Found him dead. Plenty of excitement and picture taking. Rui said this will cost a decanter of wine for natives. Couldn't have agreed more.

Spent next two hours removing twenty some wire snares from a three to four mile fenced area. On the snares for buffalo, poachers secure the end of the big wide loop to a big log. This allows it to be dragged and not snapped as if secured to big tree. They then track the log—sometimes for miles—until they find the helpless brute probably too exhausted to fight. They are also aided by the ever-present vultures and tick birds. Poachers finish him off with their poison arrows.

Went back to village. Had lunch. Started back to main camp. Broke record. Had six flats in twenty-five miles. Caused by thorns from trees. Bitched and patched tubes. Three after dark. One hell of job, takes forty-five minutes to remove patch and inflate. Got in after dark. Fred and camera crew to greet us. Couldn't believe that we left only yesterday noon for the elephant hunt and were back already. With forty-inch buffalo to boot. Much toasting and celebrating. Measured tusks—over five feet. Real respectable size for this part of country.

All plans changed. In a.m. Fred asked if Rui could take Zoli the camera man out. I went lion hunting with Fred, Halmi and Walter Johnson Sr. No lions. No signs at water hole. Back for lunch. Halmi wanted to take me fishing to get movies of catching tiger fish and talapia. Spent two hours. Caught no fish! Had four strikes. Came back before dark, first time in three weeks, and caught up on jobs at camp. Werner out after a notorious native snare poacher.

A ritual before leaving camp is to put your name on the wall of the lodge. The wall is covered with the names of famous people from all over the world.

June 25, 1965

Rui made me a bracelet from the hair of elephant tail, a ritual always observed by a white hunter when an elephant is killed. Also it is a custom to chant a certain victory song when coming back to camp. This lets everyone know that you have been successful in killing an elephant. Sort of like running up a flag when you catch a marlin or sailfish I guess.

Fish, one of the white hunters, returned at midnight with the Scourses (Barb and Spearo). Both got fine elephants. Rui took Zoli out on an elephant hunt. They got within forty yards of two large bulls. Rui whispered for him to load his gun. Put one in chamber. In his excitement he pulled the trigger and scared hell out of elephants and Rui too. Shot passed over Rui's head. He was deafened for some time. They walked two more hours and found herd of elephants. Sneaked up close for shot. Large bull standing in middle. Rui pointed for Zoli to shoot this one in the ear for brain shot. Zoli fired and down he went. Rui congratulated him. They all ran over to the spot where he fell. Real small tusks. He had shot at the wrong one—a cow. "Poop!" said Rui.

Zoli is very low. Demonstrated his humorous nature by inscribing on the wall of lodge a picture of rear end of elephant and the words "She was lovely."

Fred spent last night in blind near dead buffalo—a lion kill. Hoping to get a shot at daylight. Said lion roamed all night. Was within fifty feet of them most of night. At daylight the lion left. Fred has gone back to spend tonight there again. Knick and George came back here to main camp today. He's real happy. He got his two buffalo that he wanted and a zebra.

Rui measured my largest buffalo and bush pig. Both will go in the *Rowland Ward's* record book. The bush pig is number two according to him.

There must be a billion stars out tonight. Halmi got word today by radio that his wife had heart attack. First plane in here Sunday. Halmi will go directly to New York instead of continuing with Fred and I as planned, to India, China and Japan, Hawaii, and home. He is going with me today to film my shooting game with bow.

Went at 7:30 this a.m. with Rui across river for water buck. Found what he said was a tremendous bull. Hit him in leg at sixty yards. We tracked him for three hours. Stopped bleeding.

Came back and got six dogs. Spent two hours trying to find him. No luck. Left boy to stay in area and watch for vultures. Rui and Warner think that it must have been a minor flesh wound, that he will survive.

Went back for another try on water buck. Made one of my crazy lucky shots. Lead him about ten feet. Had space about six feet wide to shoot through. As he came out of the brush I shot. Hit him in lungs at forty yards trotting. We tracked him seven-hundred yards and found him dead. I had a $5 bet with Rui that I wasn't ever going to get one. While Rui went back to get Toyota I put a $5 bill on the arrow still in the critter. We took pictures. These large animals weigh six to seven-hundred pounds. His horns were twenty-six inches. They are dark brown with some white on their face and neck, and have white ring on rump. Look something like size of elk. Had a heck of a time loading him in Toyota—four of us with use of lifting pole.

Spent the rest of the day filming. I would sneak as close as I could. Halmi would take pictures of me pretending to shoot at game with his telephoto lens. The native tracker we used in the pictures was reported to have been a rehabilitated mental patient. He carried a big long knife on his belt. Halmi suggested that he pull it from the sheath and hold it pointed above my back. Halmi said this would make one hell of a picture—provided he didn't have a relapse and bury it in my back. Halmi thought this was real funny. I didn't.

We got some fabulous shots of me shooting at sable, water buck and Cape buffalo.

Saw reedbuck on way back to camp. Took a shot at him. Darned if he didn't run into the arrow. He went about two-hundred yards. Rui says these are the toughest of the antelope family to get. They normally live near very thick cover and don't allow you to get close. His horns are about ten inches long. Weighed probably one hundred and twenty pounds. Resembles our white tailed deer. Took more pictures at sundown.

Took waterbuck to native village.

This was a fitting climax to the end of my safari. It still seems like a dream. This makes fifteen different species of big game trophies taken with bow and arrow. Twenty-six animals in all taken in twenty-seven days with bow.

Asked Rui about who his next client was. Says he's some guy from Europe, flying here with his own private jet.

The beautiful Baobab tree grows in this area. It's a huge tree, sometimes twenty feet through and a hundred feet tall. No leaves. Limbs of structure resemble roots. Looks like tree is planted upside down. Juice runs from soft bark when shot with arrow. Natives drive sticks in trunk making ladder so as to climb up and set their honey bee traps. Natives claim the gods were angry when they made the tree so they planted it upside down.

No mail out for week now. Word by radio that we will have two twins and a couple of single engine planes to pick us up Sunday a.m.

Tore seat and knee out of my heavy corduroy pants on elephant hunt while dashing through brush. Bibla, the baron's attractive wife, sewed them up for me.

Warner is thinking about spearing buffalo. This I want to see.

Today we stopped at a native house. A man and his wife and twenty or so kids sat in the sandy yard that looked like a chicken park. Rui asked him how he would like to have our six hundred pound water buck. His eyes lit up and he made all kinds of gestures. I'll trade you for one chicken, Rui said. A responding nod from the native and the waterbuck was dumped out on the ground. Rui started after his part of the bargain in a cloud of dust and chicken feathers. As he collared the largest rooster, a violent complaint came from the native's wife. She insisted that Rui let him go and take one of the smaller ones. A big argument followed that I couldn't understand, but when our trackers started loading the water buck back in the Toyota I figured that Rui had lost his chicken.

This brought a screaming protest from the old man. With the water buck half in and half out of Toyota, further fast negotiations were made. The kicking off of the water buck again indicated a settlement in Rui's favor. Rui again gave chase and came up with the prize rooster.

Roast chicken, dumplings and gravy for dinner. The native's wife was very mad.

June 26, 1965

Went out with Dick and Wally. Took pictures and shot nothing. Dick got eland and kudu. Bill shot sable antelope yesterday. Rui is having my trophies—waterbuck, zebra, eland, buffalo, warthog, kudu, sable, nyala, leopard and elephant ear—mounted and taken care of in Laurenco Marques. Will ship rest of stuff to Michigan. Rui gave me native bow and arrow set. Went with Fred to shoot a hippo with bow in nearby lake. Plane in this morning to pick up Halmi.

They had two boats for the hippo hunt. One with motor. Had about five back-up guns. I was relieved to find that there was not enough room for me. I was observer from shore. Watched them at one hundred yards with binoculars. Close enough. A big hippo will weigh over two tons. They are known to be real mean. Fred got arrow in one's back. He submerged for a few minutes then tried to go up on shore. Fred tried to get close enough to put another arrow in him. He charged the boats and there was a bevy of rifle fire. Water spouting all around—twenty feet in air. He surfaced. Wally had to finish him with 375. Very exciting to watch. The hide is about one and a half inches thick.

Going after buffalo this p.m. One has been chasing natives. Zoli is going to try him with gun. We are just going to watch the fun. Maybe assist with a shot or two. Werner is taking his spear and six dogs. When Zoli wounds him Werner will finish him with his spear. We all went together after the rogue buffalo yesterday. It killed a native. Real thrilling. In swamp grass eight feet tall. Only way you know a buffalo is near is by the tick birds following him. We had three Toyotas, thirty trackers, bows, spears and many guns. Also six dogs. We jumped him with our Toyota. Then immediately sank the car three feet deep in mud. Scratched from the race temporarily. We had other buffalo around us. About all you could see was the tall grass moving, their dust and tick birds, until they got about twenty yards from us. We were standing up on hood for a better and safer view. Zoli spotted him and screwed up the fun by shooting it dead on the head as he charged the Toyota. Fred had one ram his Toyota. Nearly tipped it

over. It threw one of native trackers out of rear end. He had
to run like hell for a tree. Wally shot him at ten feet just
before he got a native. The impact of the charge sheared
off the spare wheel that was bolted on the back of Toyota.

Well, we said our good-byes this morning to Safarilandia. Real sad. Had twin Commanche, twin Aztec and single
Commanche to pick us up. Fred decided to stay until he
got a lion. This knocked out our round-the-world return
trip. Fred wants a lion really bad. He got an arrow into one
the other day. Lion pulled arrow out with its teeth. Bit it
into five pieces. Fred told me he guessed the lion didn't
like his arrows. He showed me the pieces.

We flew back to Biera. This was on a Sunday. The shipping company's office was closed. We decided to send back
our guns and bows by airfreight, collect to Halmi's studio
in New York. This proved to be the wrong thing to do. The
five guns and eight bows came to a whopping $486. We got
the bill when we stopped in to pick them up on the way
home. Halmi warned us to "sit down" before he presented
us with it.

Rui talked me into leaving my trophies with him. He
would have a friend of his mount them at a special
reduced price. This proved disastrous. I paid him $500
down when I took off for home. A year passed with no
news. I wrote to Rui. He responded that he had been to see
the taxidermist and assured me that the trophies would be
shipped in the near future. Another year slipped by. Again
I wrote to Rui care of Safarilandia. I received word he
wasn't with them anymore. I began to panic. I tried calling
the taxidermist by phone. This didn't work because he
only spoke Portuguese. I got $500 worth of nothing. Next I
tried my attorney. He wrote and received a prompt reply
from the gentleman. He explained that he had a problem. It
seemed that he had completed the taxidermist's work.
However, his wife had divorced him and attached his business assets which included all of my trophies, in a settlement fight.

After numerous letters and sweating off twenty pounds,
I finally got notice that they had been shipped. Several
months of boat and rail rides and they eventually arrived. I

should say most of them. Fred and I were each going to have a coffee table made from the elephant's ears. We had paid $200 extra for these. However, they never showed up, along with about five other head mounts that I had coming. This, plus the fact that they started cracking open, rounded out the lousy "Good deal."

June 29, 1965

Knick and Halmi left for direct flight to New York. Bill Wright, Zoli and I stopped in Narobi for a spell to pick up gifts. Narobi is the second largest city in Africa, a center for native art and best place for curios. Expect to go to Kruger Park tomorrow. Do some filming of animals. Then to Lake Rudolpholf to try fishing for one-hundred pound Nile perch.

Bill Wright and I flew from Rome to Geneva. Rented a car and toured Austria, Germany, and Switzerland for a few days. Then to Paris. Then on to New York. Bill and I had a super time on our ten days in Europe visiting many famous manufacturers of sporting goods. Bill was a treat to be with.

When the trip was over, Fred remarked that we had seen twice the animals on this hunt than he had seen the year previous in the same area.

X

Nebraska Whitetails
1966

In the fall of 1966 Fred, Knick Knickerbacker, Ed Bilderback, Fred's son-in-law Mike Steiger and I were invited on a deer hunt in Nebraska with Dick Mauch. Dick lives in the small town of Bassett, about two hundred miles west and a little north of Omaha. He had been a salesman with Fred's company, covering the mid-western territory. Dick had lived in Bassett all his life, and had been in the hardware and lumber business, as well as ranching. Through the years he learned of many good places to hunt in that area, known as the sandhill country. There are rolling plains where trees are sparse. About twelve miles north of town is the Niobrara River. Along the river and the canyons that drain into it are sparsely timbered areas, making for good whitetail and mule deer country. I had hunted this area before and found that both species were very plentiful. It was also good hunting for pheasant, sharp tail grouse and coyotes.

On our last trip to Alaska, we tried to talk our guide,

Ed Bilderback, into coming to Nebraska to hunt with us. It seemed since we had gone to Alaska and paid him a big fee on several occasions, it was his turn to joint us for a hunt in Nebraska.

One day in October I was at my office working when the phone rang. Picking it up I heard Ed Bilderback's voice saying, "Where are those damn mule deer you want killed, Bob?" I told him about the arrangements I had just made, and he agreed to meet me at the airport in Omaha in a couple of days.

Dick was there to meet us with his plane, when we arrived in Omaha. It was sure good to see my old friend Ed again, as he disembarked from the plane. Dick and I couldn't help but grin a little at the sight of Ed coming down the ramp, in a pair of old blue jeans and a well patched camouflage jacket, carrying his bow—without a case—in one hand, and a handful of arrows in the other.

Fred and Knick arrived two days earlier and were already out hunting. Dick said that we were to join them that afternoon, so we loaded our gear in Dick's plane and took off. As we approached a brushy area near Bassett, Dick pointed out where Fred and Knick were hunting, and spotted them sitting on a rock on the edge of the canyon near Dick's pickup. Dick decided to give them a buzz job, and as we did, I'll be darned if Fred didn't throw an arrow at us. Fortunately we were out of his range. The arrow fell far short, but I could see it all the way up. He didn't lead us enough.

Fred and I were anxious to see the reaction when Ed and Knick met for the first time. We had made it a point not to tell either of them that the other was coming. Over the years when Fred and I had been on Ed's boat, whenever he did something wrong, we always pointed out to him that it wasn't the way Knick would do it on his boat. When I had been fishing with Knick on his boat in Nassau, I likewise made the point that it wasn't the way Ed Bilderback did it.

They both hated those comments. Over a period of several years Fred and I had created quite a bit of hatred in them toward each other. Even though they had never met, they would cuss and swear whenever Fred or I mentioned the other's name. We both enjoyed stirring up a little hornet's nest on their respective boats.

That evening when Fred and Knick came in, we put Ed in another room. Then at the proper time, we had him come out and meet Knick. They were both very shocked and surprised, but pleasingly polite to each other in spite of the feelings they had built up over the years.

We had a big steak fry that evening and discussed the hunting plans for the next morning. This brought to mind last year's hunt when I had hunted the area with Dick, my son Rick, and Dick Turpin, the local warden. We were in a large field bordering the Nebraska River early one evening and had selected blinds in the various corners of the field. Somehow I happened to be the last one to start to my blind from the car. Rick and Dick were already settled in their blinds. As I headed across the field, a deer came into the field directly in front of the spot where I was going to make my stand in a haystack. The bales were in stacks about twelve feet high, which makes a beautiful spot for a blind. You can get high enough so the deer can't wind you, and build yourself a little fortress of haybales over which you can peek out.

I wasn't sure what to do about the deer, and didn't want to fowl up the situation for the others, so I walked around the edge of the field, in the brush so the deer couldn't see me. As I got to the corner where the deer was standing, I was stymied. It was a large doe, and I was hunting for a buck. I decided the best thing to do was spook her out of there, so I took a shot at her from about ninety yards away. To my surprise, the arrow hit her behind the front shoulder. She ran violently for a hundred yards then flipped over dead.

Dick paced off the shot. It was eighty-seven yards! I would like to take the credit for one helluva good shot, but all I wanted to do was spook her.

That evening Dick showed us a huge set of white-tail antlers taken by his friend, Al Dawson. Al had left it with him to have it measured for the *Pope and Young Record*

Book. Dick is an official measurer for this area. We learned later that these antlers went in as Number 2 in the all-time record book of *Boone and Crockett,* and Number 1 in *Pope and Young.*

A mutual friend of Dick and Al's, Del Austin, had been pursuing this deer for three years, and had hit it twice, but each time it got away. He had a collection of the antlers the buck shed for the past three years. He never told anyone where he hunted, and hoped to bag this big trophy for himself. One day when Al was calling on Del, Del invited to go hunting. Del put Al up in his favorite tree blind, he took another blind. As fate would have it, the big buck showed up and Al shot him.

The next morning Dick, Knick and Fred's son-in-law headed east out of town. Fred, Ed Bilderback and I drove ten miles northeast and parked the car on the rim of a large canyon. It was a bitter cold morning and Ed was wearing only a thin pair of blue jeans and a light camouflage jacket. He was the first one out of the car, and peeked over the edge of the canyon. He motioned for me to come and look at the deer in the bottom of the canyon. Fred stayed in the car. We spotted several nice bucks down in the canyon.

Fred wanted to stay in the car until the sun warmed things up a bit, but I reluctantly went with Ed. Ed had never seen a mule deer in his life, and was gung ho about getting one and having it mounted.

We picked the wind to our favor, headed down into the canyon, working our way into the direction we had seen the bucks disappear. We were about fifty yards apart, sneaking along, when I saw Ed drop to his knees and crouch behind a small bush. Over to his right I could see a large buck walking slowly away from him.

Now Ed is a pretty resourceful guy. Fred and I have seen him call deer in Alaska by stretching a blade of grass between his two thumbs and blowing on it. This particular morning, however, the grass was frozen stiff, but it only took Ed a minute to figure out how to make a call. He took out a package of gum and stretching the celephane wrapper between his thumbs, blew through it, squawking just like he does for blacktails in Alaska. The buck stopped and raised its head. I hid behind a clump of bushes and watched as the buck curiously looked in Ed's direction. Ed would give a little squawk, then stop. The buck walked slowly towards him.

The wind was perfect for Ed's position, and the buck came to within thirty yards of where he crouched. He stood facing Ed, making a poor target. Then, hearing another sound, the buck turned his head and looked back. When he did this, Ed let fly with an arrow. It struck the big mule buck between the front legs and buried deep in his chest. The buck made one lunge, slid about fifteen feet and keeled over. He kicked a little bit and that was it.

I went over and slapped Ed on the back, congratulating him on a terrific shot. Ed said, "There's sure not much to killing one of these damn things, is there?"

We hadn't been gone more than fifteen minutes. I looked up at the high rim of the canyon where the car was parked and wondered how we'd ever get the deer up there. Ed field-dressed it, and I mentioned my concern to him. Ed just said, "Well, stand back and I'll show you how it's done!"

He took his hunting knife, slit the flanks of the rear legs wide enough to allow the front hoofs to go through. Then he stuck the front hoofs through, and broke the bones in the front legs, forming a locking device like a T in a slot. He slipped into this just like a guy would put on a back pack, and threw it over his shoulders. The chin of the deer was resting on top of Ed's head with the rack sticking up in the air. Then he said, "Well, if you can carry my bow equipment, let's go!"

It was amazing that he was able to stagger along and keep the deer on his back. But I had seen him haul out my big brown bear hide in Alaska. That hide weighed over a hundred and seventy-five pounds, so I knew he possessed some kind of supernatural strength. Ed's only about five foot seven inches tall, and weighs about one-hundred and sixty-five pounds, but there's no fat on him. It's all muscle.

He stopped to rest once on the way up to the car.

Topping the canyon rim we came out directly at the car. Fred had been dozing in the front seat, and woke up to see this huge rack of antlers coming over the horizon. He jumped out of the car, then saw it was fixed on Ed's back. Ed dropped the deer at the rear of the car, and smiled at the surprised look on Fred's face, seeing us back so quickly with the big buck. It was a three point, as they are known out there. Three long tines on each side, with the longest one fourteen inches. It was a symmetrical rack, and would make a beautiful mount.

Ed commented, "Well, I got it this far. Seems like you guys could at least put it in the car for me." Believe me, Fred and I had all we could handle between us to get that fool carcass in the car trunk.

On the way back, Ed said, "Boy, that sure was a lucky shot." Then he added, "I wonder how come I keep doing it all the time?"

This brought a chuckle from Fred and me.

I've seen Ed do some outstanding shooting in Alaska, and make some fantastic running shots on wild boar and sheep in Hawaii. I recall the time he gave Fred a lesson in Alaska, on how to shoot a bow and arrow when Fred missed a fox perched on a rocky cliff on a little island. Not once, but twice. Ed said to him, "For God's sake, sit down and let a man shoot that knows how!" We were tossing around in a skiff with the waves near this rocky cliff. Ed picked up his bow, and whammo, put the arrow right between the eyes of the fox. Ed added, "We can't fool around with you all day, Fred!" Fred got a big kick out of this, even though he was a bit embarrassed. Fred says that he thinks Ed is one of the best game shots he has ever seen with a bow.

This incident reminded me of still another time I was hunting with Ed in Hawaii. We had sneaked up on a wild boar, and Ed was able to get an arrow into him, but it was a little too far back. The boar started to circle back around toward him on the run. Ed jumped up on a large chunk of lava, as he sensed the boar was getting ready to charge. As it came rushing at him, Ed pulled back and let an arrow fly at the charging boar. It hit him right between the eyes. This might be called luck the first time, but what about the second and third time? I don't know. It's got to be a lot of skill too!

We took Ed's big buck into Dick's lumber yard where he put in on the scales. It weighed 178 pounds.

That afternoon, Dick put Fred, Knick and Fred's son-in-law at the bottom of a big draw in a brushy ravine. Ed, Dick and I made a drive for them to try and push some deer out the other end. We pushed out several whitetails and mulies. The whitetails seemed to follow the valley of the canyon better. Quite often we were able to place a person where they could get a shot. Mule deer seemed to squirt out in every direction over the rim, and it is quite difficult to drive them out the end of the canyon.

Mike Steiger happened to be in the right spot when a nice buck came trotting by. He hit him in the chest cage and downed him. Ed, Dick and I arrived on the scene about the same time as Fred and Knick, and we all congratulated him. As Mike started dressing the deer, he was handling the knife in too dainty a fashion, or in a way that bothered Ed. Ed stepped forward and took the knife from him, saying, "You guys get back and keep the hell out of the way. I'll show you how to dress one of these dudes." Then he added, to Fred, "Check your watch." He tore into the job with both hands. After a couple of slashes, rips, a jerk, a pull and a kick, he had the deer completely dressed out. It took less than a minute. Ed grinned, "That's the way to dress out a deer. You don't want to fool around. Now let's go kill another one!"

The next day Knick shot a nice buck through the heart at about fifty yards. It ran seventy-five yards, then dropped. Again, Ed gave us another lesson on how to dress out a deer.

That afternoon, Ed and Dick volunteered to drive to an area of wooded timber down near the Niobrara River. Dick showed us a spot where the timber narrowed, and he placed Fred, Knick and myself there. Dick and Ed went half a mile up the side of the canyon to begin their drive. On the

way to my stand, as I stepped over a large windfall, a bob-
cat ran out and stopped about fifteen yards away. I slid an
arrow over his back and he scooted into the heavy brush.

We had spent only a few minutes on our stand when
we heard the brush crash and two bucks came into view
running full tilt in Fred's direction. One was about seventy-five yards ahead of the other. They passed within thirty
yards of Fred, one going on his left and one on the right.
He drew a bead on the one on his right. He must have lead
him six feet. He let the arrow go shortly after it got past
him. It looked like a perfect hit in the buck's chest cage.
We waited until the drivers showed up, then started tracking the blood trail.

We found the buck some two-hundred yards down the
canyon. This demonstrated Fred's quickness and his
uncanny ability on a moving target. One day on another
occasion I saw Fred pin a cock pheasant on the run at forty
yards.

Dick asked me to stay on for a few days after the gang
left, to join him and some other friends he had invited up.
Two of his friends were Rick and Dick Cooley from Illinois.
Dick was an airline captain of a 747 jet. His wife, Rick, was
an avid bow hunter too. They had flown their small plane
to Alaska last fall, and both had been successful in getting
moose, caribou and black bears. Rick's black bear was
large enough to have the Number 1 spot in *Pope and
Young*, the record book for bow and arrow at that time.

The other guests were Art Lahaha, his wife and her
girlfriend from Winchester, Wisconsin. Art ran a deer camp
for bow and arrow hunters, and claimed to have taken over
a hundred deer in his lifetime with a bow. He has written a
book on tracking wounded white-tail deer. He can tell, he
claims, by the hair, the blood or some part of the deer on
the arrow, where the deer has been hit and how far it is apt
to travel. Art has also hunted polar bears with a bow. He
had a harrowing experience one time when a polar bear
knocked him down, either in an attempt to get to him or
get by him. I guess that experience satisfied his whim to
hunt polar bears.

I went with Dick Cooley, his wife and Dick Mauch the next morning before daylight. It was a real crisp, cold morning with frost on the cornstalks. We drove down the road toward the ravine, passing a recently picked cornfield. Silhouetted against the rising sun stood a huge buck mule deer about fifty yards from the road. We stopped, Dick Cooley got out, strung up his bow and took a shot at the deer which obligingly stood motionless. He buried the arrow between the front shoulders right into the deer's heart. It took one lunge and piled up.

The following day I went out with Dick for the evening hunt in a hayfield near the Niobrara River. We were sitting on top of haystacks, two hundred yards apart. Just as it was getting dark, a large buck came out in front of Dick and he took a shot at it. When I went to pick him up with the car, Dick was looking for his arrow. We got a flashlight and found the arrow with blood the full length of it. We decided to go back to his place, have dinner, and then come back later. Dick and I thought that with a pro like Art Lahaha in our group, it would be interesting to see him try to retrieve the wounded deer.

We went back out to the spot about 9:00 P.M. and looked for the track. Using a Coleman lantern, we soon found the blood trail. At the beginning of it, there was quite a bit of blood. Art and his friend, the woman who works for him at the hunting camp, and known to be an excellent tracker, led the way. We trailed the deer through a thick, wooded area where there was a heavy growth of brush for perhaps a quarter of a mile. Soon the blood signs became less and less. It was slow going, and Dick, my son Rick, and I let Art and the woman do the tracking. It was interesting to watch them, as they were well experienced at this. At Art's camp he has a rule that if one of his clients hit a deer, they should come back to get him. Then he and the woman would track down the deer. They claimed that they had tracked down and recovered over a hundred deer. Whenever we came to a tree with the trail leading on the side of a hill, Art would ask me, "Well Bob, which side do you think that deer has gone?" I'd invariably pick the wrong side, and he would comment, "No, he went on the other side I think." After close examination, he'd pick up the trail on the side he predicted.

We tracked the deer up the side of a large hill, a sloping grade probably half a mile from where the deer had been hit. As we neared the summit, our gasoline lantern ran out of fuel. After a brief conference, Art said he thought the only thing we could do was go back and get more gas. So Dick, Rick and the woman took the car and headed toward Bassett, some ten miles away. Art and I continued by flashlight, up the slope at a snail's pace and eventually topped the ridge where there was an open area. We stopped to rest. I swung my flashlight around to the left, and there was the huge buck, laying about twenty yards from us. He was still alive, with his head up and looking directly at us.

Art whispered to me to turn the light off. We sat there in the dark for an hour, whispering to each other, trying to decide how to handle the wounded buck. We had no bow or any weapon to finish it off. Art said that when we saw the car lights, he would backtrack down into the timber and find a club. Then when they returned with the lantern, he would rush the deer and hit it on the head, hoping to do him in. This sounded like a far-fetched plan to me, but seemed to be the only solution.

We soon saw the lights of the car coming down the valley, and signaled them to come up. Dick was elated to discover we had located his trophy. By the Michigan scoring system, it had seventeen points and was a huge, magnificent, symmetrical whitetail.

Enroute to the airport to have Dick fly us to Omaha, we passed a spot that brought back some memories of a coyote hunt. I had jumped a coyote while hunting pheasants, and shot him. He ran out over a small hill and disappeared.

I thought I saw him falter as he ran out of sight. I had shot him with number 7-1/2 shot, standard bird shot, with my Remington 12 gauge trap gun. It had a beautiful, burly walnut stock and ventilated rib. As I topped the hill on a dead run, I nearly hurdled the coyote to avoid landing on him. His rear-end was down but he was trying to stand on his front legs. He was growling and showing his teeth. I didn't want to finish him off with the shotgun, because I wanted to have him made into a rug with a head mount. I very foolishly walked up to him and, with my shotgun stock gripped firmly in my hand, took a golf swing at his head with my gun barrel.

This did the trick alright. It killed the coyote, but also killed the shotgun. It bent the barrel and split the stock. It cost me $140 to have it put back into good shape. After paying the taxidermist to have it mounted, it had to be one of the more expensive coyotes that ever came out of Nebraska.

Deer

Jerry Anderson, Bob Munger, and Fred Bear at Grouse Haven.

Water buffalo shot by Fred in the Amazon.

Dick Mauch.

Phyllis Munger.

Joe Engle at Grouse Haven.

Bob with a rabbit shot behind Fred's house.

Nebraska bow hunt with Mike Streecart, Fred, Knick Knickerbocker, and Ed Bilderback.

Ed Bilderback and Bob with crows.

Bob with a Cape buffalo he shot with his bow.

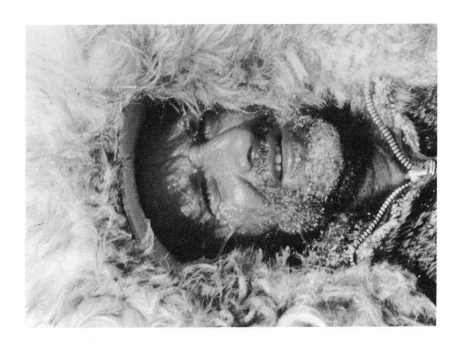

Bob taking a dog sled for a ride.

XI

Tenting on the Arctic Ice Pack 1966

Fred had it in the back of his mind since 1962, when we had our second failure on a polar bear hunt, to someday go back and accomplish his goal. In 1966, Fred made arrangements with ABC American Sportsmen TV film series to go back to the Arctic. He again asked me to be his personal cameraman. A friend of ours, Don Johnson, a local pilot, flew me to Grayling to pick up Fred at the airport. Fred and his wife Henrietta, and his plant manager, Al Mitchel, met us at the plane.

While loading Fred's gear in the airplane, his wife called me to the side, and said, "Bob, I want you to take good care of Fred. I don't want him smoking any cigarettes or breathing any of that cold air." In order to follow this request during the weeks to follow, I had to remind Fred about breathing cold air several times.

We arrived at O'Hare at a busy time, and it was a problem with a small twin to slide in between the big jets in a landing pattern. Don held the plane at a high altitude until we got landing clearance, and then practically dove it down and slid in behind two jets. The tower immediately told us to swing off the first ramp, which we did, so the jet wouldn't suck the tail off our plane.

On our flight to Anchorage, Fred and I were the only two people in the first class section who were not members of the cloth. It turned out that a big catholic conference was going to be held in Anchorage. The most Reverend Joseph T. Ryan was on the plane and sitting right in front of us. We got acquainted with him. He seemed intrigued with our challenge of camping on an ice pack to find a new polar bear hunting method.

At that time, the state of Alaska began restricting polar bear hunting because of the use of airplanes. Some thought they should be put on the endangered list and the season closed entirely. It had been customary up to then to use airplanes to track and hunt the bears. Fred had a special permit from the Fish and Wildlife Department to take a polar bear in May or June. The purpose for this was to try to prolong the sport and prove it could be done without the use of an airplane, by camping on the ice and baiting the bear. To do this with a bow and arrow is truly a challenge, especially under the Alaskan Arctic weather conditions.

We landed at Anchorage and a big delegation turned out to welcome all the priests. There was a band, television cameras, and many dignitaries including the Governor, Mayor and a crowd of other important people. The only thing that wasn't so great, as far as Fred and I were concerned, was that we were asked to get off at the rear end of the plane so we wouldn't be in the picture. This was the first time I'd ever flown first class and been asked to get off at the rear coach section.

We were met at the plane by two friends of mine, Bill Gamel and his wife, Beth, residents of Anchorage. They picked us up, drove us to our hotel, and we had dinner together that evening. This brought to mind a previous occasion when another friend of mine, Harvey Holcomb, and I landed at Anchorage enroute to a brown bear hunt on Kodiak Island in 1954. Harvey had never been in Alaska, but he knew I had. When Bill and Beth met us at the airport we had a trap all set for him. I sent Harvey down to get the luggage, while I met Beth and Bill on the main floor, and we reviewed the trick we were going to pull on poor old Harv. I went down and met Harvey dragging out the luggage. Beth, after I'd given her the cue, came running out of the crowd calling, "Oh Bob, Bob, I'm so glad to see you!" She was a very attractive gal. She threw her arms around me, giving me a big smooch, telling me how much she had missed me. After the hugs and kisses I introduced her to Harvey, then said, "Where's the other girl?" and she answered, "Oh, she's out in the car!"

Harvey just about dropped the luggage, his face turned three shades of red and purple. Before we let the thing go too much farther, Bill walked up and I introduced him to Harvey as Beth's husband. I'm sure it was quite a relief, or maybe a disappointment to poor old Harv. It was kind of a dirty trick, but we all got a big kick out of it, except Harv.

The next day, we met the TV crew, the director, Burr Smidt and Cliff Robertson, the actor. They also had a cameraman and a soundman. We got acquainted over breakfast in the hotel. Burr asked the manager what time the flight to Barrow was and he replied that it was at three p.m. Burr said that we had to get up there before that, so he chartered a C-46 and we had the whole plane to ourselves. We probably had fifteen-hundred pounds of gear with us. Fred had brought several tents which the Thermos people had provided. We had lots of camera gear and sound equipment, heavy sleeping bags and all the necessary camping equipment for the arctic hunting expedition.

Fred booked this hunt with Bud Helmerics, who lives two-hundred miles east of Point Barrow at the mouth of the Colville River. He felt that we should be off by ourselves and have a better chance to do our hunting without any one near our camp. We learned that prior to our arrival, however, there had been over a hundred bear shot out of Barrow. This gave us a bit of apprehension. If that many had been cut off at the pass, how many might be left? It would have been impossible for us to come at the early part

of the season because of the impractibility of the total
darkness at that time of year. The cameras would have
been of no value to us. We had to make this hunt in May
and June, when there was daylight nearly around the
clock. Likewise, the temperature was more compatible
during those months for tent camping.

We landed at Barrow and renewed acquaintances with
a lot of old friends that we had made on the first two trips.
There were quite a few polar bear hunters leaving Barrow
as the gun season had just closed.

The next morning they flew Fred and Cliff Robertson
out to inspect the camp that Bud Helmericks had set up.

We played cards that evening in the little lobby of the
hotel. A young Eskimo native stumbled in and wanted to
get in our game. We tried to discourage him but he insisted. Finally Burr said, "Well, let him play." We dealt him into
the game and damn if the guy didn't win the first pot. When
he started to drag it in, Burr put his hand out and stopped
him, saying, "We're playing Las Vegas rules. You have to
win two pots before you win." This perplexed the Eskimo a
little bit and me too, but he was very agreeable and went
along with it. Damned if he didn't win the next pot. I think
he won more money than all the rest of us. It was about
two o'clock in the morning when we decided to quit and get
some sleep.

We had been weathered in for a couple of days, but the
next day it cleared up and the camera crews were able to
get out to the Colville River. We had talked to Bud on the
radio, and he said conditions around that area had cleared
up. The plan was for Fred and Cliff to go out, survey the
camp that Bud had set up, and we were to follow.

There was so much gear that we had to charter another plane to fly the rest of the crew out. I flew with Joe
Vanderpoole in a Beaver so loaded with gear that there was
barely room enough for Joe and me to get in the plane. Joe
was a little worried about landing the Beaver on the ice, not
knowing whether a strip had been smoothed off near the
camp. Usually a smooth spot can be found to set a plane
down. But when you have to set it down at a certain spot,

sometimes the landing strip is not good, and the wind may be in the wrong direction. Anyway, we flew out and Joe set the plane down. We'd no more than got the skis on the ice than it bounced back in the air. Joe let out a few cuss words and damned the crew or whoever was responsible for cleaning off the runway.

We came to a bouncing, sliding halt and Joe gave Bud a piece of his mind about the lousy landing strip. I think this was about the time that I was appointed maintenance director of the landing strip, and learned that it was going to be my job for the next few days to get it smoothed out.

We unloaded the gear and stored it in one of two tents that Bud had set up a day or two previous. A bear had come along and ripped the other one in half. Normally, we would have felt badly about this, but Fred was pleased to see that we were in good bear-hunting territory. With some twine we sewed up the ripped tent.

Fred, Cliff and I went into the tent where all the gear was stored, one of us picked up a bottle of brandy and we sat down on the duffle. I looked at the label, it said, "Serve at room temperature." Well, it was about twenty-three degrees below zero that day. I asked Fred if he thought it would be alright to serve the brandy at this temperature. He agreed that it would be, so the three of us proceeded to warm our bellies. I can truthfully say that was the best tasting brandy I have ever had. Any warming sensation was a scarcity in this area.

As we stepped out of the tent I looked over to the east. Three hundred yards away, I saw a polar bear moseying along. This would have been an ideal chance for Cliff to take his bear, but the camera crew hadn't shown up yet. So we had to pass him up.

We were camped some 45 miles northeast of the mouth of the Colville River, about ten miles from an open lead to the north. This seemed to be an ideal spot, as seals like to lay and sun near the open water. Also, at this time of year, the seals were having their young. They would burrow down into the snow since polar bears would search them out. Seals are the bears' main diet.

All in all, we felt we had a good combination going for us and that we'd see lots of polar bears. A huge ice pile behind the tents gave us a spot to climb and to scan the ice pack for miles with binoculars. It also provided us with some good drinking water. When the ice lies over a period of many years, the salt drains out of it and it turns a beautiful clear turquoise color. Pieces, chopped off with an axe, can be melted for drinking water or cooking. All the snow that lies in the ice has absorbed the salt and is not fit to eat, drink or use for cooking.

Fred and I set up all the camping gear. We had four Prairie Schooner tents and four pup tents which were about seven feet in diameter. Cliff and the camera crew used the larger Prairie Schooner tents. Fred and I had two of the pup tents, which we set up one inside the other. Fred thought it would be a good idea to insulate these with snow between them.

The snow in the Arctic is dry, and the drifts are packed hard. We used a carpenter's handsaw to cut pieces of insulation from the snow just like styrofoam, about four inches thick. These we slid between the flaps on the tent, about five feet up. We had nothing to put on the floor except our air mattresses. The first night we discovered this was not the thing to put on the ice under a sleeping bag. I had a large Eddie Bauer sleeping bag and I slid a lighter mummy bag inside of it. We put a box in between us on which to set our Coleman lantern and our catalytic heater. This practically took up the whole tent. We slept with our heads near the zipper flap, so if we had to get up during the night—perish the thought—we could handily unzip the tent.

Incidentally, whenever mother nature gave us a nightly call, we took my 375 Browning rifle with us, just in case we bumped into a polar bear that thought we were a tasty seal.

We complained so much about the cold that first night that Bud brought out a couple of caribou hides on his next trip. These we laid down with the fur next to the ice. The hide of the caribou, like all of the deer family, is hollow and acts as a good insulator. Our sleeping conditions improved one hundred percent.

The first night was quite an experience. We slept with all our clothes on except for our heavy insulated boots. We even kept our hats on. Fred had a down insulated hat with flaps which he pulled down over his ears. He also wore his seal skin mittens. I pulled down the earflaps on my own seal skin hat, too. It was twenty-two degrees below zero that night. I didn't sleep very well and finally decided to light the lantern. I thought it might warm up the tent a little bit. I tried to read, but it was almost impossible to turn the pages of a magazine with my mittens on. My ice-cold reading glasses sent shivers up my spine. I gave up and settled for a snort of Early Times, which I fortunately had tucked beneath my pillow. Thought this might ward off any cold I might catch.

When I woke up the next morning, I was accused of doing a powerful bit of snoring. The inside of my sleeping bag, by my head, was covered with a thin layer of ice near my nose and mouth where the ice had formed from my breath. I hit it and it flicked off like peanut brittle.

It was really quite a test, we learned, to live under these conditions for five and a half weeks. Bud told us, prior to our coming, that in the month of February they had three days that were sixty-two degrees below zero. The reason we took our hunting trip in May and June was so we could endure the temperature in a tent at that time of year. Likewise, the sun was up most of the twenty-four hours of each day during May and June, enabling us to film the hunt. I asked myself, why the hell I was there. My purpose was to be a backup cameraman for Fred and take some still pictures that he wanted to use in preparation for his book. I was working for Fred, not hunting!

Our experience with commercial cameramen had not been too good in the past. I don't claim to be a professional cameraman, but in a pinch a little something is better than nothing. Twice before, Fred had arranged for professional cameramen. One weighed nearly three hundred pounds and couldn't climb a mountain. Another time, he simply didn't show up. So I got the job. There are also some cameramen who take a dim view of walking to within a few yards of a bear with nothing but a camera to defend themselves. With a bow and arrow you have to get very close. It is frightening to think what might happen if your guide, who was backing you up, made a poor shot when the bear came charging after you. On the two previous polar hunts, the guide had to shoot the bears to save our skins when they charged.

On our arrival, Bud told us it was a shame to shoot a polar bear. He said he had taken a cameraman out once who wanted to get a closeup picture. Bud said that he hit the bear on the nose with a shovel in order to move him closer to the camera and the bear cried like a baby. This was a little hard to swallow after Fred and I had been charged twice. Bud had corresponded with Fred several times about a polar bear hunt and assured him that he would have no problem getting a bear with his bow. We learned later that he had told Burr, our ABC director, Cliff shouldn't have any problem getting a bear with a gun but he didn't know how Fred was going to get one with a bow. Needless to say this didn't make a big hit with Fred and me.

After several incidents with a polar bear at close range, you become sort of callous to the situation. You also develop confidence in your guide who is backing you up with a rifle. Trouble must be expected when you are harassing a bear that is minding it's own business. And if you put an arrow in him, he is apt to take defensive objections. Unlike rifle hunting, you are invariably so close that the bear sees you before you shoot, and when hit, he identifies his pain with you. You are his enemy!

Cooking in the tent camp was a real problem. Everything starts out frozen, including the water, which comes from blocks of solid ice. My first cooking job was to cut up the caribou leg shanks that Bud had brought. All I had was an old dull hand saw. It took me an hour and a half to cut some steaks for the gang that first night. This was the only time my hands had been warm since we had arrived.

The next day, we started to get things under motion for the Cliff Robertson movie. He was complaining about the loss of his gun. It never arrived in Barrow along with his gear. I told him he could use my 375 if he liked. He asked me to give him some instructions as to the operation of it, and I went through the routine with him several times. Every time he left to go on a hunt, he would call me over and say, "Hey, Pappy, I want to show you how to do this again!" He would then repeat the process of loading, etc. One day he managed to slide a shell into the barrel by mistake. He was holding the barrel down and had a loose grip on it. Somehow he got his finger on the trigger and exerted too much pressure. There was an ice shaking explosion! Fortunately, I had just stepped back a little. The bullet went between Fred and me, and just missed the airplane that was tied down by the tent. The gun flew out of Cliff's hands and slid on the ice about ten feet behind him. Fred looked just about as white as the snow. I was shaken up too, and was stone deaf for awhile. Needless to say, Cliff didn't pass the gun inspection test that morning.

That evening, Burr was telling us about some of his experiences in the service. He described a buddy who went berserk and ran around the camp with a rifle which he would fire in the air and holler, "Yellerbird!" Just as we were settling down in our sleeping bags, Burr sneaked out of his tent with the rifle and fired a shot right near our tent. Then he hollered, "Yellerbird!" The camp came alive immediately, and everyone shouted some choice remarks at Burr. I suggested to Fred as a result of this incident that we should call our camp "Camp Yellerbird." This met with the whole camp's approval. We had a yellow towel that I rigged up on a flag pole. The next morning we ran the flag up on "Camp Yellerbird."

We started that morning to film the picture of a polar bear hunt starring Cliff. It was to include Fred, Cliff, and the Eskimo, Simon. By this time I had worked my way up to chief maintenance man on the airstrip. I was busily leveling it off, the best I could, with a snow shovel when I heard the putt putt of a skidoo. It was Burr. He drove his snow sled up to me and said, "Munger. We're going to elevate you from airport maintenance man to movie star." I said, "What happened?" "Well," he answered, "Every time I point the camera toward that Eskimo he just melts and won't say anything. So you're going to be Simon, the Eskimo." This was my first experience doing anything like this, and I felt a little shaky about the deal. Bud had two Eskimos drive the skidoos out fifty miles to our camp, to ease some of our problems.

The film was done with synchronized sound and we had microphones in our shirts. The antenna wires ran down our legs and we kept the batteries in our pockets. We spent the next two days working up different phases of the hunt, with the intention of dubbing in the kill scene at the end. This gets rather monotonous when you don't have too much to do, and you sit on the ice and pretend you're an Eskimo looking for a polar bear. You get to shivering and shaking after awhile.

The camera crew was a bunch of young guys from New York. This was their first exposure to the arctic weather and they hated it! Fred and I were amused at their remarks when we began filming. They held a slate in front of the camera noting the title and the number of the take. They labeled it, "Ice on Your Balls Bikini Party"; Take #1.

The crew started grumbling a little bit about the food we were eating. Burr and Cliff didn't care for caribou meat. Fred hinted that Bud was sending us all the shanks and keeping the choice cuts for himself and his wife back at the house. We didn't get very good steaks out of the meat he sent us.

The next day, Burr approached Bud about the idea of having something different to eat. Bud started to whine a little bit and said, "Well, you know, when you are in the Arctic you gotta put up with a lot of things." This comment made Burr pretty ticked and he said, "Bullshit! I want some steaks." Bud replied, "Well, I can't get you any steaks." So Burr came back with, "Okay, if you can't get any steaks, I'm gonna get in your damned airplane and I'm gonna fly to Barrow and call New York and have some steaks flown out here." He added, "I want them sitting right here in front of this tent, tonight!" and he pointed to the spot. Then he said, "And they're coming off your bill!"

Bud's temperature went up about twenty degrees. Quite an argument ensued. Burr remarked that he thought Bud was a pious fake. This went over like a lead balloon with Bud. Cliff made it clear that he agreed with Burr, and from then on, there was not much harmony or cooperation as far as Bud, Burr and Cliff were concerned. This made for big problems because Bud had it in for Cliff and Burr, and wouldn't do hardly anything they asked. Fred and I were the only two that he'd talk to after that incident.

The next night Dick McIntyre, from Fairbanks, also a polar bear guide, came into camp with his 180 loaded with New York strip steaks. For the next three days we ate steaks and more steaks. Apparently Burr got his point across. Actually, it was a good thing this happened, because it gave us an extra airplane. Dick had had lots of experience flying in the Arctic, so we used his plane to hunt for bear with Cliff. Cliff shot a big ugruk seal one day while he was looking for polar bears. They skinned it out for him and he planned on making a rug out of it. These are the largest members of the seal family, weighing around one-thousand pounds.

We finally started Fred's film. We spent a day filming the loading of the camping gear on a large sled and pulling it to our new camp site a mile away. There was a block of ice that had been heaved up by the tremendous ice pressure, probably fifty feet high. The beautiful turquoise color made a very colorful back drop for our campsite. The huge block was a good wind break.

We set up our tents, then shot footage of our arrival to our home on the ice pack. Fred did some fancy shooting of flying cardboard discs I threw up for him and the crew filmed it.

In the film, Cliff was supposed to fly in and meet us for Fred's hunt. Bud, on cue, landed in front of our camp and taxied up near our tent. He taxied the plane too far and Burr said he'd have to do it over. He redid this scene six times. Each time it didn't suit Burr. Once we screwed up our lines.

Fred and I were to go out to greet him. When we thought we had it down pat, Fred blew it again. It had not yet been established what my name was. I played the role of the Eskimo guide. When Cliff got out and shook our hands, Fred introduced me to Cliff as Simon Kill-A-Bear. Well, this cracked Cliff up and they had to throw that strip out and do it all over again. They made three more takeoffs and landings before they had a wrap up on one that could be used.

That afternoon a plane circled our camp and came in for a landing. Much to our surprise, it was George Theile, the guide that Fred and I had on the two previous polar bear hunts. Fred and I walked over to the plane and found still another and more pleasant surprise. George introduced us to his polar bear hunting pal, Nina, a gorgeous red head who was Miss Alaska. When the word was out about our new guest, all tents emptied. Cliff was very impressed with the looks of the best dressed polar bear hunter. This was the best thing that had happened to us yet. Burr Smidt, our ABC director, tried to negotiate a contract for her to star in the movie. We learned later that Nina shot a bear on the way back to Barrow. Fred wondered if George gave her a discount on the hunt.

Filming in the Arctic, as Fred and I had found out in our two previous trips, presents many problems. The kids from New York, who were the ABC crew, had never been exposed to anything like this. One can't imagine just how many things don't work. Light filters in from every angle. Film, camera, batteries and photographers freeze. It's hard to work with gloves on, and impossible without. Patience wears thin.

As time went on and Cliff was having no luck in getting a bear, Burr suggested that we film two endings. One that we could work a bear into later, and one without.

We spent the next three days on Cliff's film, riding the sleds and trying to build up to our stalking of a bear. Cliff and I sneaked up on several fake bears as the crew filmed our actions. We crawled in and out of huge blocks of ice, with Cliff pointing and whispering which way the bear was going. I followed him, like a commando with my rifle, as his guide who was backing him up. Many times we almost froze to death waiting for the crew to work on the cameras or sound equipment. On our final sneak I got Cliff up into a huge jumble of ice and pointed to the fake oncoming bear.

When he appeared, Cliff whispered, "Bob, he doesn't look very big." I responded, "He's not a really big one." Cliff tapped me on the shoulder and said, "I guess I'll pass him up. I didn't come up here to shoot a small bear. I'll come back next year for a big one." I turned and congratulated him on his good sportsmanship, and that was the end of his movie.

Simon told us that when the spring breakup occurred, the arctic char congregated around the icebergs. These are excellent eating fish. I asked him if he thought they would bite now, assuming we could make a hole in the ice. He said he thought that they would. We were all anxious to supplement our caribou diet with fish. Bud brought out a spud and Simon and I started spudding. We got down four feet and had to put a four-foot extension on the handle.

After two hours we had a breakthrough at seven feet. It proved to be a real gusher, bubbling up about a foot high. Before we realized what was happening we had the supply tent flooded with four inches of water, and it was headed toward the other four tents. It also was headed toward Jim's airplane. We didn't want the skis to freeze in the ice. Jim moved the plane and we talked Simon into wading out in the water and capping the hole with a chunk of ice.

The next day, I got up the courage to punch a small hole where we had spudded to try a little ice fishing. We were in seventy feet of water. I couldn't catch anything with my bacon except some small shrimp that clung to the bait. Apparently, the tide had been coming in while we were spudding the day before, and forced the water up through the hole. We had to continue on our caribou diet.

One day, we were all sitting in the cook tent when Jim

jumped in his plane and started his take off. He was heading to his house to pick up some supplies. Suddenly, the engine roar stopped. Mike, the cameraman, stepped outside to take a look. He came running back in the tent and said, "Jimmy crashed on takeoff."

We all rushed outside. Sure enough, the new super cub lay on its nose with one wing up in the air. Fred and I jumped on the skidoos and ran to the rescue. He was out of the plane before we arrived, and stood looking at his poor new Super Cub. Fortunately, he was not injured. A strut that supported the ski buckled and let the prop down on the ice. The prop was bent and a wing tip ruffled. Other than that it appeared okay. Bud came out and inspected it. He went back home, got his tools, a prop, some bolts and bailing wire. After a short time they had it standing on its two legs again. Jim took it for a short, slow and low cruise to see how it handled. Bud concluded that Jim should fly it into Fairbanks to get the wing fixed.

Jim took off the next morning on his six-hundred-mile flight over the mountains. Bud asked me if I could do the job of cooking in Jim's absence. I told him I thought that I could. Cooking is one of my favorite pasttimes and never bothered me, but I got a liberal education under these arctic conditions and with this pack of hungry guys. When you start with everything frozen, it's a different ball game.

We had a bottle gas stove in the cook tent. The first order of the routine was to get some ice. I had to climb a big chunk near the tent. I would chop off the peak of the iceburg with an axe.

The next thing is to thaw out your hands and the cooking utensils. All the food, of course, is frozen solid. It's hard to crack an egg when it's like a billiard ball. As you can imagine, I took much more time to get things going. Likewise, cooking for eight people in the small tent made it a lengthy procedure. It seemed that the cold weather made us all hungrier than usual. Everyone wanted a full course meal three times a day. Steak, vegetables and potatoes for lunch and dinner. If you didn't get right at the dishes when the meal was over, all the silverware would freeze to the dirty plates. After each meal I had to change into my hunting clothes to assume my role as the Eskimo guide. It kept me busy just changing clothes.

We ran out of meat in three days. Bud flew me to shore where I shot a caribou. Seems strange to see a herd of caribou this time of year. All, except the large ones, have small antlers now. I asked Bud, "Where are the big bulls?" "Those big ones without antlers are the bulls. They have shed their antlers." When you take off the caribou hide you discover that it has many blotches about half the size of an egg. If you cut the skin covering this, you find large white grubs that have spawned from the bite of a large fly in the summer. These are about an inch long and nearly as large as a cigarette.

Fred felt sorry for me one morning and offered to cook the pancakes. He made several attempts to get them to rise, but couldn't. He added some ingredients that he was told would help. Nothing worked. Just as he admitted defeat, his knee hit the big platter of bacon that I had cooked. It slid off the stove and dropped in a bucket of dishwater. I kicked his butt out of the kitchen and started all over.

Fred and I noticed that, each evening after supper, the soundman would jump on a skidoo and disappear for an hour or so. We both were curious, so the next scouting trip we took we followed his tracks. About half a mile from camp we found a polar bear carving made out of a huge block of ice. He had learned sculpture at a university in Rome. It was a real good likeness of a bear and just about the same size. He told us he had done it with a machete.

Some days the weather was too bad to film. I talked one of the camera men into helping me build an igloo, using a hand saw and a machete. We would saw blocks out of a snowdrift, set them on each other, and rub some snow in the cracks. At twenty-five degrees below zero, they freeze together solid in a few minutes. I tried to interest Fred in sleeping in it one night, but he didn't think much of the idea.

The next evening after supper when Fred was in the

cook tent watching the boys play cards, I took the sleeping bags out of our tent and put them in the igloo. Fred was surprised and shocked to find the empty tent. He tracked me over to the igloo where I had a sign saying, "Welcome to the end of the world!" Reluctantly, he crawled in and we had the distinction of being the only guys in the group that night to be sleeping in an igloo. It was as warm as the tent.

We spent half of the next day riding the snowmobiles past the cameras through the jumbled chunks of ice. This proved to be quite a spectacular part of the film. They got an angle shot of Fred as the skis were off the ground. Another day was spent following Fred and me sneaking up on imaginary bears. Fred sneaked through the towering chunks of ice with his bow and I followed him with my rifle. We were both dressed in full white suits and were wired for synchronized sound. This recorded all of our whispered conversations. We used the film that I had taken the two previous trips to dub in bears walking past us. We wound up filming Fred's movie in three days and the crew packed all the equipment and readied themselves for their departure. They were ready and anxious to leave.

The next day proved to be a whiteout and we all knew that the Beaver would not be able to fly. This caused much discontent and put the boys in somewhat of an ornery mood. They had thirty pieces of equipment packed in aluminum cases sitting at the airstrip. They spent the day playing cards, drinking booze and bitching about the weather. They had just returned from a balmy trip in South America and were scheduled to make their next film of General Doolittle hunting in sunny warm Africa.

The thought of this increased their hatred for the Arctic.

The next day was the same, weatherwise. Fred and I hated to face the crew, who we could hear cussing in the next tent. I recall that one of them vowed his only conversation was going to be "Shit!" We tried to console him, but all we got was "Shit!" Fred and I started praying for good weather.

The next morning was clear and they were all smiles,

knowing they were leaving this miserable spot. They briefed me on the camera equipment that they were leaving for me to use to film Fred's killing of a bear. The drone of an engine brought ecstatic yelps as they ran to the landing strip.

I recall Fred's remark as we stood watching, "My God! When they all made a rush for that open door on the Beaver, I thought they would come out the other side they were going so fast!"

I think Fred and I both housed an envious feeling as the plane lifted off the ice and disappeared as a speck in the sky. It had been nearly three weeks for us in this cold, bleak country, and I can't say I was too wild about staying on. Especially with the shortage of bears. No telling how long it could take. Anyway, now it was Fred, me, Simon and the polar bears. The first order of the day was to move our gear into a bigger tent.

We spent hours sitting and discussing how we were going to find a bear. Having seen only one bear so far and Fred not wanting to use an airplane, posed what seemed like an insurmountable situation.

The days that followed were both long and rather lonesome. The sunlight now lasted for practically twenty-four hours a day. You could read a newspaper anytime of night.

Fred figured the best way to find a bear was to bait one into camp and Fred could shoot him from the tent. This sounded good on paper. We organized a series of seal hunts. Fred and I would strike out daily, going north about twelve miles to the open lead where the seals were.

We used the same trail daily, mostly to help our navigation on cloudy days, and to sweeten up the trail with seal blood. Fred drove the snowmobile and I sat on an eight-foot sled that we built out of two by sixes. After shooting the seals, I sat on the sled and carved them up in little chunks and sprinkled the trail with bait all the way back to camp.

We also made a cooker out of a fifty-five gallon drum and boiled the seal fat to make a scent that should be sniffed for miles by any passing bear. Our trail ran north and south. We were told that the bears work from west to east. The idea was that when they come upon the baited trail they would nibble their way to our camp.

We kept the camera mounted on a tripod focused on some seals stacked in front of our tent. We kept the tent flap open for any night visitor. Fred had his bow ready and I slept with my 375. During the many hours of bad weather, Fred and I sat on our cots and tried to entertain each other by telling stories of two lifetimes of hunting experiences. After we had told each other the same story about three times, they ceased to be funny anymore.

Time dragged and we both wished we were back home. On hunts in the typical mountains and woods, one can lessen the monotony by going fishing or hunting some other kind of game. Here, it's limited to one monotonous pasttime. I guess the real test of one's nerves and compatibility is to spend five and a half weeks in a small tent looking at each other.

Many seals gave us a problem as they were in flat areas of ice and we had to take long shots. I recall Fred's telling me about Bud flying him to an area where there was supposed to be a lot of seals. They pulled a sneak, but couldn't get closer than two-hundred yards. Fred shot the seal and Bud patted him on the shoulder saying, "Lucky shot, Fred." "Good" would have been the word Fred preferred.

Fred had Bud bring out a kid's sled and some plywood. He had the idea he could rig up a shield on the sled, cover it with a white sheet, and leave just a small hole to shoot through. He then planned to lie on his belly and paddle the sled with his hands in hopes of getting closer for a shot. Fred spent about two hours fixing up this shooting device. I told him he should put this in the next year's catatog.

Bud spotted the sled as soon as he got out of the plane. "What's this, Fred?", he asked. Fred proudly remarked, "That's my new seal hunting rig." Bud leaned over and put his hand on the plywood shield. He said, "Fred, this is not going to work," and to Fred's shocked astonishment, Bud ripped the shield off the sled.

This was one of the three times that I ever saw Fred get mad in thirty some years. He stomped around like he had his pants full of ants, and his face turned as red as a beet. He didn't say a thing. I think actually he was too mad to talk. Bud got the unhappy drift, got back in his plane and left.

It took an hour for Fred to cool down and stop sputtering. I thought it was funnier than hell myself, but I dared not show my emotions, except in a sympathetic fashion. Well, he finally did pick up the pieces and patch it back together. In spite of Bud's opinion, Fred was able to put it to use and kill a few seals.

On one of the drag trips I was on the back end of the sled, Fred was pulling it with the skidoo, and I saw two strange black objects. It was rather fuzzy that day, with visibility not too good, and these objects were behind us about one-hundred yards, and about three feet off the ice pack. I kept watching as they gained on us. It turned out they were a couple of eider ducks trailing us in our snowmobile tracks.

We wound up with some carcasses in a pile in front of our tent. Fred fixed a string to the seals and ran it into the tent where he fastened it to a cluster of empty beer cans for a night alarm system. The only time it worked was one night when I had to get up and go outside. I reached down and jerked the string. I got a response from the tent, "How big is he, Bob?"

In the two weeks of dragging, we discovered one bear track that had hit our trail, but he went in the wrong direction—out to the open lead. I noticed that he left the trail several times. On close inspection, we found that he had eaten our cigar butts that we had thrown out previously. I told Fred we were using the wrong bait and we should have Bud bring out a few boxes of Tipperillos.

Jim came tooling in from Fairbanks the next day with the repaired Super Cub. He flew Simon back to the mainland.

Fred and I kept wondering when Cliff Robertson would show up.

We kept up the seal hunt on days we could travel.

Some days it blew so hard we didn't dare leave the tent. These days were not what I would call fun and games.

Bud came out the next morning and Fred suggested we take both planes and go on a scouting party. Fred went with Bud and I flew with Jim. We had flown only a few miles from camp when Fred spotted a bear. He was walking along a pressure ridge that led to the open ice to the north. It had been twenty-five days since we had seen one. We almost forgot what they looked like.

We decided to land several miles ahead of him on the pressure ridge and set up an ambush. Bud left Jim with us and flew back to the mainland. The thought of whether or not this nineteen-year-old kid could handle the job of backing us up with his rifle if the bear charged us worried me. Having had two bears gunned down when they charged has made us a little jumpy.

Fred picked out a spot that looked good to him. He placed Jim and me twenty yards behind him in some chunks of ice. We waited, waited and waited. It seemed like an hour and a half. Fred peeked over the huge block of ice that he was using for cover and spotted the bear coming our way. When he was four-hundred yards from us, he veered to his right. This fouled up our ambush position. Fred whispered for us to follow him. We hurried in a hunched-down position behind some rough ice to a spot about one-hundred yards to the east and took another stand. Fred did all the looking. One head is better than three. He signaled to Jim and me what was happening.

A situation like this always presents a problem. I knew I shouldn't raise up before Fred was ready to shoot, for fear the bear would see me and spook. On the other hand, Fred wanted a movie of his shooting the bear. I asked myself, which was the more important thing? The bear or pictures? Once down on Kodiak Island, I raised up too quickly and all we got was a picture of a running bear. We had tried so hard for so many days and I sure didn't want to be the one to screw it up.

I had eyeballed a large chunk of ice near me that I tentatively chose to jump behind if the bear charged. I had the camera trained on Fred and decided that when he raised up to shoot, I would stand to catch the action.

The bear came shuffling toward us almost on a trot. When he got within about fifty yards from us he stopped. Fred raised up and so did I. The bear was standing broadside looking at us. He acted as if he may have winded us. Fred knew this was the moment of truth and released the arrow. I saw it bury deep behind the bear's front shoulder. He spun around, trying to grab the arrow shaft.

He quickly shifted into high gear, running the other way, thank God! I could see a red blotch on his white fur as he hurried over the next pressure ridge. Fred turned and smiled at me. I slapped him on the back and shook his hand. Jim came over and congratulated Fred on the perfect fifty yard shot.

We waited about five minutes, then started after the bear. We hit a good blood trail as we topped the pressure ridge and saw the bear down about seventy-five yards from us. Finally the three of us walked up to within thirty-five yards.

Fred and I were both beat when we reached camp. Fred finally spoke, as he threw his parka down on the floor. "Bob," he said, "I hope I never have to kill another bear!" The next day we stretched the nine and a half foot hide on a rack to take pictures.

Bud flew out the next day and said that he had received a message about Cliff Robertson, but it was not clear. The transmission was not good that day, and he couldn't determine whether they said he was, or wasn't coming. Fred suggested that they fly into the Dewline site, which was on the shore about forty miles directly south of us. This is an early warning system operated by the military. So Fred and Bud flew in and landed on the ice in front of the building.

The man in charge of the site was surprised to have callers, and started quizzing them about who they were, what they wanted, and how they got there. After putting them through a third degree, he finally allowed them to come in and let Fred use the radio to call Barrow to try to get a communication through to New York to ABC to find out about Cliff. It was quite a shock to the military to learn that we had been flying past the place for the previous five weeks and their radar system had not picked us up. It makes a person wonder whether those things really work.

We got confirmation through Bud's radio on the fifth day that Cliff was coming back, so Fred and I felt we might as well go to Bud's house and stay, as it would be a lot more comfortable. I told Fred that we had one more task to perform, and told him to follow me. We jumped on our skidoo and took off. Fred was puzzled but followed. When we arrived at a spot about two-hundred yards from the sculptured bear, carved out of ice, I stopped and said, "Fred, we've got to kill one more bear!" I flipped a coin and Fred won the toss. I handed him my 375. He took a shot and missed. I took the next shot and blew him into a thousand ice cubes. I finally got my bear, too!

Fred had quite a bit of gear with him, so Jim took Fred in the first trip and I stayed behind and waited a couple of hours for him to return for me. It's hard to describe the lonely, isolated feeling I had when that little plane disappeared as a speck on the horizon. Being on that vast ice pack all alone for the first time was a rather frightening feeling. I was quite relieved when at last I saw Jim's plane coming back to pick me up.

When I arrived at Bud's place, Fred had already showered and changed his clothes. He'd made plans to have a little celebration in honor of Cliff for his arrival. We were mighty glad to leave that ice camp. Before too long Bud's voice came over the radio, "This is the Arctic Tern, estimate arrival in twenty minutes. I have Cliff Robertson." In twenty minutes the voice came back on, "I'm on the final approach." I looked out the window and saw the Arctic Tern touching down on the strip.

I was the first one out to the plane and opened the door for them. Cliff hopped out and greeted me with a "Hi ya, Pappy." It was good to see him again.

Fred and I slept in the barn. It was pretty crude. It had an old stove in it which we had to keep pouring fuel oil into it to keep things from freezing. There was one window that was a pretty good size. I peeked out the next morning and directly below us were several ptarmigan nestled down in the soft snow. All I could see were their heads sticking out with their little black beaks and eyes. I thought this would be a real good opportunity to shoot some for our evening meal.

Fred helped me remove the window pane, and I got my bow and leaned out the window. Fred hung on to my belt so I wouldn't fall out. It was about a fifteen-foot shot straight down. After shooting several arrows, the birds still sat there. I had them fenced in with arrows, but I couldn't seem to hit one. I got down to the last arrow in the box, and missed again. Fred promptly took the box and threw it out the window hitting one of the birds and the flock flew away.

In the meantime, the weather closed in and we all were frustrated by the wait, and we finally gave up. Fred chartered a Beaver to pick us up and fly us back to Barrow. That evening we took the Wein flight into Fairbanks and put up at the Fairbanks Inn.

The next day, we had to go to the game commission and turn over the bear hide which Fred had taken on the special permit. We were tickled to death to catch the first flight to Seattle and get out of that cold, miserable country. We were both getting quite homesick, too. In fact, one day Fred took a five-gallon can and fastened a sign on it which read:

DONATION Please help support the financing of the divorce of two overdue polar bear hunters.

We were both pleased to get back to Michigan after that long stay in the Arctic, not to mention completing our third, and our last, try at polar bears. I hope.

ABC ran Fred's movie on their Sunday national program twice. They never did show Cliff's film.

Covering the three trips on the icepack, Fred and I have spent over three months hunting polar bears. We have probably looked at nearly a hundred. I question if any one will ever exceed this record. I hesitate to attempt to convert this into dollars and cents. Maybe this should be spelled sense.

XII

Take a Girl Hunting 1967

Fred contacted me in the spring of 1966 and asked how I'd like to star in a TV film. My first thought was, what does it pay? But my answer was "Hell yes!" It seems that Bob Halmi, director of Fred's tiger film in India and the buffalo film in Africa, wanted him to do a grizzly bear film in British Columbia, Canada. Fred had previously agreed to do a deer hunt for the TV show "American Sportsman." Bob Halmi had teamed up with Joe Foss to do a series called the "Outdoorsman for TV." Fred told Halmi to contact me. He called later that day and I tried to play hard to get but I gave in quickly and took his offer. We did the show in the Kispiox River in British Columbia during September.

Afterwards I got a call from Joe asking me to join him at the Kispiox film premiere in New York. I took my friend, Harvey Holcomb with me as he was with us on the grizzly hunt. It was a fancy bash, held at Toots Shore's Dinner Club in the Big Apple.

There were about one hundred fifty guests from the

219

Outdoorsman, American Sportsman, Outdoor and *Travel* magazines, travel agencies, airlines and gun manufacturers at the premiere. We were all asked to drop our names in a box as we entered the club. After the show, awards were presented. Joe was the M.C. and drew the names out of a hat. I was shocked when the first name drawn was Bob Munger! Beautiful gifts like fancy rifles, shotguns, bows and many other items littered a twenty-foot table. As I came to the table, Joe introduced me as his hunting buddy and proceeded to tell a story about me to try to make me a hero.

I noticed an airline ticket on the table, picked it up and read the caption: "good for one free trip to Africa." I said to Joe, "Is this for real?" He assured me that it was and I said "I'll take it." I have since admired Joe's ability to draw names out of a hat.

After the drawing, Toots Shore invited Joe, Harvey and me to join him at his table. I called my wife after we had a couple of drinks. I woke her up at 1:00 a.m. and asked her if she would like to go to Africa. I guess she thought I said "Honey I'm going to Africa." She gave me a gruff answer. When I finally rephrased my offer she was very excited and happy.

The ticket was presented by Pan American Airlines and was good only on their inaugural flight to Dar es Salaam, Tanzania, a seaport town on the Indian Ocean. The flight would leave Friday of that week. The drawing was held on Monday. Let me tell you, it's quite a trick to get back to Michigan, get shots, a babysitter, and dog and cat sitters, visas, money, pack and arrive at Kennedy Airport by 4:00 p.m. on Friday.

Everything happened so fast that I had no time to make any hunting arrangements. I just threw my bows and arrows together. I wanted to take a lion and a rhino to complete my big five: the ultimate of African hunting achievements. We made it to Kennedy on time and were paged by Pan Am. We met the manager who was traveling with us on our flight. He asked for my tickets. Upon examining them he said, "One is for first class (mine) and one is in the tourist section." I said I would drop back and visit my wife occasionally. He laughed and said, "Give me those tickets." He reappeared in a few minutes with two first-class tickets.

Shortly after take off I was paged by a Mr. Roman Houpolski of the Safari Outfitters Travel Agency in Chicago who wanted to meet me. He had heard of my travels with Fred and sat down with us. He was going to Tanzania to set up a hunting complex and asked if I had made any arrangements. I told him I had not. He then asked us to join him on a ten-day safari at the base of Mt. Kilimanjaro. I hastily thanked him and accepted his offer.

We arrived at Dar es Salaam at 1:00 a.m. There was a hang-up with the immigration people and they kept my bows and Houpolski's gun at the airport. We went back the next morning to pick them up. I got my bows but they confiscated his gun and he never did get it back. Houpolski was very upset. I stopped to pick up my license and was shocked to hear that they didn't allow bow hunting in this country. This really changed the water on the minnows. I had taken twenty-six animals the year before while with Fred and wasn't about to repeat the act with a gun. I was very disappointed and Phyl sensed this. I said I had so wanted for her to see Africa in the wild state, unlike in the parks, where the four o'clock beasts meet the 4:00 bus for a hand out. There the animals are wild all right, but not like in a hunting area and you are protected by bars on the bus windows. It's just not the same. The wild ones dodge a bullet now and then, and kill their own food and react much different toward humans.

The best way to tell it is, it's like tenting out but the wild areas are different and more thrilling such as when you see the tracks of a lion that sniffed your camping gear during the night. Animals are spooky when hunted. Phyl saw the disappointment in my face and said, "Well, I'd like to go and camp out. I'll hunt." I just about dropped my teeth! About the only thing she ever hunted was mice with a trap in the kitchen. Well I kissed her and rented a 30.06 rifle for her. I rented a 20 gauge automatic shotgun for myself and vowed that I would keep the camp in meat. We got outfitted in Arusha and with four trucks and two Land Rovers loaded with gear headed out for the base of Kilimanjaro. Ten natives and two hunters accompanied us. We set up camp under a huge akasha tree with the mountain in the distance, its peak blanketed in snow.

As soon as we were settled in, Keith McCormack, one of the hunters, tried to teach Phyl to sight in her 30.06 rifle. It was a disaster. She couldn't come anywhere near the target with a scope! After many tries, Keith discovered that she couldn't shut her left eye. Phyl shoots right handed. Keith took her shooting glasses off and taped the left lens shut with some electrician tape. She tried again and "BINGO," the bucket went flying. No trouble now. "She's ready" said Keith.

The next morning we embarked on Phyl's first safari. I was thrilled and she was too! The weather and the countryside were beautiful. This area reminds me of the plains around Las Vegas. Keith soon spotted a Grant's gazelle feeding near some akasha trees. He took Phyl with him and they sneaked behind some brush to within eighty yards of the gazelle. I stayed back about two-hundred yards. Phyl leaned against a tree to use it for a rest. She was wearing her shooting glasses and squeezed off a shot. Down went the Grant. I ran over to congratulate her and tears were flowing. She said, "Oh! I've killed him." The ink hadn't dried on my safari check yet and she wanted to call it quits! I had to have a serious fatherly talk with her. I don't remember how I convinced her that she should continue the hunt but she finally agreed.

On the way back to camp she shot a Thompson's gazelle. I picked off several guinea hens for the pot.

The next day she got a beautiful Garnuk or Waller's gazelle. I was amused when the Garnuk jumped just as she shot. Phyl was a little miffed. Up to now she was two-for-two. She got off another shot and knocked it down. But the Garnuk got up and ran a short distance. With the next shot he was down for good. Roman brought in a big cape buffalo that evening. The next day Phyl got a record-book impala. One of our black trackers was so elated that he kissed Phyl on the cheek. I thought this was touching!

On the way home we saw a large python trying to catch a Dick-dick. He slithered up in a thorn bush. Keith asked me if I wanted him for the hide which could be tanned and used to make some leather goods. I said I did. He didn't want to fire a shot because there were some lesser kudu in the area, so the trackers, Keith and I each found a club and surrounded the bush. When the python stuck his head out near me, I whapped him on the head, and did him in. That snake measured 18 feet in length.

Then we saw a kudu, but Phyl didn't get a shot. Actually she saw it and we didn't and Phyl scolded us for not doing our job. She said we were spotting game like a bunch of women.

Back to camp for "sundowners." Cocktails around the camp fire at sunset are known as "sundowners." The cook fried up some tasty tidbits of guinea for hors d'oeuvres.

We started out at daybreak and ran into a herd of zebras. Phyl made an outstanding shot and dropped a zebra at one hundred yards. I was real proud of her. On the way back to camp we came upon a deserted Masai village. Phyl wanted to take a look inside one of the huts. These are made by putting sticks in the ground and bending them over to make a dome top. Then a coating of cow dung is added. They look like an Eskimo igloo with a tunnel crawl space at the entrance. Phyl is quite adventuresome and so she crawled into the hut on her hands and knees. She came out quicker than she went in, followed by a swarm of bats.

At last we were back at the sundowner campfire where Roman was just starting a big celebration. He had returned to camp with some huge elephant tusks. We enjoyed a feast of mixed game for dinner that night. All of the antelope family is delicious eating. Tomorrow would be our last day on safari.

Keith wanted Phyl to get a fringed ear oryx—a large antelope about the size of an elk with three foot spiral horns. These are considered a prize trophy. At about 11:00

we located a large bull, but were not able to get a close shot. Finally Keith said, "I think this is about as close as you are going to get." The oryx was about one hundred seventy-five yards away. Phyl leaned against a tree and took a shot. To my amazement he bolted to his left, flipped and was down. He was dead on our arrival. I couldn't believe it. Keith was real tickled and so was I.

This made six trophies, a very respectable bag for a short safari. I was very proud of her. I picked up some lesser busters—like a turkey and a few sand grouse for camp. We hated to think about leaving Africa.

On the way back to Nairobi the next day, we met two Masai tribesmen tending their cattle. Their only means of defense is a crude shield from cowhide and a six-foot spear. This hardly seemed the right equipment to ward off a lion attack.

I asked Keith to have them come over to our car. I wanted one of their spears and a shield. Keith said, "Your money is no good." A six-foot-five Masai came up near the car. I took an aluminum arrow out of my quiver and threw it like a dart near his feet. It stuck in the ground. I said, "Keith, tell him I'll give him six arrows for his spear." The Masai handed me his spear. It cost me another six arrows to get the shield. I trust he had a back-up supply of spears and shields.

After the safari we visited some of the highlights of Kenya, Bill Holdens Safari Club at Mt. Kenya, Kikerek, and Tree Tops, a famous hotel built in the trees for observing wild animals.

When you leave Africa you feel like you are saying goodbye to an old friend.

XIII

Barefoot Moose Hunt
1967

Fred and I made arrangements to return to Alaska hoping to shoot even a larger moose than the one he had taken the year before. Again, we agreed to meet in Chicago.

From there we flew nonstop to Anchorage. The month before Fred had made reservations for us at the Captain Cook Hotel, a beautiful highrise structure outside of the downtown area.

We checked in at the desk and were surprised to learn that they had no reservation on file for us. Fred asked to see the manager, Dick Lowe. He and Fred were old friends. He was real pleased to see Fred. After a jovial chitchat, Dick asked if there was anything he could do for us. Fred said, "Yes, there is Dick. Bob and I wondered if we could pitch our tent out on the front lawn." Dick said, "What are you talking about?" "Well," Fred said, "they seemed to have lost my reservation."

A puzzled look came over Dick's face, he promptly reviewed the guest list, but came up with nothing. His face flushed and he said, "You guys come with me." He took us by elevator to the top floor. As we stepped out, he explained that this floor was known as the Crows Nest. It consisted of three suites, number one, number two and number three Crows Nest. He asked if we thought we could put up with one of these for a night or two? Fred turned to me and said, "Golly, I don't know, what do you think, Bob?" I tried to answer him in a way that camouflaged my enthusiasm with a calm, "Yes." Dick and Fred both smiled—the deal was made.

Fred selected Crows Nest number one. Dick explained that this was the Governor's Suite. He further explained that Governor Hickle owned the hotel. Fred and I tried to make the necessary adjustments to fit into the environment. The view out of the all-glass walls was breathtaking. The west looked out on Cook inlet with snow capped mountains in the distance, to the north was Mount McKinley, Alaska's tallest mountain blanketed in snow, and to the east the city of Anchorage. To go along with our facilities was a beautiful glassed-in dining room and bar a mere 50 steps away. Fred and I spent the next two days just looking out the windows with an occasional break to visit the dining room to get in our exercise.

The next morning, we met Hank Taylor, a friend of ours who had been on several hunts with Ed Bilderback, our brown bear guide. We invited Hank to join us for breakfast. Hank told us he could line up an American bison hunt for Fred. He said that it would make a thrilling movie. All Fred would have to do was to ride a horse over the rough tundra at full tilt and shoot the buffalo while sitting in a saddle. Fred replied, "Hank, don't you like me? Why do you want to get me killed?" I guess I shouldn't have to say that Fred turned the offer down flat.

We ate in the plush dining room. Fred and I sat side-by-side in a booth and Hank sat across the table. A man and his wife sat at the table beside us. During our conversation, I inquired about Ed's wife. Hank answered me in a booming voice, "My God, she's huge!" and he pointed to the lady sitting across from Fred, saying, "Why she's almost as fat as that lady right there." Well, the lady jumped up about four inches in her chair and pointedly replied, "Young man I want you to know that I'm just pleasingly plump." Fred and I both wished we were on the top of a mountain somewhere.

After breakfast, we broke company with Hank and strolled to the lobby. The whole place was teeming with excitement. Everyone seemed to be on the run. Fred asked the desk clerk what was going on and he said Governor Hickle and some dignitaries from Washington, D.C. were coming in. We watched the procession of limousines pull up in front. Fred and I stood by the front window puffing on our tiperillos, watching the show.

Governor Hickle was the first to make an entrance. He walked directly to the front desk where Mr. Lowe, the manager, was standing at attention, and said, "Dick, I would like number one Crows Nest please." Dick, with a red face and quiver in his voice said, "I'm very sorry Mr. Hickle, but number one Crows Nest is taken." With this Fred broke out with a chuckle, almost swallowing his cigar. He said, "Bob, as far as I'm concerned the hunt's a success!" It's not everyday that you can bump the Governor out of his room, in his own hotel.

Well, as you can imagine, we thoroughly enjoyed our stay at the Captain Cook. We were reminded of current world problems when we learned that the huge jets we watched from our living room window were carrying wounded soldiers from Vietnam. A constant string of military aircraft landed at Elmondrof field.

The next day, Dan Oldham picked us up at the hotel to take us to our hunting camp. High Lake is about an hour's flight northeast. He had flown in from his High Lake lodge and brought his seven-year-old son with him. We stopped for supplies then headed for the airport. We had a rough ride back to High Lake, bouncing around with the wind currents.

When we approached the dirt landing strip, we noticed the surface was very muddy and slippery from a recent rain. Ken had to come in against a crosswind, which was tricky. He had to crab it in the approach, and as we dropped below the tree tops he realized he couldn't mush it in with the wind gusting forty miles per hour. He had to fly the plane with power practically to the ground. The wheels set down, we rolled a little ways, then the plane swerved to the right as a strong gust of wind hit us, and Ken lost it momentarily. We slid down the runway sideways, heading towards his lodge, which was adjacent to the runway. About two-hundred feet away from the building, Ken gave it a burst of throttle and spun the craft around a time or two. One of the wings dipped down into the mud and the plane came to a stop.

Fred, in his inevitable calm fashion, said, "Ken, you don't have to put on these exciting exhibitions, especially for us. Bob and I are having a good time as it is." Ken was pretty shaken and concerned about the damage to his plane.

We left the next morning with Ken's Super Cub on floats. We touched down on Swimming Bear Lake. Ken went back to High Lake and returned shortly with Don, another guide. We stayed the night at Ken's cabin on the shore. The next morning, we started our five-hour trip to our favorite moose pasture. We arrived about five o'clock and were lucky to get our tent up before dark. We made camp on a high peak on the rim of a mountain.

It was a lousy spot for a camp site with no windbreak and a long trip for water, but Fred felt we should stay out of the valley where the moose were and keep from spreading our scent. I was the first one up at daybreak and I took a bucket to fetch some water.

I was filling my pail and noticed a black spot about a mile away near the spruce trees down in the valley. On my return to camp I got my binoculars and glassed the spot. Sure enough, it was a large bull moose. I reported to Fred and he got up for a look-see. "He's a good one," Fred exclaimed, and asked Ken what he thought. Ken said, "Why don't you and Bob go down and chase them around. I'll take Don and we'll go on a scouting trip with the thiokol." We had breakfast, then Fred and I got ready.

Fred and I started out about eight a.m., working our way down the slope toward the timber line where we had last seen the bull. It was a beautiful September day. The high mountains to the east threw a shadow in the valley below. It took us a half hour to work our way down to the timber line. Checking the moose tracks, it looked as if they were headed into the timber to bed down for the day. The valley ran north and south. Fred checked the slight breeze that was coming from the east.

"Bob," he said, "We've got to cut north for a while, then we can swing east down in the timber, and we can work crosswind to the south and hopefully spot the bulls."

We went about half a mile to the north, then swung into the timber. The area had blotches of spruce trees with small openings filled with low brush. Fred had chosen arrows for both of us that were painted white. We each had a bow quiver. He pointed out that these would be our signaling devices. He said, "Let's keep about one hundred yards apart and work slowly to the south. Be sure to check in my direction so you don't get too far ahead or behind. Signal me every few minutes by moving your bow back and forth. The white shaft of the arrows will tell each of us where the other one is."

This worked very well. I could not see Fred but I could see the arrows. We worked south on tiptoe, so as to spot the bulls laying down. I was lower in the ravine than Fred. We spent about a half hour stalking slowly through the willow brush and cedars, checking and signaling each other every few minutes.

It's important that one guy doesn't get too far ahead. I was working my way, measuring every step, when a cow appeared nor forty yards away, broadside and looking me right in the eye. How I ever missed seeing her I don't know. I did know that this could be the kiss of death for our sneak on the bulls. A cow acts as a lookout, and will alert the sleeping bulls of any danger.

I didn't know whether to signal Fred or not. I chose to stop and stare her down. Surprisingly, she turned and slowly swung to the east without making any noise or fuss.

I breathed a sign of relief as she disappeared and signaled to Fred, who stood motionless, watching my problem about eighty yards from me. He motioned to keep going. I soon came to an alder thicket that obstructed my view of Fred. I was slowly picking my way through the thicket when the silence was broken by snapping brush. I crouched down on my knees. Through the brush directly ahead, not more than twenty-five yards, was a huge bull moose. He had been lying down, and apparently decided to get up. He was black, about the size of a large steer, and sported a huge set of antlers.

My first impulse was, "Aw, poop!" I've spooked him. But to my surprise, he started scraping the brush with his rack. By then I was flat on the ground with only my head peeking up to see what was going on.

He had not seen or winded me. Shivers ran up and down my spine as I watched him strip the bark off the alders. He threw his head back and forth with a crashing sound as he broke the brush to the ground. Some branches were the size of a ball bat. I sneaked a cautious peek around to see if he had a buddy lying nearby. I couldn't see any other antlers through the brush. What a deal! Here I'm twenty-five yards with a standing broadside shot at the largest moose I have ever seen. And I can't shoot him because he's not my moose. He belongs to Fred.

This thought prompted me to say to myself, where is Fred, anyway? I laid on the ground, pondering the situation while the bull smashed more alder brush. I decided to slip off my hip boots and crawl back to the spot where I had last signaled to Fred. I hoped that he had missed me and stopped for my signal, rather than continue south along the ravine.

The wind switched and was coming out of the south. If Fred got too far ahead, the bull would wind him. This concerned me, but I still had to retreat at a snail's pace, lest I make a lot of noise and alert the bull. I worked my way back seventy-five yards and slowly raised up to see if I could see Fred.

To my surprise, he was standing motionless about

one-hundred yards to the west of me. When he lost contact with me he froze in his tracks, thinking that I must have spotted something. I cautiously waved my bow back and forth and got his attention. I motioned him to come to me and put my finger to my mouth to caution him to be quiet. It seemed like it took him twenty minutes to work his way down to me. It was probably only five. I whispered to him what had happened. "I think it's the big bull you're looking for," I told him. Fred had a serious look on his face as he whispered the plan we should use to sneak back to the moose.

We crawled back on our hands and knees to the spot where I had seen the moose. I found my boots, but no moose. Oh damn, was my first impulse, I must have spooked him or something. Fred and I sat crouched there, wondering what to do next. Maybe he had swung down the slope and could now wind us. What a deal! Here we had him right in our lap, and fate screwed us up.

Suddenly Fred grabbed my arm. He pointed ahead and a little to our left where there were several spruce trees. Fred's good eyes had picked up the movement of our lost bull. I was on my hands and knees in order to keep out of sight. He whispered that the bull had just gone behind one of the spruce trees. I could not see a thing. Fred said the bull was heading to our left and should walk out from behind that spruce tree and then be in the open. Fred readied himself in a shooting position.

Sure enough, the huge antlered head and body emerged from behind the tree. I was concerned because he was about sixty yards away now, and on a downhill angle. Fred made no attempt to better his shooting distance by sneaking closer. I crouched behind him. I could look right down his arrow as he came to full draw. When he released it, it looked as if it was perfect for right and left, but perhaps a foot too high.

I should not question Fred's uncanny ability to shoot instinctively. Just as it appeared that his arrow was going to pass over the bull's back, it dropped and buried itself deep in his midsection, directly behind his front shoulder.

The bull let out a grunt and trotted forward. To our amazement, he went about fifty feet and suddenly crashed to the
ground. I patted Fred on the back and said, "Great shot!"
Fred admitted that he, too, thought the shot was going to
be too high. We paced it off, and found it really was sixty
yards with a decided sharp downhill angle.

We slowly approached the downed monster. There was
no sign of life. As I shook Fred's hand, I said, "I think this
has got to be time for a short Peppermint Schnapps." We
sat down and admired the huge antlers on the bull, and we
went back over the circumstances of events. Fred talked
about the stalk and we agreed that luck was on our side
with refinding the huge bull. Fred examined the antlers
closely and said he certainly would make a beautiful life-
size mount for the museum. We were both pleased and
grateful for his success.

We unloaded our back packs and all our camera gear,
and spent the next hour taking pictures from all angles. We
cleared the brush in front of the bull so we could get good
wide-angled shots. Then we field dressed it and tied a red
bandanna on it's antlers so that when we came back we
could spot it easily at a distance. Hopefully the bandanna
would keep the grizzlies away. It's a good idea to tie something with human scent on the kill if you have to leave it in
the woods overnight. I found out the hard way when a bear
ate the nose of a moose I had shot. This, of course,
destroys the chance for a life-size mount.

On one hunt I tried eating some moose nose. Our
guide told us it was the delicate part of the moose. We
boiled it and found it didn't taste too bad, something like
tongue.

We packed our gear, started up the slope, and headed
toward the camp. It was a long steep climb, and we had
gone about a half mile and were pretty well tuckered out.
We stopped to rest just above the timberline, catching our
wind for the long climb back up to camp. We could see a
mile north down the valley, and I looked in the distance
toward the brush area. My eyes picked up what could be a
moose about one mile away. I glassed him and, bingo, it

was another big bull. Fred checked him out and agreed. He then said, "Bob, I'm sorry but I've got just enough steam to make it to the camp. He looks like he'd be worth a try, but you're going to have to do it alone."

I deliberated a moment, then said, "Well that's what I'm here for and I guess I'll give him a go." Fred wished me luck and I struck out.

It took the better part of an hour to cover the rough terrain, stopping several times to check the moose and the wind. I finally got within one-hundred yards and noticed that my hip boots were making lots of noise scraping on the willow brush.

I sat down and took them off. I also removed my socks so they would stay dry for the walk back to camp and rolled up my pant legs. The barefoot sneak was not too comfortable through the rocks and brush and mushy tundra. I worked my way to within sixty yards of the moose. I could see his body quite plainly. The terrain was barren of trees for about two hundred yards. The willow brush provided no place for an escape route and nothing to climb if he decided to charge me. This concerned me a little bit as I thought, if I infuriate him with a poor shot he might do just that. Anyway, I had gotten myself into this soup, so it was up to me to get myself out of it. It was too late to turn back.

I came to a small clearing and was on my hands and knees. There was a twenty-foot opening ahead, but to get to it I had to crawl through the fence-like brush. Once through that, I could move another fifteen or twenty feet closer. If I could do that without disturbing the moose, my shooting range would be greatly improved.

I put an arrow on the string and raised up slowly. Still in a crouched position I tried to move the brush, but couldn't do it. My bow was in my left hand but I needed both hands to get the brush out of the way. I used my right hand, opened up a path like a swinging door, and started sneaking through. The willow brush I was holding slipped out of my hand. I had been biting my tongue, squinting my eyes and holding my breath, hoping I could make it through this obstacle when kerslap, the willow brush hit my side with a loud noise.

The moose jumped to his feet and stood broadside staring at me. This was now my moment of truth. Forgetting to be frightened I instinctively snapped a shot at the very impressive looking beast.

The arrow hit him mid-section behind his front shoulder. I froze in my spot, hoping he would go the other way. Thank God he did. He trotted to my left, stopping about sixty yards from me. He again gave me a broadside shot. I was much braver now. I decided to give him another shot. The arrow struck close to the first one. He trotted toward the cedars. In about one hundred yards he had to go over a small ridge and he then would be out of sight. I ran as fast as I could in my bare feet to reach the top of the ridge. At the top I stopped to catch my breath. The moose was one hundred and fifty yards away heading for the timber when he collapsed. My hopes shot up one hundred percent. I made my way to him as quickly as I could, huffing and puffing. He was stone dead. I sat on him and admired his rack. Measuring with my arrow, I guessed he was sixty inches. I patted him on the side and complimented myself on my stalking and shooting. My arrows were six inches apart. I field dressed him, tied my handkerchief on his antlers and headed back in search of my boots.

I decided to save some hiking, I would cut cross lots. I tried to find the place where I had left my boots, but couldn't locate them. The bushes all looked the same. Everything seemed to be foreign to me. I walked all around the area, trying to find something familiar, but I couldn't. The clouds were getting heavy in the west and I noticed snow was starting to fall. This prompted a quick decision. I could either stay here and perhaps find my boots for a comfortable walk back to camp after dark, or start walking now to camp barefooted.

It was about 4:30 P.M. In September, especially if there is a mountain in the west, it gets dark in a hurry. Heavy clouds were moving in. I could faintly see our tent flapping in the wind against the skyline on the mountain about three miles away. Since I didn't have a compass and this was my first time in the area, I decided I had better head for camp while I could still see it.

With my pant legs still rolled up, I struck out up the mountain for camp. I don't know whether anybody else ever shot a moose in their bare feet, but I wouldn't recommend it if you ever have the chance. There were no trees between me and camp, but one hell of a lot of rocks that made the going rough. There were also many low willow bushes that obstructed my view of the tent from time to time. The tundra patches had pockets of water in them, and these had skim ice on them. The willow roots cut my ankles, so I couldn't go very fast. Many places I had to pick my way by feeling with my feet. I finally made it to camp. It was dark as hell when I opened the tent flap. Fred was lying on his cot. "Don't you wear boots?" One look at the blood running down my bare legs and he said, "What the hell happened to you?" "Well," I said, "I lost my boots." He then said, "I wondered what happened to you. I saw you screw up the shot at the moose through my glasses. Then you disappeared out of sight." I said, "You better have your glasses adjusted. That moose is lying dead down there at the edge of the timber."

Then I showed him my bloody hands, shirt, and pants and he began to believe me. "I think it's time to have another celebration toast," I told him, and I took my Peppermint Schnapps out of the back pack.

Our guides were not back yet. We thought it would be great fun to play a joke on Ken when he returned. We conjured up a story that when we got to the moose area we found all kinds of tracks made by other hunters. We heard the thiokol returning and I covered up my bloody legs. Ken and Don came in our tent and sat down. They had gone south several miles along the ridge but hadn't been able to locate Fred's big moose. Ken was sure they would be able to find him the next day.

We gave them a drink and sat having a little chat. Fred finally brought up the story we discussed and said to Ken, "Do you suppose there is another area that you could take us to? One that is a more remote and isn't hunted quite so much?" Ken sat up like he had been hit by a needle in his butt and asked, "What the hell do you mean?" Fred went on, "Gosh Ken, when Bob and I got down there we found empty beer cans, cigarette butts and a deserted camp site. Ken hit the roof and exclaimed, "That's the bastard to the north of me. I'll bet he has seen me checking this area and moved in ahead of us. Hell, this is the most remote spot in Alaska for moose."

We let him fume for a little, then Fred said, "Bob and I have been lying here feeling sorry for you guys. Here you are busting your butt to find me the monster moose and the hunt's all over." Ken replied very puzzled, "All over, what the hell do you mean?" Fred said, "Well, I shot the monster and Bob got himself a big bull too!" Ken nearly dropped his drink. He wasn't too pleased to get the news and said, "Well, I'll be damned." He acted like he didn't believe Fred and stomped out of our tent. Fred said we probably shouldn't have dropped it on him so hard.

In the morning we took the thiokol and picked up the two moose. Fred said he had never seen a moose hanging from a tree limb and asked Ken if he could do this so we could get a picture for his book. Ken said, "Hell yes." He picked out a fair sized spruce and dragged my moose over to it. He shinnied up the tree and fastened the cable from the thiokol. He then jumped on the machine and gave it power. Much to our surprise the thiokol went up the tree, with Ken looking straight down and hanging on for dear life. The moose was still on the ground. Fred said, "That's O.K., I don't care what goes up the tree, either one will make a hell of a picture."

The next day we returned to Swimming Bear Lake and back to the main camp at High Lake.

Ken flew us to Fairbanks the day after. We ran in to George Theile, our polar bear guide. He told us of a hot spot for caribou and asked if we'd like to try for one, I told him that I would. Fred said he wasn't interested, but go ahead. George picked me up before daybreak. We went to the commercial airport where George had his plane down near the end of the run way. The fog was nearly down to the ground. We got in his plane and warmed the engine and George requested permission to taxi his plane to a hanger across the field.

I was shocked when he spun the plane around and sped down the runway away from the tower. The next minute we were airborne and fog bound. George apparently knew the situation. We left the fog as soon as we were two-hundred feet off the ground and found that the fog was only over the river.

We flew about one-half hour, sometimes going through a near-blinding snow storm. We came to a large rocky gravel bar where George spotted a small migration of caribou. He set the plane down and directed me where to set up an ambush.

I walked half a mile across the large gravel bar with many small streams in my path. I selected a point of brush near the edge of the gravel bar, peeked over the brush, and spotted a big bull heading my way. He walked past me at thirty yards. I shot him in the neck. He dropped to his knees, then tumbled on his side. I had hit the jugular vein.

George had been watching me with the glasses and brought the plane over. I told him that I wanted to save the whole thing for a life-size mount to put in the museum. We had started skinning when a tremendous explosion broke the silence. I almost dropped my knife, and exclaimed, "What the hell was that?" George with a half smile and half frightened look replied, "We're not exactly where we're supposed to be. See the other side of this gravel? That's the boundary of an artillery target area. That was an artillery shell burst." This news speeded up the skinning.

Before we were done, another explosion occurred. We made haste, chucked the hide and meat in the Super Cub, tied the antlers on the strut and got the hell out of there. What an exciting caribou hunt.

XIV

The Swamps of the Amazon 1967

When we returned from the long siege in the Arctic on our polar bear trip we stopped at Jonas Brothers in Seattle and visited our friend Bert Klineburger. These people are the greatest taxidermists in the world and have done much work for both Fred and me. As we were seated in Bert's office, a huge set of horns lying on the floor caught Fred's eye. Fred asked Bert what they were. Bert said, "Oh, that's an Asiatic Buffalo. I just returned from a hunt in Brazil where I shot this huge beast." He told us the animals were planted there eighty some years ago in the hopes of having a huge beef animal. They are commonly used as a beast of burden in the far East. However, the project hadn't been successful and these animals had reverted to a wild state. Bert asked us to step into the other room and see what he really had in mind when he went on his trip to South America.

In the show room which is also a trophy museum, a display contained a huge jaguar. He explained that these were the largest jaguars in the world. They looked almost as large as a tiger from India and were a beautiful brown and black spotted animal. He told us that they also have black ones which are considered a rare trophy. Fred looked at me and said, "Bob, don't you think we ought to have one of these for the museum?" And in a weakened moment I agreed with him.

In addition to being in the Taxidermist business the Klineburgers are outfitters for safaris and shikars throughout the world. Bert would go to a country and make necessary hunting arrangements. He would then stage a hunt of his own and bring back a trophy with him to display. He neglected to emphasize the fact, however, that these animals were taken on the first and only trip made to Marajo Island in the Amazon and that we would be a couple of guinea pigs on our hunt. He had not totally set up the organizational methods of a good hunting camp—supplies, food, equipment, etc.

At this point, Fred questioned him about when would be the best time to go on a hunt there. Bert told us that the month of October would be the best, so Fred booked a hunt for us for the month of October.

This was the start of another trip, I guess the measure of success of any trip is to plan another one before you get back home from the present one.

At this point I would like to say that if anyone ever offers to take you on a free trip to the swamps of Marajo Island, for God's sake, turn him down. This proved to be one of the most trying and painful ventures that had ever befallen Fred and me. Absolutely miserable!

Early in October of that year, Fred's company experienced some labor problems which delayed our departure date for two months. We should have cancelled out because this is the start of the rainy season. It's also summer down there and hotter than hell—120 degrees is not uncommon—but Fred was determined to make the trip, so we took off. I met Fred in New York. We spent one day making arrangements for our passage and picking up last minute items we might need.

We left Kennedy airport at 9 a.m. the next morning for the long flight to Belem. The trip involved four stops on the way. Our first stop was Barbados; second, Port of Spain; third, Georgetown; and fourth, Paramaribo; then on to Belem, Brazil. Each time we stopped, Fred and I took the occasion to get off the plane and stretch our legs, buy a few postcards and take a few pictures at the airport before our flight departed. By the time we reached Paramaribo on the northeast coast of South America, it was ten o'clock at night. Our flight had left at nine in the morning so the day was beginning to drag out. We took a stroll in the moonlight at the airport before boarding for our final destination. Every stop we made, the temperature seemed to get a little bit hotter. Fifteen hours after leaving New York we arrived in Belem at midnight. We concluded that even with a jet it was a hell of a long way to South America and through two time zones.

We were met by our white hunter, Dick Mason, who was employed by the Klineburgers. He had previously been a white hunter in several countries in Africa. Dick was about 28 years old, tall, dark and very handsome.

He took us to the Vanja Hotel where we sat and got acquainted at the cocktail bar. The only thing that they sold at the bar was rum and gin. I ordered the gin. They asked if I wanted a Singas cocktail. Singas is Portugese for carbonated water. It sounded like the best thing they had to offer, as rum didn't really turn me on. It turned out to be a "yuk" drink. Fred and I were beat and we turned in shortly. I don't know how this hotel was rated, but they hadn't appropriated any funds for air conditioning as yet. By American standards it was quite antiquated.

The next morning, after a skimpy breakfast of rolls with coffee that you could float a spoon in, we decided to take a walk around town. Fred felt we shouldn't leave on our hunt until he got word from his factory that the labor problems had cleared up.

The town of Belem is a rough and tough seaport city. It reminded us of Mexico. Practically no one speaks English. Instead they speak Portugese. We noticed the unusual Christmas decorations on display in the store windows. A strange looking Christmas tree was made out of blue and aluminum tinfoil, its straggly limbs sticking straight out of the trunk. Unlike the trees we have in North America, they don't trim it to a point at the top. They are the same length from bottom to top. That afternoon Fred and I took a trip to the local zoo. After observing the hundreds of various types of snakes and other crawling and creeping reptiles we almost wished we hadn't bothered to take the tour. There are many poisonous insects and snakes in this part of Brazil. All of this added to our uncertainty of the outcome of our venture.

That evening Dick Mason came to our hotel and asked if we would like to take in a locally famous cocktail lounge. Inside the lounge we both had a feeling that it was good to have Dick as our bodyguard. It was a pretty raunchy place. I unscrewed my Rotary pin, and after gulping one drink, Fred suggested we go back to the hotel. We spent the evening hearing stories Dick told about the dangers involved in hunting these buffalo. He told us about the experiences of some of his friends who had hunted them. They all agreed that it was the most dangerous hunting they had ever experienced. The big problem is terrain. It is almost like hunting in a sugarcane field. The huge swamp grass grows ten feet tall and it is very thick. The buffalo wallow through this to feed. The water is from a foot to three foot deep. The only way you can tell a fresh track is by the fresh mud on the larger blades of the grass. This tells you that the buffalo is not too far ahead. Sometimes the hunters use a dugout canoe where the water is too deep to walk, and pole it along to sneak up on the buffalo. He related stories of several people that had been killed by a close, quick charge, when the gun bearer was not able to gun down the buffalo.

Fred and I went to bed that night wondering if we had done the right thing coming on this hunt. Our guide finally told us that we were also there at a bad time as this was the start of the hot summer season. We would experience some uncomfortably high temperatures. Likewise, the rain had preceded us and much of the island was flooded. He was concerned as to whether we would be able to set the airplane down in one of the open areas Dick had picked out near the hunting camp.

The next day Fred received word that the labor problems had been settled in Grayling. We contacted Dick Mason telling him that we were ready to leave. Dick said there was two places where we might be able to set the plane down.

When Dick came to pick us up we were dressed in our camouflage hunting outfits. He was shocked when he saw us. He said, "You can't wear that. They'll think we are some gorilla outfit or military group to overthrow the government. You'll have to wear your other clothes and put your camouflage outfit in the suitcase."

We went out to the airport and met our pilot who was to fly us to our camp with a Cessna 180. He spoke only Portugese. As we climbed to four-thousand feet we could see Marajo Island in the distance. This blocks the mouth of the Amazon and makes it two-hundred miles wide where it floods in the ocean. The south fork of the muddy Amazon looked like it was about ten miles wide at this point, about the same color as a cup of strong coffee with a little cream added. A few sailboats dotted the horizon. Dick said these were used to ship the cargo from the Island to Belem.

We flew nearly one-hundred miles over the heavy vegetation which was filled with water. As we came to an open spot that he had in mind, we could see that the grassy area was covered with water. However the pilot felt that he could set the plane down near the shack where the rancher lived. He made several low passes trying to determine the depth of the water. As we touched down, the wheels pushed water out sideways from the plane about twenty-five feet, much like a speed boat. We came to an abrupt halt as we settled several inches in the mud and water. The ground underneath, however, seemed to be firm and we were able to taxi up to a little higher spot where we could get out without getting wet. It was decided that the pilot would fly over the area where our hunting camp was located, several miles away, and signal our arrival to our Amazon Indian guide. The pilot would drop out a can which was the signal for the guide to bring the animals to this ranch and pick us up. As the plane took off, the 180 looked like it was on floats, water squirting all over the place.

I turned to Fred and said, "I wonder what would happen to us if the pilot got hit by a taxicab this afternoon when he gets back to Belem. How long do you think we would be here?" He and Dick Mason both looked at me and Dick kind of smiled and said, "Well, it would be probably fifty miles to a river where we could hitch a ride on one of those sailboats that might be going back to Belem."

The term rancher was used very loosely. A small shack nearby was assembled much like what you would see in the hills of Kentucky. A man and his wife, along with several kids, took care of a dozen head of cattle. He was called a rancher. We went in and were introduced to the man and wife. The kitchen was actually part of the living room. We noticed pigs, cats, and dogs were part of the kitchen fixtures. The chickens had a roost next to the stove. It looked like quite a menagerie.

The lady cooked us a fried chicken dinner which really wasn't too bad. Fred and I had to be careful about drinking the water. We had brought some Halazone tablets to ward off the malaria or whatever we might catch. These were dropped into the water and diluted. Fred and I both, on previous trips to Africa, had contracted malaria. Fred had a very serious attack and wound up in a hospital in Washington D.C. I had experienced two attacks in the last three years.

Shortly after noon our native guide came with our transportation. He had two horses for Fred and me while he and Dick rode Brahma bullocks. We also used Brahmas to pack our gear on. I wasn't looking forward to the five mile trek. The trail led us through the swamp that was filled with water. Occasionally there were some open grassy areas. The sun was hot and it was very humid.

In one of the clearings I noticed a cow laying near the

trail. It was on its back with its feet up stiff in the air. I asked Dick what happened. He said, that probably the cow had been bitten by a poisonous snake or had stepped on an electric eel. As neither Fred nor I had boots, this didn't enhance our desire to start the hunt. The electric eel was something I had never heard of. It wasn't mentioned in Bert's brochure. It lives in the mud under water and we were told that if you step on it, it kills you immediately—a consoling thought indeed. Like many of the trips Fred and I have taken, you don't really find out what things are all about until you actually get started on the hunt.

It took us four hours to make the trip to our campsite. A tent that was mosquito-proof and reptile-proof (we hoped) had been set up for Fred and I. There was the native guide, his wife, and two children. The water was so deep that they had sidewalks built out of logs between the tents. Five large dogs, used for tracking jaguars, were tied to palm trees surrounding the area.

We learned that our water supply was an open well with surface water seeping into it. Fred and I were really quite concerned about drinking the water. Our camp had no refrigerator. Before dinner Fred and I had a shot of gin mixed with this warm, muddy water. As the days went by we found that this was the highlight of our day. The most we could expect to look forward to at the end of the day was this lousy drink of warm gin and warm muddy water, yuk. We found a wild lemon tree with scrawny fruit and we squeezed this into our drinks to enhance the flavor. Even with this juice, I would have to say the gin and muddy water made the absolutely worst drink that I have ever had in my life.

As the camp had no refrigeration everything had to be shot or come out of a tin can. We ate mostly from the fat of the land—kite, doves, parrots, monkeys, and alligators. The dogs were fed palm hearts. Raimundo would shinny up a tree and chop the top off. This provided all of the dog food. Likewise they made a salad for us out of the tender shoots which wasn't to bad. It tasted something like ripe avocado.

In the evening, bird life becomes lively. There are huge flocks of doves and various types of exotic birds. As we were eating dinner in the evening quiet we could hear a sound like the screeching of tires on a race track some distance away. I asked Dick what the sound was and he told us it was howling monkeys. He says that a half dozen of these monkeys will make all that racket.

They rigged up a shower for us and this was the best thing that had happened to us all day. Dick told us we were going to start early in the morning and that we had better turn in. Due to the intense heat we were obliged to hunt early. We began walking to our hunting area around 3:30 in the morning. This business of walking without boots on in the dark, wading in the water, and not being able to see where you were going was for the birds. It was a beautiful moonlight night, but I wondered if I was going to step on a snake or an electric eel. I could still see that dead cow with its stiff legs in the air. This gave me something to think about, to help pass the time while we sloshed through the swamp.

The method of hunting the buffalo is to try to intercept them as they leave the swamp area at daybreak and retreat back into the forest where they lay during the hot part of the day. What they refer to as a swamp is covered with ten foot high reeds. It's very thick and dense like a sugar cane field and lined with paths where the huge animals come out at night to feed. The forest is a combination of palm trees and other types of bushy trees that grow about forty feet tall. There is also a heavy cover of low brush. It's very shaded and dark.

We wore ankle high boots that Fred had designed, and he had planned to put them in his catalog with the other hunting gear. However, this was shortly after he had sold the company to Victor Comptometer and they took a dim view of him going into the shoe business. As a result, Fred and I have the only two pair of genuine Fred Bear hunting shoes in captivity. He never was able to put them into his catalog. We sure put them to a test in South America. I'm going to will mine to him for his museum.

We stopped at six o'clock and waited for daylight, hoping to spot a buffalo sneaking out of the swamp. We followed a fresh track that led into the forest, saw lots of birds and monkeys but no buffalo. Dick and Raimundo decided that we should head back to camp. It was a thrill just to sneak through the forest even though we didn't run into a buffalo.

We got back to camp at 12:30 P.M. with red, sweaty faces and mud up to our knees. It was too hot to hunt the rest of the day. We took a shower, had lunch and a nap. It was beastly hot, must have been over one hundred and twenty degrees and humid. We both got burned a little. Tonight we are going to try to shoot some doves near our camp with the 20 gauge shotgun that Dick has.

Our native tracker had been working for several years for $1.00 a month. Dick disrupted the whole economy when he offered him $4.00 per month. I took another look at the well where our drinking water came from and kept my fingers crossed that we didn't contract malaria. I would have given plenty for a good cold glass of water and twice as much for a bucket of ice cubes.

We had chicken—called wild turkeys—for dinner, which Raimundo shot. They don't look like our North American variety. Fred and I got eleven doves and three parrots to help fill the pot for tomorrow.

The next morning we started out about four a.m. This time we took horses, headed for the swamp and arrived at daylight. Throughout the swamp there was an occasional tall palm tree. Raimundo would tie pieces of a burlap bag on his bare feet so he could shinny up the tree. This made a good lookout from the top of these palm trees.

That day we tracked three huge buffaloes through the swamp. We were in water over our knees and Raimundo with his bare feet could feel the hoof prints down in the mud and we could see fresh mud on the sides of the reeds where the huge beasts had wallowed through. We followed them into the thick forest for about twenty minutes. We would always go single file, Raimundo first, Dick Mason second, and Fred and I would follow up the rear. I would catch myself from time-to-time peaking around to see if there was anything sneaking up behind us. All of a sudden we heard a terrific crash. The buffaloes had apparently winded or heard us and started to run. Its difficult for four people to be quiet, sneaking up on any animal while slopping through water.

We soon picked up another track at the edge of the swamp. Dick Mason carried a 375 for back-up and Raimundo a 404. This is a British rifle that shoots a ball over 400 grains.

We lost track of the buffaloes in the tall grass and decided to turn back to camp. The natives, as in Africa, eat almost anything. Last night we had fried parrots and doves. We were both a little skittish about giving the monkeys a try, but they were scheduled on the menu for that night. After our evening dove shoot and a few shots of gin and muddy water we had our dinner and turned in. Parrots and monkeys are not my idea of an adventure in good eating.

The next morning we were up and at it again around four o'clock and headed for the swamp. As we worked ourselves through the thick reeds we heard a sloshing sound to our left. It sounded like it was coming closer and headed in our direction. This seemed to be the chance we had been looking for.

Fred got an arrow on the string and we stood motionless waiting for the buffalo to walk into our view. A path in the reeds was leading directly to us. A terrific splashing noise told us the buffalo had winded us, switched directions, and run. Raimundo climbed a palm tree and spotted him a hundred yards away. This would have been an easy rifle shot but with a bow you can't hang on to a tree and shoot. We tried another sneak on him, but he spooked the second time. Dick said we might as well give up on him. If you jumped him twice forget him.

We picked up another track and followed it into the forest for two hours. We came to a water hole in a small clearing in the forest and decided to take a rest. Fred was seated on a log across the pond which was twenty feet wide and I was on the opposite side looking in his direction. I glanced to Fred's left and saw an alligator about eight feet away with his head pointed toward Fred. I said to Fred, "Why don't you shoot that alligator there?" He thought I was kidding and said that he was pretty busy and didn't have time to right now. I got up slowly, walked to the opposite side and said, "I'm not kidding you. There's an alligator pointed toward your foot." Fred casually glanced in that direction and was quite shocked when he saw the seven-foot reptile laying motionless looking at him. Fred got up and put an arrow on the string. He placed the arrow directly behind the alligator's left leg. The arrow went completely through to the feathers. Fred took a step or two towards the alligator to retrieve his arrow and Raimundo grabbed Fred from the back and shook his head. At the impact of the arrow, the alligator had given absolutely no reaction to being struck. His eyes never blinked. The native tracker took his machete and cut a palm branch that was about five foot long and about two inches thick. He walked over to the alligator and waved it over his head. As he did so the alligator jumped up, grabbed it and snapped it in two with his powerful jaws. Fred was pretty lucky that he hadn't removed the arrow.

He took another arrow and placed it between the alligator's eyes. This shot penetrated the brain and killed him instantly. Raimundo then dressed it out and laid it on its back. With his machete he whacked a large palmetto-type palm bush and stripped off the leaves. He proceeded to weave a backpack much like an Indian basket. In about fifteen minutes, he had the neatest little backpack that you ever could imagine, complete with carrying straps for over his shoulders. He also left a hole about eight inches in the bottom. We picked up the alligator and slipped him tail first into the carrying pack until the lower jaw of the alligator rested on Raimundo's head. He secured the arm straps and we trekked back to camp. We didn't arrive until nearly three o'clock that day and it was hot, hot, hot. Fred and I made a beeline for the shower.

Dick entertained us again with tales of his experiences with the Indians in the Matagoros area. This is the big bush country in the western part of Brazil. He maintains that there are lots of wild people there who do all their hunting with spears and bows and arrows and that some of them are cannibalistic. Sounded like a poor place to book a hunt.

We feasted on the alligator tail that evening. It is a transparent meat in the raw state, when boiled turns white the same as lobster, but has a more mild taste.

We headed for the big swamp the next morning before daylight and heard the sloshing of an animal walking near the trail we were following. As it stepped out in the moonlight we could make out the unmistakable hump of a Brahma bull. It was one of our bulls and had gotten loose. Fred was just about to zap him with an arrow when he stepped out from behind the brush.

We found a large lone buffalo track that led to the forest. Dick said it was a fresh track and the buffalo had not been spooked, so we decided to track him.

Its almost a lost cause to try to sneak up on an animal when you're wading through the water. We tiptoed the best we could. It takes a long time to cover any ground when you have to plan each step so carefully.

After about a half hour of tracking we were suddenly attacked by a bunch of howling monkeys. They jumped from limb to limb directly over our heads screeching bloody murder. This halted all hunting proceedings. Then the damnedest thing happened. They started bombing us from both ends. They must have thought we were toilet bowls. We all suffered direct hits. This went on for about ten minutes. I was pretty disgusted when one crapped in my face and I vowed to get even. He came down the trunk, probably to laugh at me. This was too much. I drew a bead on him with my bow and let fly. The arrow struck him in the chest. He grabbed the arrow with his front paws, then keeled over like they do in the western movies. That's the last monkey I'm going to shoot, but at the time it seemed like the proper thing to do. We gave up on the buffalo and started out of the forest.

On the way out we found a waterhole with lots of

tracks, and it looked like a good place to build a blind. We spent an hour getting a blind built nearby. We built a machan in the palm tree about fifteen feet high. On our way back the horses bogged down in the mud, and we had to get off and lead them in water over our knees. We returned to camp again without seeing a buffalo.

The highlight of the day seemed to be the evening dove shoot. Fred and I had things well set up by then. We knew when and where the flight would take place. So, after our shower, we both took a camp chair and waited for the doves to fly by. We took one box of shells with us, and applied a few rules. One guy could shoot until he missed; then it was the other guy's turn. It proved to be quite a contest. Usually we would wind up with six to twelve doves, plus a couple of parrots and maybe a toucan or two. A toucan looks very much like a goose when it is in flight. They are black in color, their beak sticks out about twelve inches and it looks almost like the long neck of a goose. They have bright orange, red, and yellow color on their beaks. These are likewise good eating.

Dick Mason always plugs the rifles and shotguns with rags each night so that the hornets don't get in them and build mud nests.

We noticed a couple of dogs were missing an ear, and quizzed Dick about it. If a dog looses the trail of a jaguar, Raimundo takes his machete and chops his ear off. He claims that this punishment really works—sounds like something our courts should look into for drug addicts.

It looks like we are out of luck for jaguars. The dogs can't track in the water. These highwater conditions prompted us to concentrate totally on buffalos.

The next morning we left at five o'clock. We rode our bullocks into a deeper water area as the split-hoofed animals don't sink into it as bad as horses. It's almost a sea sick ride to travel on one of the Brahmas because you sit directly behind the huge hump and watch this sway back and forth as you wallow very slowly through the water. They have a brass ring through their nose and the reins are a piece of leather which you try to keep between the bull's horns in order to steer him. There is no "gee" or "haw" to it. You simply lean one way or another to get the animal to turn, jerking on the ring. We tied the Brahmas up to some brush and went back into the swamp where Raimundo thought he heard a buffalo. Again the buffalo spooked on us. This made four days and no sight of a buffalo.

We decided to build a blind or machan up in the trees. Dick feels that this method has to work or the hunt will be unsuccessful. These buffalo are far smarter than the cape buffalo we hunted in Africa. When trying to trail them the advantage was all in their favor. We sneaked for hours through the swamp and didn't know whether they were thirty feet or two miles ahead of us. The dense forest makes it very difficult. By ten thirty it was so hot that we had to quit. We saw our first tarantula spider that morning and millions of ants crawling all over the ground.

Dick suggested that we forget about the morning hunt the next day and go over to our machan late in the afternoon and spend the evening trying to intercept a buffalo. We arrived at 4:30 and stayed until dark and saw or heard nothing.

About daybreak the next morning the parrots came screaming in, flying into a huge palm tree that had the top blown out of it. The noise was so loud that I couldn't sleep. I grabbed the shotgun and sneaked beneath the tree. The palm tree was literally lined with parrots hanging on like locusts on a stalk of grain. I fired three quick shots through the bunch, and it rained parrots. After the feathers cleared I picked up fourteen parrots.

It always disgusted me to see Raimundo pick each feather off by dry picking these birds and it took him almost an hour to do it. I called him over and told him to watch me give him a lesson on how to clean parrots. I taught him to take the skin off the same way I would a bunch of partridge. In a matter of twenty minutes I had all fourteen parrots ready for the pot. Raimundo just shook his head. He just couldn't believe that it could be done that way. The next time we shot parrots the jerk plucked them again his same old way.

The natives also hadn't learned how to cook parrots. They put the parrots on a flat block of wood and chop them crossways with a machete. This splinters all the bones in the breast, and you have to be very careful eating them. I wanted to give them a cooking lesson too, but I thought I had better keep my mouth shut and stay out of the kitchen. They boil the breast for hours because the parrots live to a ripe old age.

In the afternoon Raimundo shot six howling monkeys for dog food. He mixed the meat with chopped palm shoots and the dogs had a feast, gobbling it up in no time.

We decided to spend the night in the machan, leaving camp around four that afternoon. On our way we ran across one of Raimundo's friends who was coming to see him. He told Raimundo that he had seen buffalo near an abandoned shack in a clearing about a mile from us. Dick told Raimundo to make arrangements for several cowboys to meet us in a couple days with their horses and we would use them to make a drive.

We decided to check the shack out and found several large tracks in the clearing that he had told us about. The shack had a covered porch on the front which we thought looked like a more comfortable spot to spend the night than in the machan we had built in the trees.

As dusk settled in so did the mosquitoes. Fred and I decided to stretch out and try to get some sleep. Dick cautioned us to cover up our bare ankles as this was a popular spot for the bats to light. He said they would suck the blood from any exposed area. Fred and I covered our ankles by tying our pant legs with small vines. We put our jackets over our heads. Dick and Raimundo stood watch.

It was a calm evening and the only thing to break the silence was the hum of the insects and the flapping of the bats as they flew by. Needless to say, we didn't spend a very good night. I couldn't sleep thinking about the bats and mosquitoes. Plus, the thought that continually went through my mind was, how were we ever going to get a shot at one of these darn buffalos. We hadn't even seen one of them yet. I cursed the thought of staying on until we got one. I likewise hated to leave empty handed. I had learned from past experiences that when Fred Bear goes hunting, his admirers expect him to drag something back. I knew he'd want to stay until he got one of the critters and I'd have to stay too! These thoughts cancelled any chance for sleep.

Fred has concluded that the biggest problem we are confronted with is that the natives have the buffalo all spooked trying to capture one of them for themselves. Dick says they could get $50 if they shot one. This, compared to the $1.00 per month wage, looks pretty attractive.

Fred thought it would be a good idea to sneak into the water hole where we had our machan. We started single file into the forest which was shrouded with early morning fog. We were pleased to find evidence that some buffs had visited the wallow during the night. Raimundo thought we should follow their tracks as he said they had just been made. We tiptoed further on into the forest following their tracks. We had gone about two hundred yards when Raimundo held up his hand. He motioned for Fred and me to come up behind the brush near him. Dick whispered, "Two good bulls," holding up two fingers. Fred and I edged cautiously to where Raimundo crouched. Fred peeked over the brush, then signaled me to get ready. I worked my way up beside him and peered over the brush. There were a dozen buffalo feeding in a small clearing. The closest two were about sixty yards from us and seemed to be feeding our way.

These were not the world's largest bulls. My bow hunting experience has taught me that many times we have to settle for a smaller trophy. I sensed that Fred was about to draw his bow back.

I edged to his right and got into a position to shoot. Just as the bulls emerged from behind the brush something caused them to stop some fifty yards away. They looked directly at us and stood motionless. I have sensed the moment of truth many times in my bow hunting experiences. I knew that they were about to run, and in a split second sure enough they whirled and headed for the thicker cover. Fred and I both wasted an arrow on them as they disappeared into the thick brush.

We were disappointed, but yet encouraged that we had finally seen what we had been searching for, for so many days. There are buffalo here! We made the long plod back to camp and voted to give ourselves the day off tomorrow.

Raimundo made plans for his cowboy friends to put on a drive the following day. Fred, Dick, and I rode bullock for about two hours to a clearing on the edge of the forest. We waited there for the cowboys to put on the drive for us. The only thing that came out were the cowboys. I wasn't totally disappointed as I have been on many unsuccessful drives before. We headed back for camp, cutting through the swamp.

I always carried my camera gear in a light-weight, waterproof pack on my back and would snap shots as we went along. Fred hadn't planned for any movies on this trip. We came to a spot in the tall reeds where the trail was filled with water.

I had just put the camera in the pack when my bullock became mired in the soft mud, the water deep enough that it came up to my knees. The bullock stumbled and threw me, sliding off over his hump. I quickly threw my bow and grabbed the backpack. Sliding into the water, I held the pack as high as I could.

I wound up in three feet of water holding the camera gear up over my head so it wouldn't get wet. This gave me just one arm to balance myself. I was wallowing around in the mud like a sow when Dick came to my rescue. My bullock had fallen and was trying to get up beside me and I was trying to keep out of his way so he wouldn't crush me or step on me.

Fred was no help at all. He was laughing so hard he could barely stay on his bullock. We had quite a time rescuing my bullock and getting me remounted. It made Fred's day. He laughed all the way back to camp. I think my acts of entertainment may have prolonged his life.

That evening Raimundo told us that we had been invited to a celebration taking place tomorrow on a big ranch to the north.

We decided to take them up on their invitation and take a look at one of the island's largest ranches. It took us five hours to make the trip with our brahma bulls.

The owner could not speak English so we used Dick as our interpreter. This occasion was to celebrate the two-hundredth year of the family's ownership of the ranch. Our host was very genial, but his supply of liquor was worse than ours. He had two large shack-type buildings, most of which comprised sleeping rooms. A plane landed in his pasture and we got our first view of a Brazilian beauty, a beautiful redhead in her late 20's I'd guess. By my standards I would label her as a "keeper." She was our host's date for the celebration. Also present was a man who was one of the owners and business advisor.

Small groups of natives drifted in from the swamps, mostly riding bullocks or horses. These were ranchers and cowboys who had come from the surrounding area. They had a record player powered by a gasoline fed generator, with several loud speakers, hanging in various parts of the house. Fred, Dick and I drew the room directly above the ballroom. You could drop a cigarette through the cracks in the floor or peek through the floor and watch the dancers. By the time the sun set there must have been a swarm of nearly three hundred people—most crowding into the dancing area or on the huge front porch. When they all got brave enough to dance, the building shook.

We had smuggled a little gin in with us for an evening nightcap. As we sat visiting on our bunks the door opened. A big two hundred and fifty pound native pushed the door aside and stepped in. He was darker than our black room.

He was all grins and I am sure he knew that we had some booze. Dick spoke to him, but he did not answer. Finally Dick went to the door to invite him out and close the door. He was not about to leave. It looked like storm clouds might be brewing. My first thought was, "How long is his knife?" The grin left his face, and we all wondered what was going to happen next. We were afraid to share our gin with him, and also afraid to refuse him. A scuffle seemed to be the most ill-advised method of negotiation. We would definitely have been fighting out of our weight class and probably with a weapon disadvantage.

This was the most exciting part of our buffalo hunt thus far. As we all stood wondering what was about to happen next, another large native stepped into the room. This made the situation look even worse, but he took the big guy's arm and pulled him out into the hall. Dick leaned over, fastened the door latch, and we sat down with a sign of relief.

After this the blaring music and sweaty dancers kept us up all night. We left at daybreak with the dancers still dancing and sweating.

The next day Fred decided that we bunch the day hunt and go back to one of our machans late in the day and try our luck again at night. I had mixed emotions about sharing my night with the mosquitoes and all the other swarming insects and bats that seem to take great delight in harassing us as soon as the sun sinks. The great forest is full of many strange noises. This type of hunting tests your patience to the straining point. When there is no wind and its deathly still, all sounds seem to be amplified. You feel like you're shouting when you whisper. For me it's hard to sit and stare at someone without talking. A cough would sound like a small explosion. The slap of a mosquito sounds like a .22 rifle. Fred's biggest worry was that I might doze. Not that he cared about me falling out of the machan, but my reputation for snoring had followed me to several continents. Fireflies blinked in the darkness. Mostly to keep awake, we would share a cigarette, but also in hopes, that it would ward off the mosquitoes. We were ever so careful, cupping it with our hands. The flash of a match in the darkness was like a bolt of lightning. Once in a tree stand in Michigan, my lighting of a cigar signaled an oncoming buck. I felt like a kid with his hand caught in a cookie jar. The spark of the match was all it took—he looked me in the eye for an instant, then bolted.

The night was long and monotonous. The only highlights were a few sips of warm gin and muddy water between yawns. Who said hunting was fun?

Eventually dawn tried to make its appearance, along with it a misty fog. All at once the silence was broken. In the distance we could hear a loud sloshing sound and the cracking of brush. Fred and I attempted to get on our knees. It's surprising how stiff you can get by just sitting on your butt. We knew we had to take this position in order to get a shot. The noise of several beast behind the thick brush became louder and told us that they might be heading for the wallow below our machan.

The first thing I saw was one horn that looked like it was four foot long. With the next step I could see the whole head and both monstrous horns. He was headed our way. Chills ran up my spine. I could see another huge hulk following him. The first buff belonged to Fred. I had told him before that if a situation like this ever arose that I was going to switch weapons. I'm sure if I stayed a few more days I could have taken one with a bow but I'd had it and was ready to get the hell out of there.

My part in the trip was to take pictures for Fred. However, he had agreed that if he got a good hit it was O.K. for me to take one of the critters too!

I didn't want to foul anything up. The lead bull ambled past the brush and into the opening. I watched motionless as Fred drew a bead on him with his bow. The arrow buried deep behind the front leg. It was a fatal shot. A quick glance told me that the other buffalo was now on the alert. Fred's bow string made quite a twang sound. I already had the .404 sighted on the bull's chest. I fired and absolutely nothing happened, except it almost knocked me off my perch. I couldn't believe it. I racked another shell in and gave him another in the same area. This time he lurched backwards and started trotting towards the thick brush. I gave him another parting shot for good measure. He stumbled and fell just before reaching the thick reeds. Naturally I would have preferred to have taken him with my bow, but I had convinced myself I would never return to hunt these beasts. EVER! And, if my chance came, I'd better take it. I especially wanted one of these trophies for my museum.

Fred and I walked over to my buffalo. We waited for the sun to rise a little higher to give us better tracking light. We found that Fred's buffalo had travelled about two hundred yards into the forest. Fred and I were real pleased. I think the greatest feeling for both of us was that we were going to get out of this hot, miserable mess. When Dick saw the buffalo he was quite excited. He claimed these were the largest he had ever seen. He and Raimundo returned and took the horses and several Brahmas back for the horns, capes, and meat.

We cancelled the dove and parrot shoot for that evening. Again we had some of our delicious gin and muddy water cocktails before dinner. We hoped that this would be our last dove and parrot dinner. We rehashed the hunt that evening, but I'm sure Fred and I were thinking mostly about the plane that was scheduled to check on us tomorrow.

In the morning we said our goodbyes to Raimundo and his family and rode back to the pasture where the plane was to meet us. Our concern now was, will the plane show up? Did the pilot get run down by a taxi or something?

We sat on our duffles scanning the sky. About two o'clock we heard the drone of a motor and I don't mind admitting I was thrilled to death to see a small speck in the sky heading our way. I could have kissed the guy when he landed. We loaded the gear, skull and horns into the plane. Like all horned animals the outside shell slips off. We taped them together.

We again said our goodbyes. The pilot tried to start the engine and would you believe he couldn't get the darned thing started. We didn't need this at this point! The pilot gave the engine a Portugese tongue lashing. He fiddled with the carburetor and gave the engine another try. It coughed, sputtered and belched out a puff of blue smoke. What a beautiful sight! Fred and I kept out fingers crossed that we could make it nonstop back to Belem.

We were checked in by the Belem officials who had to

tag our trophies. Fred and I watched a big hassle with Dick and the officials. Finally Dick came over and said, "These guys claim these trophies are new records for Brazil and they want to keep them for their National Museum." I think both our hearts stopped momentarily.

We had a short conference and decided to see if a few cruiseiros (about a hundred bucks worth) might change their minds. Dick came back smiling and said, "It worked. Let's get the hell out of here." It didn't take long for Fred and me to book a flight on the next jet for New York.

As we strapped our seat belts and waved to Dick through the window, Fred let out a sigh and said, "I've never been so glad to get out of a place in my life." I wholeheartedly agreed and added, "Goodbye to gin and muddy water."

XV

Old Mossy Antlers
1967

Fred and I returned to High Lake for another exciting hunt. Lots of game, lots of moose, and lots of fun. The fun part was doing the hunt our own way.

Our guide left on a scouting trip to set up things for another day. We were left sitting on our duffs, watching it snow. We had had some cold nights, only five degrees one night. The food on our dirty dishes froze—too pooped to wash them—from the night before. Water buckets and the coffee pot were covered with a half inch of ice. We had been walking from eight to ten miles a day and we were ready for the sack after dinner.

As last year, Ken flew us to Swimming Bear Lake and we took the Thiokol about eight miles to the Valley of the Big Moose. Even though Fred had taken a sixty-four inch monster the year before, he was determined to get one that stood seven feet at the shoulders for his museum.

The country is beautiful with spruce timber in the valleys, willow brush above and snow on top. We had shooting every day, but most of it long shots and some of it moving. I spent one solid day shooting and gained some confidence. Fred's shooting never ceases to amaze me. He can hit a fifteen-inch target at one hundred yards.

I'm still counting on my hunting skill of stalking up close for a shot, plus *luck,* to score. I passed up a monster bull standing at seventy-five yards, gambling that I could shorten the distance, but lost. A cow saw me and spooked the bull. No shot and no bull.

I had several running shots the first three days at some real big sixty-inch plus bulls, but seventy to ninety yards is too far for a hit. Another guy I saw missed 'em too. On the way back to camp Fred found one of the arrows I lost last year shooting at caribou. It was badly bent by moose, trampling during the winter.

One day we spotted a herd of moose at timber line on the next mountain, about four miles from us. We could see one nice bull. As it was only ten a.m. we decided to give them a try. We had to go down through a valley, and cross a good sized stream filled with boulders covered with ice. This was where I got my foot wet. It took us until 12:30 to again locate the herd on the north side of the stream, figure out the wind and the proper approach.

I decided to stay high in the alders, where the grizzlies like to hang out. Fred took the edge of the spruce timber. We kept within sight of each other, approximately one hundred yards. It's sure a different feeling hunting alone. You never know what you are going to meet up with in the brush. Without a guide for back up, hunting becomes a completely new ball game. It prompts you to look at everything that moves, *twice.* Hunters have taken eight grizzlies here so far, but neither Fred nor I wants to tangle with one. Ever since I had one come after me in British Columbia and the guide shot it at fifteen feet, I've felt a little jumpy about grizzlies.

There have been many exciting stalks every day. Once, a bull practically ran over me as I lay on the ground just twenty feet away.

Our guide was Bob Sedlock, manager of Anchorage

Jonas Brothers Store, six-feet, five inches and as rugged as they come. He just came out for the fun of it for a few days because he wanted to watch Fred shoot a moose or caribou with a bow. Bob is real good company, with twenty years guiding experience, but he had never been out with a bow hunter.

One day I had a large bull caribou standing at twenty yards, but the darn cow stood beside him and completely shielded him. I didn't shoot! Maddening! One morning I climbed a tree by our tent and spotted some moose about three and a half miles away on the next mountain side. We took a lunch and started after them. It took us till noon to cross the stream and climb the mountain. After lunch we glassed the area and I spotted a bull as he disappeared into the spruce timber from a clearing.

We worked into the general area, discussing his location in the timber when we heard the crashing of antlers. Two bulls fighting about one hundred fifty yards ended our argument and we scrambled to get in on the fight. Working into the timber we spotted them. They stopped momentarily and trotted away from us. We separated and I lost track of Fred. I saw four cows sneak out to my left and a wind change on the back of my neck told me the bulls had spooked. I heard the gutteral grunt of a bull some distance down in the timber and figured that was where the action was. So I thought I'd better hunt up Fred to tell him they had run off.

I hadn't gone far north when I heard some brush snap to my right. I wondered how Fred had got around me so quick. Four hairy legs stepped out of the brush and they didn't look like Fred's. A large cow was trotting out of the brush directly towards me.

This set the stage for one of the most exciting moose hunting experiences in my life. The cow passed me on the run at thirty yards. Then I heard the darnedest crashing of brush and timber, sounding like a bulldozer knocking down trees, and coming my way. Along with it there were many grunting sound effects. I dropped to my knees, partly from fright and for some concealment.

The brush opened with a crash. Out came the apparent winner of the battle of love that Fred and I had broken up. This bull sure looked mean. His antlers were filled with brush hanging like grapevines. His hair stood up on his back like a cat that just saw a dog. At this moment I didn't know whether he had winded me and wanted to fight another battle, or whether he was thinking about his girlfriend. He came directly at me on the run. I was just about ready to trade my bow for a spruce tree. The red in his eyes told me he meant some kind of serious business.

I gulped and hoped he didn't see me. All this happened in a flash, but time seemed to stand still. At this point the bull veered off to his left and I quickly got the idea who he was after, and I was glad it was the cow instead of me.

I made a fast fumble with my bow. Up to now I'd been concentrating on methods of tree climbing—the hell with the bow!

He really made a lot of noise and that added to my excitement. I had quite a time knocking an arrow and watching him at the same time, to see if he hadn't decided to switch targets. I don't know how, but I finally got an arrow on the string. I tried to second guess which side of a large spruce tree he was going to pass. If he turned right I had a straight on-coming shot. If he went on the other side, he would pass at about thirty yards. Then my only choice would be a ten foot opening, as he ran past the spruce trees. Fortunately, and with considerable relief to me, he went on the other side of the spruce. I've thought several times since about what would have happened if he had busted out on my side and spotted me crouched in his path.

When he disappeared momentarily on the other side of the spruce, I came to full draw. As soon as he appeared in the opening, I released my arrow. I was pleased to see my arrow bury itself just behind his front shoulder while he was on the run. I'm not noted for running shots so I mentally patted myself on the back. The bull let out a large "oomph" when the arrow hit and looked surprised. He kept his trotting pace for a spell, but stopped at eighty yards, and glanced back in my direction.

Oh! oh! what's he thinking now, I wondered? I took a wild shot at him, the arrow went through his antlers and made a loud whack as it stuck the palm. He took off away from me on the run.

Just then I caught a glimpse of a flash that came flying high off the ridge behind me. I thought it was an arrow. Fred came out of the timber, grinning from ear to ear. Apparently he witnessed my moose hunt episode. However, he had not seen my first shot and began giving me the business for sticking the bull in the antlers. Because he didn't see that first arrow he was real surprised when I told him I had a good hit in the mid-section. We sat down and had a rest. Fred complimented me and we toasted ourselves with a short nip of peppermint schnapps.

We looked for Fred's arrow and couldn't find it. That told us that it must also be in my moose. We paced off Fred's shot at one hundred twenty yards, down hill and on the run.

There was a good blood trail and in fifteen minutes, we found him dead—carrying my two arrows—the one that killed him buried in his ribs, the second one gone through his ear and stuck in the antler—and Fred's arrow buried in his hind quarter. One antler tip had been broken off in the fight with the other bull.

We took a bunch of pictures and I dressed him out. He was not a real monster but a fifty-four inch respectable bull and a fitting reward for our efforts.

We sat down and ate our sandwiches. Fred thought the other bull had gone to the north and suggested we take a swing in that direction. Traveling north about half a mile, we came to a spot with lots of fresh signs. The trail headed east, into the wind.

We worked into the wind slowly, checking on each other often. Just as we came to a patch of willows, I saw a cow moose with a large pair of ears looking at me. After staring her down for about five minutes she dropped her head. She must have thought that I was another moose and went on feeding. Slowly I worked my way around the edge of the brush toward Fred who was about sixty yards from me. He had spotted a bull, away from the cows, and he was moving, in a sneaking position for a close shot.

It was impossible for me to move as the two cows were within thirty yards of me and between Fred and me. I could only see the bull's back and antlers above the brush since he was lying down. Fred spotted him at about two hundred yards and cautiously tiptoed toward the bull, working to within twenty-five yards. He slowly drew back and released an arrow. The bull jumped to his feet and crashed through the brush, the arrow sticking in his side. Fred shot at him again while he was on the run. The second arrow hit the midsection.

The bull didn't leave much of a blood trail on the dry ground, and we played hound dogs to follow him. After two hundred yards we found lots of blood where he had stopped, and from then on we could tell that he was starting to stagger. We found him dead in another one hundred yards.

He was a nice big bull, sixty-two inch rack—Fred always carries a cloth measuring tape—with nice palms and brow tines. I field dressed him while Fred rested up. I was blood from one end to the other. We hung a white rag on his antlers in hopes of keeping the grizzlies from eating him. It was time to start our hike back home, through a big wet marsh, then up a mountain for a four mile hike. We dragged into camp at 7:30 p.m., and hardly had strength to eat. Truly a good day's hunt!

The next morning we took off for Swimming Bear Lake. Ken came in with the plane about 4:00 o'clock and took us back to the main camp. It seemed good to get back to civilization. Ken kept a big husky dog in camp. Just as we arrived the dog cornered a big bull moose. He put him in the shallow water and the bull was standing about ten yards from shore while "Ranger" gave him a good barking. This went on for an hour. Too bad I'd already shot my moose.

Ranger is a movie star. He played the part of the "wolf"

in a movie Roy Rogers made last year at Ken's High Lake camp. Ken showed us the movie. Clairol hair dye was used to give him the proper wolf color.

During this trip we had nobility in our midst: a Prince and two Counts from Germany hunting out of the main camp. They were quite impressed with our bow and arrow skills, and want to buy some bows. They had very expensive over and under rifles with set triggers, and covered with engraving. Of course, they used nothing but silver bullets and dressed like a bunch of Swiss Alpine mountain climbers.

After dinner we entertained the royalty with Fred Bear films at the lodge. He brought a half dozen reels. It was snowing like mad and a good night to stay in the lodge, listening to Ken's stereo music, watching hunting movies, with a nice fire in the big fireplace and a few tasty drinks. Tough life in the bush.

Ken mentioned that there was a big migration of caribou about thirty miles to the east of us. Fred and I quickly accepted his invitation to take a tent and some supplies and chase them for a few days.

The next morning Ken flew us about thirty miles to the east of the migration. We landed at what he called "Tight Lake," a small lake high in the barren mountain range. There were no trees for miles. He explained how it got it's name. It seems that there's no problem landing, but on takeoff it's "tight" to clear the cliffs.

As we came in for our landing, the plane spooked a sow grizzly with cubs. Ken said we'd better stay clear of her. We threw our gear out and kissed Ken goodbye. We set up our tent and cooked some moose steaks for dinner. It was dark by the time we finished eating and we turned in rather early.

In the wilderness, we rough it. Fred and I share a small pup tent, the supplies are just two frying pans. This was truly a beautiful spot. The mirror-like lake reflected snow capped mountains to the north. Just over the ridge, a huge basin about two miles across was covered wall-to-wall with caribou.

Daybreak the next morning, Fred and I climbed to the top of the ridge. It took us a half hour—puffing—but the climb was well worth the effort. As we topped the ridge, a great panorama unfolded below us. We looked several miles to the east and could see many small herds of caribou slowly making their way through river flats in our direction. There were hundreds of them.

The nearby small patches of willow brush were from three to seven feet tall. This makes a good blind for intercepting the migrating caribou. We caught a glimpse of a huge set of antlers directly below us midst a group of large boulders. Both of us dropped to our knees for a quick conference. Fred suggested I go to the left and he would go to the right. This way the caribou below us would be fenced in and one of us would have a shot for sure.

We lay on our bellies in the snow for about ten minutes watching him. Finally he came to within about fifty yards of Fred. Fred raised up on one knee and made one of his typically famous shots—zonk—right through the chest at fifty yards. The arrow stuck out fifteen inches on the opposite side. The caribou whirled and ran about seventy-five yards then toppled over dead.

We dressed him out and took pictures. Then I left to pursue the caribou herd while Fred skinned the bull. He wanted to take the whole hide for a life-sized mount.

I started down the valley, hiding behind the willow brush. Caribou were all around me grunting and chewing their cuds. While trying to sneak up on a dozen or more good bulls, I passed up lots of small ones at twenty yards. Something always happened in their favor. I hoped my day would come to take one of those big racks. Later Fred said he could always tell where I was because the caribou were running away from that spot. I ran many caribou past him as he sat chuckling, watching me chase the damn things all over the valley. We must have seen a thousand caribou that day. I met Fred back at camp about dark. I was beat. My fingers were sore from shooting so many arrows, most of them at least seventy five yards away.

A lost arrow buried in the shovel of an antler was my

only score for the day. Fred offered to be my guide the next day. He said that if I didn't get one then he was going to cut my bowstring.

We started out early the next morning and climbed the ridge. It looked like there were more caribou on the flats that day than the day before. Just sharpening broadheads for me was going to keep Fred busy. Knowing this was our last day fired up my enthusiasm and prompted me to try just a little harder.

This experience taught me one thing though: you can't be quite as selective with a bow as you can with a gun. I've had many chances at small racks, but passed them up for the big one that was coming my way, but somehow never got to me.

I spotted several good bulls working my way and tried to think where I would walk if I were the caribou approaching me, some three hundred yards away. With a final check of the wind, I picked out a large clump of willow brush to make my stand. This time I'd single out one caribou that looked like the easiest to approach rather than choosing the biggest bull. Most small herds have one respectable bull.

After what seemed like an hour but was probably only fifteen minutes, the first of the herd came into view at fifty yards. They were feeding slowly and carrying on a grunting conversation. It was apparent that, finally, things were going my way. Two nice bulls walked slowly past me at fifty yards. I debated taking a shot, but a quick backward glance prompted me to wait. Four-foot antlers extending above the willow brush were headed my way. If he'd keep coming like he was, he would pass me at twenty yards.

As the bull started to pass me, he turned to a quartering angle and stopped. He was about ten feet lower than me. This had to be my chance. The arrow passed through his neck and into his chest, severing the jugular vein. He stood perfectly still for two minutes, then trotted about fifty yards and collapsed.

I had long lost Fred, so I had to dress the caribou by myself and pack as much of the meat out as possible on my back. Fred gave me hell for shooting the wrong one when he saw the crazy rack. It was four feet high, but had few points and shovels. I was pleased anyway, to hell with Fred. The next day Ken came in and picked us up. I'll never forget those two memorable hunting days.

Back at the High Lake Camp Fred and I were sitting out in front of our cabin one morning, enjoying the view of the lake and the mountains behind it. I thought I saw a movement high up near the top of the mountain. With my glasses I started scanning the side of the mountain. Soon I found a black spot and focused my binoculars. It looked like a cow moose with her head stuck in a driftwood stump with the roots extending into the air. Suddenly both the moose and the brush pile moved.

"Hey, Fred, get your glasses! I think I've got something!" I said. We both watched this strange looking beast for several minutes. We couldn't believe our eyes. We hollered for Ken and he took a look. "I've never seen anything like this before, let's take a closer look," was his comment. He set up his spotting scope and continued looking. It was the darndest set of antlers we had ever seen. There must have been over 1 hundred points on the huge beam that looked seven feet across.

"Bob, we've got to have that beast for the museum" Fred said. Doug Walker, Fred's west coast salesman, still had an unfilled license and he was quick to volunteer for the task of running this moose down with his bow. I offered my guide services.

Doug and I made a stalk up the side of the mountain. We got to within one hundred yards of the spot where we last saw the bull. We were closing in on the brush pile where he was lying, when the wind switched direction. The bull charged up the side of the mountain and disappeared over the rim.

We made our way back down to camp feeling dejected. What an animal! We had been so close to getting him. Doug could have easily taken him with my rifle, but wanted to take him with his bow. The chance was gone, Fred and I were scheduled to leave the next day. Walking out of the cabin the next morning, I was dumfounded to see the black spot, in the same place, on the side of the mountain. I checked it with my glasses and sure enough, it was old Mossy Antlers.

All plans to leave were cancelled as Doug and I prepared to give another try at taking the moose. Doug and I climbed back up the mountain and again reached the brushy area where he lay. This time we decided to go up to the rim, spot him and sneak down on him. We topped the rim and sat down to glass the area. At that very moment the brush crashed and our prize bull went trotting down the side of the mountain.

What had gone wrong? Again, there was a long trek down the mountain with our sad tale. Doug had to leave the next morning, so it looked as if old Mossy Antlers would live another year.

I know that this is going to sound as if I made it up, like a Hollywood script writer, but so help me, old Mossy Antlers was back in his same spot when I checked the mountain the next morning. Fred claimed that old Mossy Antlers was the smartest moose he had ever seen and said, "I think that moose looks down at our camp and counts the hunters, if they are all there, he lays down and takes a nap." After breakfast, Fred and I planned to leave with Doug, but Fred called off our departure again. We bid poor Doug goodbye. He had tears in his eyes, having to leave old Mossy Antlers.

One of the guides, Bill Fisher, still had a moose license, so Fred told him to shoot the moose. We marked him down the best we could, and Bill and I started our trek up the mountain.

As we reached the bottom part of the brush patch where we had last seen the moose, we decided to separate. Bill took the east side and I took the west. The wind was a little out of the west, so if he winded me he would run toward Bill. The patch of brush was about one hundred fifty yards wide and two hundred fifty yards long and shaped like a pyramid. I started my sneak up the west side of the brush, Bill disappeared on the east side. It took us probably ten minutes to reach the top of the patch. I had come nearly to the end of it. Old Mossy Antlers had probably given us the slip again.

All at once I was surprised to see the brush move about sixty yards in front of me. The patch wasn't over four feet high. I raised up and spotted the huge mossy antlers sticking up above the brush. He had just laid down. What a chance of a lifetime!

I sneaked to within about forty yards of old Mossy Antlers. Coming around the other side of the brush patch Bill had spotted the bull at seventy five yards. The silence was broken by the ker-wham of Bill's gun. Old Mossy Antlers collapsed and never moved.

I walked up to old Mossy Antlers and Bill was very surprised to see how close I had been to the moose. We checked him over with amazement. The huge antlers had well over one hundred points. His palms were a foot wide and ten inches thick. They almost appeared to be in velvet. We couldn't wait to get back to camp to tell Fred. Of course he had heard the shot and didn't see the bull run, so he guessed the outcome.

Fred, Ken and Norma, the camp cook, volunteered to come up and help carry out the meat. Fred took the camera gear and headed up the mountain to the moose.

After the picture-taking ceremony, Norma offered to field dress and cut up the moose. Starting to field dress the bull, Norma exclaimed, "No wonder he's got mossy antlers! He hasn't got any nuts!" This was Norma's subtle way of telling us that somehow old Mossy Antlers had got himself castrated. Both Fred and I blushed and laughed. Guesses about his condition ranged from his mother's stepping on him when he was a calf, to wolves chewing them off. At any rate, this explained why he was so spooky.

It was apparent old Mossy Antlers would have had the better part of his life looking after himself. He had no girl friends to help look after him. That's the biggest problem in hunting moose with a bow—the cows usually lay near the bull and signal any danger.

It took several hours to cut up and transport the meat

down to a plane. We packed our gear, tied the antlers on the strut and took off for Anchorage where we turned old Mossy Antlers over to Jonas Brothers, whom Fred instructed to make into a front-half full mount.

Fred helping a baby seal.

Fred's silhouette.

HAPPY HUNTING
BOB MUNGER

Bud Brow
1986

Bud Brow

WITH LOVE
TO
ROBERT MUNGER

Harry

Bob sometimes hunted and fished at the same time.

Bob in front of his two prized trophies in his hardware store. He spent more hours telling stories than selling hardware.

XVI

Brooks Range and the Arctic Slope 1969

In October I met Fred and his hunting companion, Elisha Gray from Michigan, in Anchorage, for another Alaskan bow hunt. Bud, as Fred called him, was the Chairman of the Board of the Whirlpool Corporation. He had been with Fred on a sheep hunt several years previous. From Anchorage we took Alaskan Airlines on to Fairbanks. I had my bow in a carrying case with me, and put it in the seat between Fred and me. Fred commented that it was rather embarrassing for him to be associated with someone who used such antiquated equipment. "My take-down bows and arrows are neatly packed away in my suitcase," he said, "I don't have to carry them on a plane looking like a peddler.

This had been a hang-up for both of us in years past when taking long flights, as bows take up a lot of room. Fred had come out with a take-down model bow that, when disassembled, would fit in a suitcase along with the arrows.

We went to the luggage claim and discovered that Fred's luggage was missing. Fred and Bud had flown from Chicago on Northwest Orient Airlines. Fred checked his baggage to go directly to Fairbanks at Chicago.

Apparently his luggage had not arrived in Fairbanks. The airline personnel assured him it would be on the next flight in three hours.

We checked into our rooms at the Fairbanks Inn and decided to have a cocktail before dinner. The lost luggage gave me a good chance to get back at Fred a bit. I was usually the one who won awards for losing luggage. On my first polar bear hunting trip with Fred, I lost all my luggage, and they never did find it. It took two years to get a check from United Airlines. On another trip with Fred to British Columbia, I lost all my rods and fishing tackle. After that, whenever we checked into an airport, Fred suggested that I should check my gear at a different line, as I was apt to lose it and he wanted to be sure that they didn't mix his stuff with mine. Now, I needled him a bit about the luggage, as he kept making calls to the airport to check on it.

I knew he was pretty worried, so I offered to call a good friend of mine, Charlie Willis in Seattle, who was Chairman of the Board of Alaskan Airlines. Charlie was very accommodating, and called us back in about twenty minutes, "Bob," he said, "I'm sorry to tell you this, but we have definite proof that Fred's luggage was never taken off the Northwest flight. His gear is on it's way to Tokyo."

Well, with this report, Fred lost his usual good sense of humor. I tried to assure him that everything would be O.K. and that I would loan him one of my extra bows. But he didn't think that was a bit funny—he shoots left-handed and I shoot right. I could sense the kidding stage had gone far enough so I suggested we have some dinner. This was the first time, throughout my many experiences with him, that I had seen Fred really mad, but I knew just how he felt.

Before we turned in for the night, Fred told me that

Bud had brought along the same wooden arrows that Fred had given him about ten years before. He jokingly remarked, "You'd think the Chairman of the Board of Whirlpool would be able to buy some new arrows for this hunt. That's not good for my business."

Fred and Bud had made arrangements for a pack trip, south of Fairbanks, on horseback with Jim Buzby. I had always had a dream to hunt the Brooks Range and the north slope, some of the most remote areas in Alaska. From here we split up. Fred and Bud and Jim went south, George Theile and I would go north.

George had made many trips flying supplies to Prudhoe Bay for several years from Fairbanks. He flew a Hercules cargo plane for Atlantic Richfields' oilfields. These planes will carry gear like trucks and big stuff. When he returned to Fairbanks he would fly low over the flat north slope tundra looking for game. On one of these runs he spotted a record-winning moose. The sighting of this moose triggered the hunt for me.

To hunt the north slope and the northern edge of the Brooks Range with a bow was a great challenge. Not many have ever tried it. It's remote, there are no facilities, it's expensive, and a little on the dangerous side. You also must have a good guide and pilot who knows the country.

In order to prepare for the trip, George and I had to stop at his house first. George was greatly disturbed when we went to his home and found two rotten caribou carcasses in his garage. Someone had left them for him ten days ago while he was away, and warm weather had spoiled them. What a foul smelling garage.

It took us a day to get George's gear together and have the airplane serviced. It was a long flight, and there was a lot of camping gear to pack in what George called his "family cruiser." He had assembled it by using parts of three other wrecked planes. George is a very accomplished pilot, and I would fly anywhere with him under most any conditions with great confidence.

We flew from Fairbanks to Bettles, where we gassed up the plane, then headed toward the Arctic slope, and crossed the Arctic Circle. The Brooks Range is the only Alaskan Range that runs east and west. Fred and I had seen this country in 1960 when we flew back from Barrow with George, and Pete Merry.

George said it was a gamble to be going so late in the season as the weather gets bad early in the Brooks Range. We might wake up some morning to find two foot of snow on the ground. It was necessary to take extra gas as George would have to taxi back and forth to pack down the snow in order to take off.

So we carried all the extra gas that we could from Bettles, and landed on a sandbar about seventy miles south of Anaktuvuk Pass. We stashed the gas in the brush, and returned to Bettles for some more. We saw several moose on the flight up from Bettles. In fact, one huge bull was quite near the place where we had stashed the extra gas cans. Normally I would have been tickled with him, but I had a special moose on my mind.

Flying north up the Johns River, we came to towering peaks in the mountain range and to a remote spot where George had seen sheep last summer. The snow-free range was covered with little white specks. Diving down to make an inspection, we found they were white dall sheep. George twisted and turned the plane through the canyons, trying to locate the largest ram. He soon turned to me and said, "This is the place we'd better camp."

We flew down the canyon until we came to a flat area with a river spreading out into several tributaries. The shoals were covered with gravel, three inch stones and some large rocks as big as footballs.

George had equipped his plane with huge tires. These three-foot tires were over a foot wide and were not inflated with much air so as to cushion much of the shock on rough terrain.

I think we must have made at least eight passes at the strip George had selected to land on. Finally he said, "Well, here goes. Hang on." He brought the plane in for one hell of a bumpy landing. It was impossible to miss some of the rocks, but we finally came to a bouncing halt.

The area surrounding us was beautiful and remote, with the mountain range to our south about a mile. A half-moon-shaped peak formation was covered with rocks, and on it we could see many sheep.

George taxied the plane over to the edge of a high bank on the east side of a small stream. This would give us a little protection from the strong winds so we unloaded our gear here. George would have to fly back and get some poles for the tent and some firewood, because there was no timber near the area. He asked me to clean up the landing strip that he had marked out, and pick up all the big rocks while he was gone.

It was a lonely and stranded feeling watching the plane disappear from view. I was alone in that desolate area. The realization that if something should happen to George, I would have to depend on myself to get out of there, but didn't have the foggiest notion which way to go, was very scary. To occupy my mind and forget those possibilities, I began cleaning the landing strip. I also checked and patted the 44 magnum that I carried in a shoulder holster.

It was a very welcome sound when I finally heard the drone of the plane about an hour later. I could see the long tent poles lashed to the plane's struts, looking like huge rockets. His landing this time was much smoother since I had the strip pretty well cleared, and he taxied to our campsite.

George had filled the plane with firewood which we unloaded after we had unlashed the tent poles and set up our tent. It was nearly dark by the time we had done all the necessary chores. The tent was just about big enough for our sleeping bags, plus a little gear we could stuff on the side. It was a pretty rugged camp, about thirty miles south of the pass. This is where the big caribou migration crosses through the Brooks Range, back and forth to the north slope.

While George had been gone, I noticed a lot of grayling in the stream, so I rigged up my fly rod and flipped a fly out over them. It gives you a rare feeling to know that you are probably the first human ever to drop a fly in a particular pool. A sleek grayling zoomed up, coming out of the water about a foot, and took the fly on my first cast. I had no problem catching enough fifteen-inch fish for dinner that evening.

After a breakfast of bacon and eggs the next morning, we decided to go up and give the sheep a go. I put a pair of hip boots on my backpack, and used them several times crossing streams. When we reached hard ground, I stashed them in the brush and put on my hiking shoes. The first half mile was a rugged task, fighting our way through the willow brush up to the base of the mountain. Finally we broke out on a barren rocky formation that swept up to the snow capped peaks.

We followed a ravine up the slope that George suggested we climb toward the peak. There we would have a good vantage point to check the area. It took about twenty minutes to reach the top, where we sat down, and with our binoculars started to check for our trophy dall sheep. George spotted two nice rams in the valley that extended out before us. We decided that I would climb about halfway up the side of the mountain and hide behind one of the large boulders. George would go up the valley until he was even with the sheep, then hopefully run them past me.

When I had gone only a quarter of a mile, I heard a shot. My first thought was that George had met up with some sort of trouble. He probably ran into a grizzly that gave him a hard time. I glassed the area from where the shot had come. I could see George standing with his gun up to his shoulder. Then he fired another shot at two wolves in front of him. It puzzled me as to why he would be shooting at the wolves, when I was trying to sneak up on the sheep. But I kept on going up the mountain side. It took me almost an hour to get above the sheep. When George got to where the rams were, they saw him and spooked up in my direction. They ran past me crossing over onto a ledge, and at about eighty yards stood looking down at me.

This was a little too long a shot for me, so I worked my

way back down the valley and finally found George. I asked him why he shot at the wolves. Apparently they were trying to sneak up on the sheep too, and there was no use for George to keep going if the wolves were going to beat him to the sheep.

With all the commotion that we'd made, the valley seemed to be void of sheep. After lunch we decided to go back to camp, and I discovered that we had come a lot further than I realized. It took us quite a while to get back down to the willow brush.

The ptarmigan that time of year were mottled, partly white and partly brown, and were easy to distinguish in the brush. They are a pretty bird. We ran into a covy of them and I managed to shoot three with my bow. That was plenty for our evening meal. Ptarmigan meat is dark meat and very delicious. As we sat by the campfire that evening, George pointed across the spread of streams and up the side of the mountain.

"Look at that big bull moose," he said. As I looked in the direction he was pointing, the first object I saw was a good sized grizzly mosying along the river bed. From George's vantage point, he was not able to see the bear. I said to him, "George, that's an awful funny looking moose. He hasn't got any antlers, and he's all covered with brown fur." George looked at me puzzled. I said, "Stand up, George." He stood up and immediately saw the bear working its way in our direction.

Quickly I grabbed my bow and we started across one of the shallow streams to get behind the willow brush. The wind was in our favor and the bear was just ambling along at a slow gait. He was taking the path in line with the willow brush where we were hiding, so we waited in ambush for him.

At last he came by us with his shuffling strides. We could hear his claws on the rocks going clickety click with each step he took. When the bear was about forty yards from us, walking broadside, I took a shot at him, putting the arrow about an inch over his back. The sound of the arrow hitting the rocks frightened him and he turned and ran down the stream. I tried to get another shot, but the wind fouled me up.

As we started back toward the tent, George grabbed my arm, saying, "Look what's coming!" A big bull moose was coming straight toward us. Since I was interested only in the huge trophy that George had baited me with, we let him pass us at about twenty-five yards. It would have been a cinch to have taken him with my bow. Finding one particular moose on a hunting trip to Alaska, is a real trick and a test of patience.

That night we decided we would move our gear in the morning. If we packed our sleeping bags and the necessary food up to the edge of the timberline that fringes the foot of the mountains, we would not have to come all the way down to the valley floor to sleep the next night. So the next morning, with backpacks loaded, we took off for the sheep area, dropping our camping equipment at the top side of the willow brush.

We climbed up on a high plateau just above the timber line and laid down, glassing the mountains. George spotted a large ram fairly low in the valley. To our left was a slope that went up about fifteen-hundred feet. There was a notch at the skyline, covered with snow. George glassed this area and saw lots of sheep tracks in the snow on the edge of the slope. He judged that if I went up there, hid behind a rock and waited, he could spook the ram he had seen right up to me. He was sure the ram would go over the top of the mountain and pass through that little notch.

I started my climb up the mountain, taking about an hour to get up to the snow. By that time I was so hot and thirsty that I laid down and ate two or three handfuls of snow. It took me about ten minutes to catch my breath, as I lay in the snow panting like a dragon. I was ringing wet with sweat. I looked through my glasses periodically to locate George in the valley below.

I looked around for a spot to make my stand, and there were two sites that looked good to me. One was a path that went over the top where I could see tracks in the snow. The other was a good trail that ran about seventy-five yards to my right and I could hide behind a big boulder there. I decided the first spot would be the best, and worked my way up to it, picking a small boulder to hide behind.

The top of the peak gave me a breath-taking view of the valley below, as well as the mountain peaks around me. This valley ran east and west, and the peaks made a complete circle, similar to a football stadium. It was probably two miles long and a mile across, all bare rock and snow.

I was enjoying the beauty around me, when I heard a shot. Evidently George had gotten close to the ram and was attempting to spook him in my direction. I quickly spotted him coming my way on the side of the mountain. Somewhere he picked up a second ram and they proceeded to work their way toward me. They didn't seem to be too frightened. George fired a second shot, and I could hear the bullet ricochet off the rocks. The rams came bounding a little faster, heading right in my direction.

My bow was all set and I tried to settle my nerves, telling myself to calm down as it appeared the rams were going to run right over me. They came to a spot where the trail divided, and took the fork that led them up directly past the boulder that I had just passed. They stopped about twenty yards from the boulder and looked back down at George. This was a disheartening sight, I'd spent so much time and energy climbing up the mountain, and then picked the wrong spot. The sheep were over seventy-five yards from me. I did take a shot, but it fell way short.

Shooting a bow on an angle in such a high altitude, either up or down, is awkward as it's difficult to judge distances. Those who have rifle-hunted sheep know all about this. I worked my way back down the mountain and met George. He told me he had walked to within twenty yards of the ram, and had to throw a rock at it to make it run. I should have sent George up the damn mountain and gone to the valley myself, I'd have probably gotten my sheep. That's the way hunting goes. You never can tell. It's like business. If you're not at the right place at the right time, "you don't get a shot."

We worked our way back down into the timber, decided to call it a day and set up our camp. We picked a spot by a little rushing stream, that was about six feet wide, with white water dashing down the side of the mountain. Off to the right there was willow brush and some level ground. I had brought a painter's plastic drop cloth, and we tied this up with ropes to the trees and draped it over the sleeping bags. We had nothing to eat but cold cuts from a can, and turned in early. The roar of the little brook running down the mountain lulled us to sleep.

When I woke up the next morning the yellow streaks in the sky told me that dawn was breaking. It also told me that I was damn near frozen to death. It gets awfully cold up there in that altitude in the mountains. I got up and put on everything I had. I thought the best way to warm up was to make a pot of coffee. Taking a little bucket, I went to the racing stream about ten feet away, and scooped up a bucket of water. Then I got some firewood, and was about ready to strike a match when I noticed something off to my right. I stood motionless. Then I saw it move, a pure white wolf walking in my direction. He was on the other side of the stream. I cautiously picked up my bow and worked my way slowly to a log where the wolf wouldn't see me. I knew he couldn't hear me over the roaring of the brook.

I got my arrow in place and waited. I felt the wind blowing gently in my face as it came up the mountain. It was apparent that the wolf would pass me within twenty feet or closer. I watched as he stopped and nosed around, searching for food. Ten feet behind was another wolf, this one was jet black. I asked myself, which one did I want? A white one or a black one? This was quite a privileged choice to have.

Preparing myself, I scooched down and got the bow in position. Both wolves worked their way up in my direction. As they were about to step out, directly in front of me, I pulled my bow to full draw and waited. The white one was leading, and in one more step would give me about a twenty-foot broadside shot. At this critical moment, George rolled over and in a gruff voice said, "Well, I guess I better get up!" The woods came alive with wolves running in every direction. I could have shot George!

Of course, George felt bad when he found out what he had done, but that wasn't very consoling to me. We had our coffee and decided to work our way down to the main camp. If we were going to stay on this mountain side, we had to have more food.

We started our descent down through the willow brush. As we got to the last plateau just above the streams—about six of them spread about half a mile across—we stopped to rest. As usual, George picked up his binoculars and glassed the area for a few moments. He nudged me and said, "Hey Bob, there's a good bull caribou. Take a look down the river." I swung my binoculars down to the right and sure enough, there he was. A fine bull, with a beautiful white mane, stood in the middle of one of the little streams.

We debated about the best way to sneak up on him, and George finally said, "Well, you don't need me. You'd have a better chance doing it alone." So I started down the gravel bar and walked in the direction of the caribou, checking the wind. My hip boots were making an awful lot of noise rubbing against the willow brush, so I took them off and rolled my pant legs up to my knees. Let me tell you, the water in that river was mighty cold. My feet became numb in a very short time, and I could hardly feel the sharp rocks on the bottom.

Working my way through the willow brush, I crossed several streams and got into a position where I could get a good shot at the caribou. He was facing the other side of the stream, and was almost broadside to me. I thought I should get a little closer, so in a crouched position I went as slowly as possible until I got within about forty yards of him. I figured that was about as close as I was going to get, without him hearing me.

The caribou was standing in water about two feet deep. I pulled the bow back, but my movement caught his attention and he turned and looked at me. This was a frightening sensation, and I responded by releasing an arrow before I had taken good aim. I hit the caribou in the neck, and he immediately whirled and started toward the other shore. He took about two bounces, then whirled around and came back toward me. This must have been one of the most exciting moments I have ever had in hunting caribou. I had never heard of caribou charging before, but this one looked like he was about to try it. His four-foot antlers looked very impressive and sharp.

He made about four bounces directly at me. The water was splashing up about eight feet high around him and his hoofs were clicking on the rocks in the stream bed. At fifteen yards he stopped, turned broadside and looked back the other way. When he did this, I was really puzzled. A glance over his back showed me two wolves standing on the other shore. The bull gave me a perfect shot and I put an arrow behind the front shoulder. He ran a few feet and fell on the edge of the gravel bar.

I then directed my attention to the wolves, neither of which seemed to be particularly disturbed by the whole affair. They just stood there looking at me, about forty-five yards away.

Again I thought, boy, here's a chance to get me a wolf. I put an arrow on the string, took aim, and released the arrow. It skidded over their backs. This didn't seem to bother them too much as they continued to stand, still looking at me. So I had a second chance! But I rushed my shot, hit a rock between the legs of the largest one and they both took off on the run. I could have broken that bow right over my knee at that point.

George came down and congratulated me on shooting the caribou and asked me what happened to the wolves. I told him that apparently I wasn't too good on wolves. We dragged the caribou out onto the gravel bar where we took a bunch of pictures. We field dressed him and went back after our gear. By that time my feet were so numb I couldn't feel anything, and they had turned a pretty pink color.

We picked up our gear and I put my socks and boots back on, then we sat there and rested, deciding what to do next. George looked through his binoculars at the valley and exclaimed in a excited tone, "Hey, what the hell's going on!" I responded with, "What do you mean?" He answered,

"Those damn wolves are right back at the caribou!" Later we found out that the wolves kept that caribou in the water for several days, as he was very thin. When we skinned him for a life-sized mount, he actually had water between his hide and the flesh on his legs.

After looking at the wolves by the caribou, I swung my binoculars over to the right where our tent was, about a third of a mile away across the spread of streams. I couldn't believe my eyes when I saw our tent opened up on the side and a huge grizzly stepped out. He did not bother to go through the flap in the front, but came right through the side of the tent. He was standing between the tent and the airplane that was tied down some forty yards away. I watched while he walked over to the plane and stood on his hind legs, putting his front paws up on the windshield and along the leading edge of the wings.

I told George to take a quick look, and he said, "My God! What do you want to shoot now Bob? A wolf or a grizzly?" I answered, "Well, so far I haven't been too good on wolves. Let's try the grizzly."

At this point George was quite concerned about his airplane. We hurriedly got our backpacks and sleeping bags on our backs and started working our way across the streams. Our tent was near a ledge that was about thirty feet high. We went across to a point where we could climb this ledge, thinking I could shoot directly down on the bear. He seemed content to stay in the willow brush back of our tent. We glassed the area several times, and saw that he was having a good time eating whatever food he had found in the tent.

We spooked the wolves when we went past the caribou, and George jokingly remarked, "We have to get over and kill that damn bear and get right back here, or those wolves will eat up your caribou!" What a delightful predicament!

We made our way to the side of the hill next to the river, and climbed to the top. There was willow brush about three or four feet high that we had to walk through. Again I took off my boots because of the constant scraping noise that they made in the brush. George was right behind me with his gun. We walked quietly up to the ledge where we could look down over the tent. I peered over the top but could see nothing of the bear. On closer observation of the rear of the tent in the willow brush, I saw the bear lying down. I pointed him out to George and he whispered, "Shoot him!"

I really had a very poor shot. He was only about twenty-five yards away, but on a forty-five degree angle down, and worst of all, I had to slide the arrow through some brush. Picking out an opening through which I could see a big blotch of brown fur, I let one fly. The arrow hit some of the brush, and slammed against some rocks as it hit the ground. The bear turned around and looked toward the arrow. In so doing, he placed himself in a better position for me. I put another arrow on the string and this time I hit him right behind the front shoulder.

He thrashed around in the brush. I wasn't sure whether he was going to come up the ridge, or go down toward the stream, so I quickly stepped behind George. I was very pleased when I saw him run past the tent and out toward the stream. He stopped about fifty yards away and stood looking back in our direction. He still had not spotted us. Again I put an arrow on the string. It was a down hill shot and went over his back. By now the blood was pouring out of his side and he bounded off to our right, up the stream.

George and I hurriedly took off parallel to the bear, on the ridge through the willow brush, hoping to intercept him if he came over the top. I was ahead, and running. We came to a little notch in the ridge, to our left and all of a sudden, boom, the bear broke out about thirty feet from us, heading right at us. He saw us and growled, whirled and went back down the ridge. This happened so fast that I wasn't able to stop and take a shot. We watched as the bear ran about two-hundred yards down the river basin, then climbed the ridge and started up the mountainside. He stopped as soon as he topped the ridge and looked at us. His whole side was completely covered with blood. He strolled slowly up the mountain about two-hundred yards and laid down. George extended his hand, smiled and said, "Well, Bob, congratulations. I guess you got yourself a barren ground grizzly!"

We went back to the tent to examine what supplies were left. The bear had taken all of our food. He had eaten several ptarmigan and some grayling that were laying outside of the tent. There was nothing but feathers lying around. Inside the tent he had picked up the canned foods, and crushed them with his teeth. They were so flattened they looked like they had been run over by a truck. He had sucked all the juice out of the cans of vegetables and had eaten the heel off one rubber boot and the toe off the other one.

Everything was in shambles. George inspected the airplane and found that the top of the cowling above the engine, and the windshield, had huge muddy bear paw marks on them. The windows also had paw marks. Fortunately, we hadn't left any food in the plane, or he probably would have torn the airplane all to pieces. That would have put us in one hell of a fix. I hated to think how we could have ever hoofed it back to Anaktuvuk.

My main concern at that time was whether he had eaten our whiskey bottles. On close inspection, I found that they were about the only thing that he didn't touch in the tent. He had even chewed on our sleeping bags. It would take a while to get things organized. George suggested that we have some lunch. He said, "That bear's not going any place. We might as well have some lunch, then we'll go up and get him." So we straightened up the tent and ate sandwiches which had been in our backpacks.

Now it was about 4:00 o'clock in the afternoon and the sun was fairly close to the top of the western peak. We took a route north up the river basin to the point beyond where we had last seen the bear. Climbing the ridge, we sneaked through the willow brush and circled around to come in above the bear. It took us about half an hour to climb up the side of the mountain and get on the rocky ledge to a good observation point.

George spotted him with the binoculars, and he was lying in the same spot he had been in before. George thought we should sneak down toward him because he might not be dead. We worked our way cautiously through the willow brush, watching each step we took so as not to dislodge a rock and make a noise. We were able to get to within twenty yards of the bear. We crept very quietly, tip-toeing to a small opening in the brush that gave us a clear view of him. He was lying flat on his side like a dog sleeping. He appeared to be dead. George whispered for me to shoot him again, just in case.

I put an arrow on the string, and was just about ready to release it when he raised his head and looked at us. I was surprised that he was still alive. I zeroed in on him and released the arrow, hitting him in the mid-section. George and I were both surprised when he jumped to his feet and started slowly shuffling up the mountain. He stopped about every one hundred yards and looked back at us. Now both sides of him were saturated with blood. We knew he couldn't last much longer.

His movements could be followed now by eyesight. He was walking slowly on the barren tundra above the willow brush. We watched him disappear over the top of a ridge. We followed his heavy blood trail to the top of that ridge. He headed toward a small draw with some low willow brush in it. The brush was about six feet high and very thick.

We followed the blood trail to the edge of the brush and George glassed the area toward the top of the mountain. The brush covered an area about one-hundred yards long and forty yards wide. This was the only willow brush to the top of the mountain. George said, "He's in there someplace, Bob." We knew that he could not have left the brush area.

The sun was dropping over the side of the mountain to the west, and George said, "You know, I don't think that it would be smart to track the wounded grizzly through this willow brush when it's getting dark. We better go back to camp and pick him up tomorrow." He didn't have to say anymore to convince me to quit. We worked our way back down the mountain, picked up the hindquarters of the caribou at the river and headed for camp. George said, "I can't believe that bear went so far."

That evening we sat by the campfire eating steaks from my caribou. We looked across the west bank of the river, about a quarter of a mile away, and saw two wolves sitting there watching us. Another wolf was working on the remains of the caribou carcass. George commented, "Well, you haven't done too badly Bob. You've shot yourself a mess of ptarmigan, a nice bull caribou, and a grizzly so far." It certainly had been an exciting hunting day.

George finished his last cigarette and I puffed on my tipperillo and we turned in for the night. George had suggested that we tie the tent flaps open. He said with the grizzlies as thick as they are we had better be prepared to defend ourselves as well as protect our caribou meat and our airplane.

During the night I awakened abruptly to find flames about a foot high in the tent, next to me on the side where all my gear was. One of our smokes had ignited my clothes in the tent. I woke George, and we both jumped out of our sleeping bags, and began to beat out the flames with our caps. When the fire was out, we checked the damage. The fire had burned my bow string into two sections, burned my jacket and the feathers off most of my arrows.

We didn't sleep too well the rest of the night. I realized how fortunate it was that we had left the tent flap open, or we might have been asphyxiated.

As we were having breakfast the next morning, we looked over toward my caribou carcass. George had sawed off its antlers, and darned if one of our wolf friends wasn't making off with the skull.

I grabbed my bow and tried to pull a sneak on him. I ran up ahead of him in the willow brush to intercept him. Knowing he couldn't see or smell me with that caribou head in his mouth. He had to tip his head back to handle the weight, but somehow he gave me the slip.

I had no more than returned to the tent when it started to rain. It rained all day and all night and we spent the whole day inside, worrying about my grizzly hide. Grizzlies are known to eat other dead grizzlies.

The rain let up just before sundown and we cranked up the plane to see if we could spot our bear from the air. About one-hundred yards from the site where we had stopped trailing the bear two days ago, George spotted a mound of brush and rocks near the top of the willow patch that the grizzly had entered. He said, "There's your bear. Another grizzly has covered him up. If we don't get to him by tomorrow, there probably won't be anything left of him. In fact," he said, "it may be too late already, another bear may have chewed him up before burying him." I had a very sick feeling about the situation.

The air was filled with snowflakes the next morning, and George said to me, "Bob, we've got to make a decision. We've either got to go back to Bettles or go up to Umiat and get some gas. I don't like the looks of this snow! I don't think we should stay here, it looks like the weather is going to change. A lot of snow would make it impossible to get the plane off the ground with our big wheels. We've got one problem, though," he continued, "I'm not sure whether they have any gas at Umiat. We have enough gas to get there, but if we get up there and they don't have any gas we're going to be stuck there for maybe a week or two until someone comes by."

I told him that I'd be willing to take a chance on that. So he said, "O.K., let's go!" Then he added, "I'm afraid you're going to have to settle for just the skull of that grizzly. I'm sure that other bear has chewed up the hide by now." He said he would pick up the skull and send it to me later. I hated to leave without giving it one more try, but the weather overruled us. George suggested we leave our old badly ripped tent. He said he had an extra pup tent.

We topped the mountain peaks then slid down and dipped low through the Anaktuvuk Pass. George thought we might pick up some gas from the Eskimos there. We could see the Eskimos below us, perched on the side of the pass, watching and waiting for the migration of the caribou herds. When we landed at Anaktuvuk the ground was bare.

Two Eskimos came out on a snowmobile to meet us. Anaktuvuk is a native village about a hundred miles south of Point Barrow, and is a very quaint, remote spot. George asked the natives if they had any gas, and they said they had about forty gallons that they could spare. They wanted $2.75 a gallon for it. George raised his eyebrows and said he guessed we had enough to get where we were going.

We took off to the north, where the country flattened, making a barren wasteland, referred to as the tundra. The land mass from here to the Beauford Sea extends north one-hundred miles from the north slope. You can see about twenty miles in any direction. It was a good feeling for me to return to the flat vast tundra country again. It brought back many memories of my days spent with George, and Pete Merry on a wolf hunt in this lonesome land.

We spent the rest of the day flying over the tundra hunting oil drums. In years previous, George had flown many drums of gas up for the Cat Train that ran to Prudhoe Bay, and he stashed some drums of gas in the brush. He thought that maybe they hadn't used or found it all, but after six landings and thumping oil drums, we found they were all empty. George said we had just about enough gas to get to Umiat and we had better head over there. We saw five grizzlies that day.

We flew into Umiat about 6:00 that evening, and the Eskimo who met us said they did have some gas. We both heaved a sigh of relief.

Umiat is a weather station operated by one man and his wife. They radio weather reports in to Barrow and Fairbanks. Their home was a quonset hut, and they invited us to stay with them. There was an extra room where we could sleep, so we made our headquarters there for the next few days. This area is generally not hunted by sportsmen due to the great distance and lack of facilities.

Our hosts had not seen anyone for days, and were hungry for conversation. We had a pleasant visit after feasting on a caribou dinner that we were pleased to provide. They seemed to know a lot of people that George new, and vice versa, so it was like old home week for George. When they told us they were practically out of meat, George assured them that we would shoot a moose or a caribou for them. They could not get away from the air strip, and all their hunting had to be done there around their quonset house.

After a hardy breakfast the next morning we took off in search of our big moose. We flew several hundred miles and saw lots of moose, but they were not the right one. We also saw a few caribou and four barren ground grizzlies.

About 4:00 we returned to Umiat, and George asked our host if he ever did any fishing. He said he didn't know that there was any fishing near here since he had lived there for only a month. George inquired if he had any fishing tackle. He said he did, and brought out a collection of rustyspoons and a spinning rod. We borrowed his jeep and I took my fly rod. George's parting words were, "We're going to have fish for supper, I'll guarantee it!"

George knew of a small stream east of the air strip and we caught a nice mess of fish. One of them weighed about twelve pounds. Our host was really surprised when we dumped out a gunnysack full of fish. We all enjoyed a big fish dinner that evening.

We continued our search for the big moose the following day, flying another three-hundred miles. We returned after four hours in the air, having seen nothing but a few caribou and foxes. We had lunch back at the quonset hut and decided to put off the hunt until the next day. We spent the afternoon fishing again and caught a bunch of grayling.

The third day we probably covered another four-hundred miles, flying the rivers, because that's where the willow brush grew, making cover for the game to hide. No luck again, and we flew back to Umiat. I had begun to think that it was like trying to find the proverbial needle in the haystack. I wondered which would happen first, fly the wings off the airplane, or go broke on $1.50 per gallon gas?

It was very foggy the next day, and as we sat around the table talking and drinking coffee, we heard a voice come on the radio asking for weather information at Umiat.

We were all surprised that anyone would be out in such weather, and George jumped up, saying, "Let me have the mike! I know that guy!" He told us it was Noel Wein, a fellow he had worked for. Wein recognized George's voice right away, and they were delighted to run into each other in such a remote spot. Wein said he wanted to come into Umiat for gas. George said he would talk him down by radio.

George instructed Wein to watch out for the high hill at the north side of the landing strip as soon as he got down to where he could see the ground. We went outside and listened for the plane. George put the microphone out the window and talked Wein down. He had a 411 Cessna twin engine, with five passengers on their way to Prudhoe Bay. They had to wait a couple of hours for the fog to lift so they could continue. George said it looked like this fog could last for several days and could foul up our moose hunt and it might turn to snow.

He also added that he really should get back to Fairbanks to pack up his next hunter. Naturally I hated to give up on the big moose but agreed with George that we should call it off. So we packed our gear. George said if we go "low" and "slow" to the east he felt we could make it out of the fog.

We flew about a hundred feet off the ground for forty-five minutes to the east, and were surprised as we broke out of the fog, to see another plane. It was flying directly towards us. George swerved, and it passed us about a hundred yards to our right. George remarked, "What the hell is that guy doing up here!" Then he said it probably was Jim Helemicks heading for the mouth of the Coleville River. We climbed then and flew west over the mountains east of the Anaktuvuk Pass. By now the weather looked pretty good and there was no snow on the ground, so we decided to go back to our old campsite. We had left our tent set up when we took off for the north slope. We landed and saw it had been completely torn apart by a grizzly. There was no way we could patch it up or salvage anything even to stay that night.

When we took off, I asked George to swing past my bear burial ground. The mound had been torn apart and we could see patches of fur. I said, "There goes my bearskin rug! But I would appreciate it if you would pick up the skull someday." He said that he would.

As I have indicated in the pages of this chapter I rate this the most challenging, exciting and rewarding hunt I have ever been on in my experiences around the world. I feel very obliged to my friend, pilot, and guide, George Theile for one super trip.

I checked into the Fairbanks Inn and found that Fred was not back yet but he had lots of mail waiting for him. I thought he might like to have it, so I called George and asked him to take me out to Fred's camp the next day on the little delta. When we reached the camp, we saw that some large tripods had been put on the landing strip. Busby uses horses for his hunting and doesn't like airplanes, so he had put up the tripods to discourage anyone from landing a plane on his emergency strip.

As we flew low over the cabin a woman ran out, probably the cook, and waved at the plane. George thought she was trying to wave him off, and this made him a bit miffed. He scribbled a note that said, "If you don't move those damn tripods, I'm going to land this thing right in your front yard." He made a low pass and dropped the note.

We circled for about fifteen minutes and she finally came out and moved a couple of the tripods. She was not too receptive, but after I introduced myself and told her I was bringing Fred's mail to him, she seemed to feel better about our presence. She even brought us a cup of coffee and said she expected Fred momentarily. I went outside and could hear horses down the trail in the distance. The noise of horses hoofs came closer. I went down the trail a ways and met Fred and Bud coming up the hill. Fred was leading the way, perched on one of the hayburners. He was quite surprised to see me. We exchanged a few greetings and then Fred came up with his best classic remark. He said, "If you think moose are hard to kill with a bow and arrow, you should try hunting them with rocks." It had taken ten days for him to get his lost bow back from Japan. Fred had had to watch Bud do all the hunting and settle for a bloodless hunt.

George flew me back to Fairbanks, and Fred came in the next day. We shopped around Fairbanks for a while, and I bought a prehistoric buffalo skull for my museum. Fred also purchased a few things for his museum.

We flew to Seattle the next day and made arrangements for a life-sized mount of caribou.

XVII

Whitetail Paradise
1970–1988

In 1970 I was pleasantly surprised when I received an invitation from H.R. Boyer, the owner of Grousehaven, to join him and Fred Bear on a deer hunt along with some of his other friends. Mr. Boyer, I later gained the privilege of calling him Bill, was a close friend of Arthur Godfrey, who also hunted at Grousehaven.

Fred had told me of his meeting Godfrey on his trip to Grousehaven last year. The story goes that. . . .

One evening Godfrey asked Bill Boyer, (H.R.), if Fred Bear lived somewhere in Michigan. Bill told him, "Yes, he lives about forty miles away." Arthur said he would like to meet Fred, so Bill called Fred and invited him over.

Fred accepted the invitation and the group went hunting for several days. Then, Godfrey invited Fred to appear on his television show. As a result of that appearance, Fred was invited to appear on several other national TV programs such as "What's My Line?".

These appearances contributed greatly to Fred's success story, gaining a national image and promoting his product, the famous Bear Bow.

Grousehaven has been in the Boyer family for many years. It is located about three miles from the little town of Rose City, about two-thirds of the way up on the eastern side of the lower peninsula, and about forty miles inland from Lake Huron. It covers approximately twenty-five-hundred acres of timber, both hard and soft woods, lots of spruce and some swamps. The Houghton Creek flows through the property, it is a beautiful place to hunt. There is an abundance of wild game. All three varieties of squirrels, brown, black and gray. A heavy concentration of deer inhabit the area, as well as a plentiful supply of grouse, after which it was named, and lots of wild turkeys.

There is a landing strip at Grousehaven, over five thousand feet long, a hanger large enough for four airplanes, but it is usually filled with old models of General Motors cars. Bill had been a vice-president of General Motors, and ran the tank plant in Cleveland during the war. He has an old World War II version of a jeep, that sports a sign on the back which says, "Follow me, you bastard!" Each time a plane comes in, the jeep is used to lead the plane back to the hanger. There is also a sign in the landing area which cautions the pilots to watch for low-flying grouse. Bill charges a 25¢ landing fee.

Mr. Boyer is the most genial and generous host that I have ever known. The past fourteen years, that I have spent the fall hunting season with Fred and Mr. Boyer and the other guests at Grousehaven, have truly been a highlight in my hunting career. I'll never forget the thrill I felt when I received my first official invitation from Mr. Boyer to join the select hunting group during rifle season.

Mr. Boyer had sent a map with instructions along with the invitation, but when I arrived at the gate, I found a chain across it with four padlocks on it. I was perplexed, I thought they were expecting my arrival, so I went into town and gave Mr. Boyer a call. Fred answered, and said, "Come on in, you damn fool. The gate isn't locked, those are just dummy padlocks!"

Fred told me a lot about Mr. Boyer, but I didn't know what sort of build-up he had given Mr. Boyer about me. I was almost afraid to go in and meet him. When I first made his acquaintance, he and Fred were sitting by the fireplace in the main lodge, Fred gave me quite a flowery introduction. My fears were quickly erased, as I soon discovered that Mr. Boyer was an easy-going, likeable sort of person who had the qualities to make one feel right at home, and to feel as if you'd known him for a long time.

In addition to the main lodge at Grousehaven, which has four bedrooms, there is another four room cabin plus Mr. Boyer's personal cabin. When we first met, Mr. Boyer remarked that the main stipulation at Grousehaven was if I became a member of the group that hunted there, I was to be a lifetime member. I've always felt honored to have the opportunity to hunt with such super guys as the ones I have met at Grousehaven.

During hunting season each year, we all gather at the lodge in front of the huge stone fireplace, with birch logs snapping and crackling, and have a couple, three cocktails before dinner. Hours are spent exchanging hunting yarns and experiences. Fred and I have a lot of fun telling true and not so true tales, and poking fun at each other.

One of the most colorful characters who hunts with us each year is Bill's good friend, General Hank Everest, a four star general in the Air Force. He and Bill became acquainted during the war, and hunted at Grousehaven together for many years. At the close of the war, he was in command of all the Air Force installations from Great Britain to Turkey.

Usually we arrived at Grousehaven two or three days before the season starts. This gives us time to select a hot spot to build our blinds, then target in our bows and guns. The General is a very methodical individual, and likes to have everything quite precise. He is especially particular about his firearms, it takes about two boxes of shells for him to be satisfied that the gun is properly targeted in.

The first year I was there, I remember, I was sitting on the bench while Hank was preparing to load his 300 Weatherby, a gun with a telescope sight. I had been a

Weatherby dealer in my sporting goods business for a number of years, and had experiences shooting a Weatherby rifle on many hunting trips. On two occasions, when the person shooting the gun either didn't hold onto it tight enough or leaned his head a little too far forward, I had witnessed a tremendous recoil. This is a common occurrence. The phrase "When you have a half-circle cut over your eye, you have the distinguished 'Weatherby look'," was coined as a result of this recoil. Anyway, without thinking, just as the General eased down into the lether pads to fire the gun, I said, "General, don't forget to hang onto that gun!"

He stopped, looked at me with a sort of chicken smile, as if to say, "Sonny, don't try to tell me how to shoot a rifle!", then eased back in his shooting position and squeezed the trigger. At the report of the gun his head popped back and the blood started squirting all over the table. Fred ran for the first aid kit, and we did the best we could to patch up the General and check the bleeding. I later commented to Fred that I had a hell of a lot of nerve to tell a four star general how to shoot a gun.

Fred's favorite pastime is building blinds. He will spend about two days building blinds in different areas, so if the wind changes direction he will be prepared. Fred also has blinds for evening hunts and blinds for morning hunts. He not only builds blinds for himself, but for other members of the hunting party as well. He hardly has time to hunt himself.

The first year that I was at Grousehaven, Fred also invited Joe Engel, the astronaut who had flown the X-15 many times, and who was slated for the space shuttle. Bill had a Bonanza single engine airplane, and wanted to take Joe and me up to see the property from the air. Once Bill got the plane up, he gave the controls to Joe. We went half an hour surveying the area, and got a pretty good layout of the land.

That evening, Fred suggested that he, Joe and I go together in Fred's car to our separate hunting spots. We dropped Joe off at a rye strip where there had been a lot of deer traffic. Fred had erected a blind up in a tree there. We wished Joe good luck and took off. Fred dropped me off down at the edge of a swamp.

Shortly after dark the lights of Fred's car showed up on the road as he came to pick me up, and then we went to pick up Joe. A very frustrated Joe read Fred the riot act. Fred asked what the problem was, and Joe said, "I've had a buck standing out here in front of me ever since you left. He wasn't over forty yards away at any time. There's just no way a right-handed shooter can shoot out of that blind you built!"

Fred got a real big kick out of that. It was true, Fred had built the blind for himself and he is a left-handed shooter. If you've ever handled a bow and arrow, you understand the fact that when you get up into a tree, there's only one way that you can swing a bow and still hang onto the tree.

The night before rifle season opened, Fred promoted a team program for the next day, and suggested that each member kick in $10.00. Mr. Boyer selected the team captains, and picked Fred for one and me for the other. It was a festive mood that night, with everyone looking forward to the hunt. We had a terrific meal, and lots of wild stories were exchanged. It was hard to sleep, with all the excitement and the anticipation of the hunt.

We rose before daylight and had a big breakfast. I went with Fred that morning, he dropped me off at my spot and continued on about a quarter of a mile to his favorite place. As daylight broke I could hear guns booming in the distance, and then a loud explosion closer by, which I hoped was one of my teammate's. The team with the most deer by the first night would win the contest and the money.

About 8:30 I was just sitting, waiting for something to happen, when I heard a "kerwham" down towards the spot where Fred was sitting. I knew he must have shot, and after waiting a short while, I stepped out of my blind and looked down the road. Fred was standing there, looking down at the ground. I was curious, and thinking I might be of some assistance, I moseyed down that way and found that Fred had a real puzzled look on his face. He called me over and said, "I want to show you something." He pointed to his blind. "See that blind over there?" It was about thirty-five to forty yards off the road. Then he pointed to a large track, and said, "A six point buck stood right here. I had all the time in the world and I drew down on him. I put him in my four power scope, and squeezed the trigger. And the damn deer took off!"

We spent the next fifteen minutes looking for a trace of blood, but could not find any. Fred said, disgustedly, "If I had just had my bow here, I could have got him." Fred hardly dared to go back to camp, as he knew that having told me about it, I would probably rat on him and he'd be the laughing stock of the camp. I did keep Fred's secret, for a while, but later it leaked out. Several years afterward, I presented him with a sign in the presence of the whole gang. It was to be erected at the spot where he had shot at the deer, and read, "On this exact spot, in the year 1973, Fred Bear, with his trusty rifle with scope, missed the largest buck in Grousehaven standing broadside at thirty-five yards." I labeled the sign, "HISTERICAL MARKER" and painted it the same as the historical markers which are found throughout the State of Michigan. Fearing that someone might miss it, Mr. Boyer erected the sign right outside the lodge so that everybody who visited Grousehaven would be able to see it. To this day the sign still stands.

The road we took back to camp passed a spot where we could see across an open area where Joe Engel and Alger Boyer were standing outside of their blind. Knowing we wouldn't foul anything up, we swung over to see what was up. Joe had just shot his first white-tailed buck, and Fred kidded him a bit because it only had two antlers about the size of a king sized cigarette. It was just over the legal limit. Fred insisted that Joe have his picture taken with this "huge rack." I cut some brush and cleared a spot to put the deer near two Scotch Pines. Just as Fred got ready to shoot the picture, I handed Joe a couple of sticks that resembled antlers, saying, "Here, maybe these will help you out." Joe put them on each of the antlers, and the deer looked like it was about an eight point buck—if you didn't look too close.

After a lot of kidding around, Joe said, "Gee, I wish I could take that deer back with me." and Fred answered, "Well, you can. We'll skin him out and cut him up into chunks." Joe had flown a jet from Houston to the Airforce Base near Alpena. Fred asked him, "How high are you going to fly?" and Joe said, "Probably about fifty thousand feet." Fred said, "Well, it will most likely be frozen in just a little while." Joe said, "You'd normally think so, but at the speed that an airplane goes, the skin on it gets so hot that the only place the meat would be safe would be in the cockpit with me."

When we got back to camp, we made preparations to skin his deer. We were just about ready to start when General Hank Everest came out. He commanded that we halt, and told us about a new method to skin deer. Seems he had just read about this in some magazine. "The only thing you need," he told us, "is a golf ball."

He had brought some golf balls with him, with the thought of giving the new method a try. He proceeded to instruct Fred how to cut the deer, and how to place the golf ball under the hide. The deer was hanging by its head from the buck pole. Fred made a cut completely around the neck, just behind the ears. He cut it down the chest to the belly cavity, then cut down each leg and around them. Next he skinned the back of the neck down about a foot from the ears and placed a golf ball under the hide. The golf ball acted as a holding device as he secured a rope tight around the hide with the golf ball inside.

About a dozen of us watched this procedure curious-ly. One end of the rope was secured to the bumper of a car, which Fred volunteered to drive. At the signal from the General, Fred took off with the car, like a dragster. When he came to the end of the rope, the tension was so great the deer tore loose from the buckpole and Fred dragged it in the dirt around the lodge.

This caused the General no end of embarrassment. He

gave Fred hell for driving too fast, and Fred, of course, was apologetic and said the next time he would go slower.

We tied the deer back on the buckpole, Fred again got in the car, and the General gave him the sign to go. This time Fred drove a little slower. The deer straightened out in an almost horizontal position. The hide started to break loose, and it soon ripped off. This did, indeed, prove to be quite an unusual way to skin a deer, and I have used it on several occasions since. The most important thing is to have a good, solid rope and pole, as well as a good dependable driver. I did this once in my garage at home, fastening it to the ceiling rafters, and almost pulled the garage off its foundation.

The boys cut the deer up in small chunks and put them in ice cream bags so Joe could stuff them easily around him in the cockpit. Alger drove him to the airport. About three hours later as we were sitting around the lodge, Joe called from Houston. I happened to answer the call. Joe said, "Me and the deer made it." I told him he was now the owner of the world's fastest deer. He laughed and said, "My gosh, I guess you're right, Bob." He already was the world's fastest man, once having attained a speed of over 4,500 miles per hour in the X-15 he piloted.

The next morning I helped Fred load an eight point buck into the trunk of his car. He had shot it down on Bear Circle, one of the roads around the place that had been named after a famous guest. Other famous named roads are: Curtis Circle, Godfrey Road, Lamay Road, Twining and Munger Alley.

The awards were given out that evening for the team hunt. My team won, and Fred got up and made a flowery speech. Then he called out to the kitchen for Marian Brown, the caretaker's wife, to come in. She was not in on the pool, but had shot the first deer that morning. Fred said he knew that he spoke for everybody in the group when he stated that she should have the money. Then he graciously presented her our money. This went over good with his team, but not so good with mine.

One year Fred took Bill Earl with him for the evening

hunt. Their blinds were about a quarter of a mile apart. When they came in that evening, Bill was really giving Fred hell. It seems that Fred shot a buck coming out of the swamp just before dusk. The deer ran and dropped dead practically in Bill's blind. "God damn it, Fred!", Bill told him, "I don't mind you hunting in my area, but you don't have to send 'um over to die in my blind!"

One year I stayed on after the rest of the gang had left, and hunted on the opposite side of the swamp where I had taken several deer on other occasions. There were many dead cedar trees in the area, with small branches. I was moving cautiously into the wind in a grassy area near the creek, when a huge buck jumped up in front of me about fifty yards away. To my amazement, I saw that he was pure white. I had heard about this deer, but none of our group had seen it. He whirled and ran to my right.

I quickly slammed my 375 Browning to my shoulder. I must have hit the side of a cedar tree with the gun, for when I put the sight to my eye, I could not see a thing. Upon investigation, I found I had pushed a little twig right into the aperture of the sight. By the time I removed the stick, the deer had gained about sixty yards and was going full tilt broadside to me. I gave him three of my best shots, but never parted a hair.

An albino deer would have been a good addition to my museum. Later, I learned that it was a good thing I hadn't hit him, as Mr. Boyer didn't want anyone to shot that particular deer.

Another year the General carefully arranged his blind on a point of land where oak trees were plentiful. It was a good place for deer to feed, right at the edge of the swamp. The General spent the first three days of the season there with no luck. Late one morning, Fred and I took a ride. We noticed the General's car was still in camp, he wasn't hunting this morning. After touring the property, we drove past the General's area.

As we neared the spot, Fred noticed a deer lying down nearly two hundred yards away. We both watched with our binoculars for about ten minutes. From the way the deer was lying in the brush, we couldn't tell for sure whether it was a doe or a buck. It turned its head and Fred said, "That's a buck. I saw his antlers move when he turned his head." He added, "Why don't you shoot him? Here, use my 270 with the scope."

I got out of the car and leaned against a tree and took a bead on him. When I fired, the deer sprang to its feet, made one bounce, then dropped. Fred exclaimed, "My gosh, you hit him!"

I ran over to the spot where the deer had fallen. Just as I reached the buck, he got up and started running. I took another shot at him, but missed. It headed towards the swamp, and I took after it on a dead run. Fred swung the car around trying to drive down to where the deer entered the swamp. I was going full tilt, and had just hurdled a brush pile when the General and Bill Boyer came down the road in their car. Fred and I were both embarrassed at being found in the General's area. Fred cleared himself by saying it was my idea. I guess it turned out alright that way, the General was only mad at one of us instead of both of us. We found the deer and the General even helped us drag it out.

Another hunting season, I had poor luck the first two days. Fred assured me he could take me to a spot where he'd guarantee that I'd get a buck. He let me out of the car at the chosen spot, saying he would pick me up about two hours later. I sat there for about half an hour getting cold, so I decided to stroll down the road to warm up.

I'd gone a quarter of a mile towards the swamp, when I heard a shot ring out behind me. It sounded as if it came from the other side of my blind. I stopped and listened for a minute, then heard another shot. That one sounded farther away, to the north of the blind. I figured someone must be driving a deer towards other hunters. Then a third shot rang out, about one hundred and fifty yards from me. I heard the brush crack, and the sound of beating hoofs, a large set of antlers was bounding in my direction.

I was hunting with my 375 which has a peep sight with a large aperture. I quickly lined it up with the trail that I knew the buck would have to cross. When the buck broke out of the brush into view, he was no more than twenty feet from me, running full tilt broadside. I touched off the 375, he rolled end-over-end and slid on his chin, winding up about fifty feet from me near the swamp. I racked a shell in the gun. As I brought it up, I heard the brush crack on my left again. There was another buck standing there, looking at me. I was about ready to pop this one for our camp tag, when my dead buck got up and started to run. I whirled around and gave him another one, dropping him just before he could disappear into the swamp. When I inspected him, I found that I had missed him with the second shot. He fell at exactly the same time I fired!

It wasn't long before Bill France and Keith Sammon came driving by in the car. Bill owns the Daytona Beach Raceway. He had flown up to hunt with his old friend, Bill Boyer. They had seen this deer and Bill France shot at it twice. Fred arrived just then. He had gone to pick me up at my blind, found that I wasn't there, but saw a large buck standing in front of the blind. At the same time, Bill France came along on another road and saw the buck too. He jumped out of the car and shot at it. The deer ran off and Bill took a running shot at it. These were the shots I'd heard, and Fred was an eyewitness to the whole thing.

I'll never forget the remark Bill France made when Fred and I were dragging the big buck out to where we could take a picture. Fred commented, "Boy, isn't he a beauty?" and Bill said, "Yah, but he isn't half as pretty as when he was running!" He was a respectable eight point buck. Still Fred gave me hell for leaving the blind, even though I got the buck.

In 1976, Fred came out with a book, "Fred Bear's Field Notes," so the following year I thought I would have some fun with him. One night when the gang gathered at the lodge for a party, I held up a book that I said I had written about Fred. I had told Fred that I was writing a book like his and said my version was going to tell it all. I think I had him pretty scared because he said, "The only thing I ask is that you wait until I die to have it published."

My daughter is an illustrator. She had made a sketch of Fred on the cover with his binoculars, looking up the side of a mountain. On the peak stood a well-endowed naked woman. I wrapped the cover around another book, so it looked like the real McCoy. The chapters I selected referred to some of the most embarrassing times that Fred had ever had, and never wanted to be reminded of, and they were definitely not in *his* book. I captioned several chapters as follows, "How to Build A Tree Blind For Black Bears"; "How to Build a Sled for Hunting Seals"; plus about eight other chapters of stupid things I had seen Fred do.

I read the captions to the group explaining in detail in my best uncomplimentary fashion how Fred had managed to get into such situations, and why they never found their way into Fred's book.

Charlie Coon, a friend of Fred's and Mr. Boyer's, was an old timer who had taken twenty-six deer in twenty-six years with a bow and arrow. He's known as "Dead Eye" and his picture hangs on the wall of the lodge. Charlie came in one morning with deer feet sticking out of his car trunk. He called me over to take a look, he had shot the buck the evening before. It was too late to track him, so Charlie had come back in the morning to track him in daylight. The back half of it had been eaten by coyotes. He was very dejected about it and said, "You know Bob, this is my twenty-seventh deer." I said, "No, Charlie, that's your twenty-sixth and a half deer." For some reason he didn't think that was a bit funny.

One year near the end of deer season I took my daughter up to Grayling to do a magazine illustration for Bear Archery. On the way home, we stopped at Grousehaven so she could take a chance at a deer. The snow was about six inches deep at that time, and Bill Brown, the caretaker, and Dick Mayhew, a friend, volunteered to put on a drive for Nancy, with my help.

This was Nancy's first deer hunting experience. We positioned her on a point of land where the deer were apt to cross when they came out of the swamp. Dick and I drove the swamp. Bill hollered that there was a buck coming, we expected to hear a ker-bang, but nothing happened. When we reached my daughter, she said it went past her too fast. During the course of the day we wore ourselves out trying to drive deer past Nancy. We could tell by the tracks that they were going right past her, she wasn't quick enough to shoot. About two weeks later when we were back home, she admitted to her mother that she just couldn't kill one of those "pretty deer". I never dared reveal this to Dick and Bill, they had worked their butts off trying to get a shot for her.

Keith Sammons, a local hunter, came in one evening to tell us he had hit a deer with his bow just at dark. Since there was no tracking snow, he planned to get it the next morning.

I got up the next day before dawn and went to see if I could find it. Fred and I had kidded Keith the night before that he probably missed it. To my surprise, I found some blood, and tracked it to the edge of the swamp, where I found the dead deer.

Thinking to have a little fun with Keith, I smothered the tracks of blood, got my car and loaded the deer in the trunk. Pretty soon Keith drove in, saying, "You know, I think somebody stole my deer." I said, "What do you mean, stole your deer? You never even hit that deer!" He replied, "I think I did." Then he asked me if I had seen any cars, or heard any, during the night. When I told him no, I hadn't, he said, "Well, I found some car tracks near the spot where I shot the deer." He was sure someone had stolen it, and appeared pretty miffed about the whole thing, so I suggested we have a little drink.

I poured him a shot, handed it to him, and said, "Let's have a drink on your deer." He looked at me puzzled, "What do you mean, my deer?" Then I told him, "I've got your deer in my trunk." He damn near threw his drink in my face.

One night before deer season opened, I presented a four-foot by four-foot photograph of Fred, to Mr. Boyer before the group of hunters. He hung it up on the wall with a caption below it saying, "Fred Bear, the World's Greatest Bow Hunter." It seemed to add a lot of atmosphere to the already trophy filled room. Mr. Boyer had been quite a hunter in his day, and had many trophies of his own hanging on the wall. At times when I couldn't sleep I would get up, sit by the fire looking around the room at all the trophies, pictures of famous people, and artifacts that were displayed there. A lot of history is hanging on those walls.

One season I spent a week with General Hank Everest at the lodge before the rest of the gang arrived. We toured the many roads on the property, checking the deer population. We shot a few partridge and squirrels for the pot, picked mushrooms, caught trout, and lived off the fat of the land. It was a real treat to spend some time with the General, he was a very interesting man with a pleasing personality. His son, Frank, usually comes with him during the season, they bring clams and oysters by the bushel for a huge seafood feed the night before the season opens.

I spent quite a bit of time with Frank, the son, who is also a bow and arrow enthusiast. We teamed up to make a serious attack on the abundant fox squirrels that had taken over the area. We treed them and worked them over with flu flu arrows. These don't shoot very far, so a hunter can retrieve his arrows.

During the course of the day, we took turns shooting while the others would pick up the arrows. The day following our squirrel hunt was the opening day for rifle shooting, bows and arrows were set aside. At the end of the rifle season, I discovered my bow was missing. I accused Frank by letter of hiding it, he responded that he knew nothing about it. This left me puzzled all winter. Later I learned that Bill Brown found my bow lying in the snow while he was cutting wood in February.

This gave Fred a lot of ammunition to use on me when I arrived the next season for bow hunting. I was rather embarrassed when it was presented to me, all broken and bent out of shape, having been warped in the cold winter weather. It looked like a truck had run over it. I felt real partial to that bow, as it was the one I had shot several trophies with in Alaska. It is now hanging on the wall in my home, retired from action forever.

One day I went hunting with Mr. Boyer's son, Harold. He had to borrow a gun, as something had happened to his. We went out to his favorite blind before daylight and had only been there a few minutes when I noticed a buck coming up behind him. It was forty yards away with the wind in our favor. The buck turned sideways then just stood there. I didn't dare say anything, so I slowly put my finger to my lips and pointed. Harold turned. Spotting the deer, he got the gun in a shooting position as the deer started to amble along the trail. I held my breath, waiting for Harold to shoot, but he didn't. Several times he flinched then took the rifle down, looked at it, put it back to his shoulder, drew another bead on the buck and tried to pull the trigger again. Each time nothing happened. He couldn't locate the safety on the borrowed gun.

Fred and I spent a lot of time riding around the roads at Grousehaven after we got our deer, reminiscing about the many trips we had taken together, and how times had changed. Fred mused regretfully that practically everything we had been doing over the previous fifteen years was illegal now. I had to stop and think about it myself when he mentioned it. The season is closed now on many animals such as polar bears, seals, and sea lions. There is no more importing of elephant ivory or leopard skins into this country, tigers and a number of other members of the cat family. We felt fortunate to have shared so many experiences and to have hunted these wild animals in various parts of the world. Many of the feats that Fred and I accomplished will never again be repeated due to changes in regulations.

There were times when Mr. Boyer, Fred and I spent hours sitting over in Bill's cabin before the huge fireplace, stoked with birch logs, mulling over experiences we had shared. Mr. Boyer always had his little dog, "Hoffy" on his lap. On the walls were trophies presented to Bill from the many famous people who visited Grousehaven.

This year's season, 1979, at Grousehaven, was another banner year. Fred brought a dozen of his salesmen and factory personnel up for the season opening, October first.

This was a smaller group than in previous years, as the factory had recently moved from Grayling to Gainesville, Florida. I met Fred for the second week of the season and took a good friend of mine, Jerry Anderson, who is Fred's biggest customer and owns the largest archery distributor in the country, located at Grand Lodge, Michigan. The sales staff left the day before we arrived and there was just Fred, Jerry and myself to spend a few days hunting together.

Fred's group had taken a dozen deer with bows the first week, Fred being the first one to score. He got a nice four point buck. This left Fred free to be Jerry's and my guide. Fred showed us spots where they had seen the most deer traffic during the first week. Jerry and I were each successful in getting a deer.

I had a rather unusual experience with the deer I shot. I built a stand in a spruce tree down by the river. The westerly exposure was open where the runway came across the river going past me to the swamp. I sneaked in before daylight and climbed up in the tree. It was a quiet morning, you could hear any noise for some distance. Shortly I heard movement off to my left, glancing over in that direction I saw a pair of deer legs coming my way out of the cedar swamp. They stopped at the edge of the heavy cover. I could vaguely see the deer's body. It was impossible to get a shot unless it stepped out into the open.

The deer stood motionless for a few moments, then suddenly it started stomping it's feet. The wind was blowing crossways, I didn't think he had winded me, but I quickly concluded that this was probably a parting gesture by the buck. I next heard a noise directly in front of me where there was an open area with some low grass, about a foot high. To my surprise, I saw a large raccoon coming in my direction, making his way slowly toward the tree I was in.

The deer stepped forward, out of the cedars, into an opening where I had a view of his spikes through the branches. He had his head up and ears were bent forward as he intently watched the raccoon. The raccoon spotted the deer, they both stopped and stared at each other just twenty feet apart. This gave me an opportunity to draw the bow back without the deer seeing me. I picked out a small opening in the branches and let the arrow fly.

When the arrow struck the deer he instantly fell flat to the ground on his side, much to my amazement. I shinnied down the tree and cautiously approached the deer. The arrow had broken the deer's neck killing it instantly. He never quivered. Later that day Fred and Jerry kidded me that I should have a mounted raccoon sitting in front of my blind from now on. It would make a better decoy than anything you could get.

Fred spent three days with us before returning to Florida. There were several pleasant evenings spent reminiscing the experiences of our many trips together.

As usual, each year Bill Boyer invites a number of his close friends up for the rifle season and arrangements were made for me to meet Fred and Jerry on the 12th of November back at Grousehaven. The General had come in from Virginia and I spent a day helping him get his blind built in his favorite spot. It takes about two days to get his gun sighted in properly. There were a dozen of us hunting out of the camp by the time the season started.

The following week I spent many hours visiting with a friend that Fred had invited as his guest, John Mitchell, who is an outdoor writer and a field editor of the *Audubon Magazine*. He had recently done a series on hunting for the magazine. This required a most tactful approach from both sides—the non-hunter and the hunter.

Fred came in one evening rather late and told me that he had hit a deer, but it got so dark that he had to give up the blood trail. The temperature was in the teens and we decided to wait until morning to pick up the trail. Fred and I left before daylight. After dawn broke we went to the spot where he had last seen signs of blood and we tracked it for about two hundred yards. It had headed for the cedar swamp. We hadn't trailed it but a short distance in the high grass before we came upon the deer. The coyotes had beaten us to it and they had devoured the hind quarters.

It's always a sad day when you have to pack up and leave Grousehaven. I know it is the highlight of my year to have the opportunity to hunt with Fred and see all the other hunting buddies. Fred feels the same way. This is the only chance he and I have to get together since we discontinued the exotic trips that we used to make together, and the fact he had moved to Florida.

XVIII

Hunting Friends

The Great Ed Bilderback

Space limits me from telling in detail about the many hunts I enjoyed with Ed Bilderback. I spent nine winters with Ed on the big island of Hawaii, running the sheep, goats, pigs and turkeys up and down the mountains. The island has two volcanoes standing over fourteen-thousand feet high. At times, in the winter, snow covers their summits. Ed has spent twenty-seven winters hunting in Hawaii. Hunting used to be fantastic there. It was nothing to see two hundred sheep a day, many pigs, goats, wild turkeys and pheasants. Ed has laid claim to taking over two-hundred animals with his bow.

I have been fortunate to be able to see Ed shoot many animals—several on the run—during hunts with him and his friend Bob Tonoue.

I have tried my best to get Fred to join Ed Bilderback

325

and me on one of our Hawaiian winter sheep hunts, but could never get him over there. He tells me he hasn't got the time. It must be hell to be so busy that you can't find time to go hunting. All I can say is that he sure missed some good times. Hawaii holds some of my fondest memories, especially if you're with Ed Bilderback.

Nocturnal Canoe Ride

I made the mistake of going on a deer hunt once when I should have stayed home. Jerry Anderson and I went up to Grouse Haven late in October, hunting Whitetails. Jerry and I perched cozy in our tree stands down by the Houghton Creek. Just before dark I hit a spikehorn. He ran toward the creek and I heard him splash when he crossed the stream. I checked out his tracks, the blood trail told me he would not travel far.

It started snowing and a cold wind was blowing out of the north. This is the season for the weather to get cold and nasty, when even Jack Frost goes south. Usually I enjoy hunting in the winter but a guy can only endure so much. So I went back to the lodge and found Jerry warming his buns by the fireplace.

I told him about the spikehorn and said that we had better find it after supper. In years past we had lost some deer to the coyotes by not going after them until morning. I came up with the bright idea that we take a canoe with us, and slide it down to the creek just in case the deer was in the water, or had reached the other side of the creek. A lantern flashlight would also be useful to take along.

We found that it had snowed about two inches since I left my stand and snowflakes the size of quarters still filled the air. I checked the creek where the spikehorn crossed and saw no sign of him. We slid the canoe on the snow down to the creek.

The first mistake I made was to suggest that Jerry should get in the bow of the canoe. I put the paddle in the stern and the flashlight on the floor. I cautioned Jerry that he must remain very still and that when we reached the other shore he take a firm but gentle hold of the brush. The current was quite swift and made it hard for me to keep the canoe from swinging. The water was black. I wanted to just touch the bow to the shore. I told Jerry to very carefully get out and keep the canoe in a level position. This he accomplished. I laid the paddle down in the bottom of the canoe and picked up the light. I said, "Now ease the bow slowly up on shore and try to pull me up close enough so I can get out. He followed my instructions to perfection but only half-way.

At this point he felt the urge to tip the canoe on an angle to keep from losing his balance. This allowed a small waterfall to cascade over the gunnel. Quickly I sank out of sight and rolled out, hitting the creek bottom. I opened my eyes and found that the flashlight was still on. I pushed, with my feet, on the creek bottom, and surfaced just in time to hear Jerry say, "Turn that light over this way, I can't see a damn thing." Let me tell you that my answer was not very gentlemenly. I do recall saying, "You bastard, I think you tipped the damned canoe over on purpose."

I floundered to shore as best I could. Jer was curled up like a whoop snake laughing his fool head off. I grabbed the canoe, dragged it up on the bank, flipped it and drained out the water. Righting it I said, "Get in and don't move." The water was squirting out of all my pockets. He was laughing so hard that he was absolutely no help. I quickly paddled us back to the other side and struck out for the car. Back at the lodge, I built a humungous fire in the fireplace and stripped everything off. A couple of stout bourbon sandwiches helped me stop my teeth chattering. Jerry got a mile of laughs. I found the damn deer in the morning about 20 feet from where we beached the canoe.

Time Heals Everything

I don't know why I ever invited Jerry to go hunting with me again, but I did. I guess time helps us forget most anything. The next year we were back at Grouse Haven. We went for an early morning hunt, getting up before daylight. I peeked at the thermometer as we left and shivered at the nineteen degree reading. I drove a couple miles south, parked my car and we struck out in the dark to our stands. We were about three-hundred yards apart.

It was crisp, and you could hear a deer walking for a long ways. About an hour after daylight and feeling frozen, I started up the narrow trail road toward my car. I had gone about two-hundred yards when I came up over a small hill. My car was parked on a curve in the trail road about one-hundred yards from the road. It was a white Ford Pinto. There was no snow so it really stuck out like a sore thumb. I scanned the open area to the left and was surprised to spot a nice buck staring at my car. I quickly crouched on one knee, in shooting position, behind a low pile of brush and put an arrow on the string. The buck kept concentrating on my car. All of a sudden the buck decided that he didn't like what he saw and bolted flat out for the swamp. It looked like he'd pass me at about twenty yards. I drew a quick bead and when he bounded past, I led him by about six feet and released my arrow. The arrow struck the heart area. He ran like mad for forty yards, then flipped end-over-end. I don't know which of us was the most surprised. I walked over to him and saw that he was a goner.

I don't know why but the canoe incident flashed to mind as I looked at that deer. I recalled the trick Jerry had pulled on me the year before, dumping me out of the canoe. Then I got a good idea! There were lots of dead ferns nearby. I cut a bunch of them and piled them over the buck. I left the arrow in place. It was a big mound of ferns about two feet high when I finished.

I went to the car, started the engine and turned on the heater. I knew Jerry would be along shortly. My blood got up to temperature and, sure enough, here came old Jer, plodding up the road. He got in the car and gave me hell for leaving my stand too soon. He said a nice buck came in after I left and stood looking at my stand. This of course made me feel bad.

We sat and listened to the radio, soaking up some more heat. I said, "Jer, did you notice that big mound near the road just over the hill? He said he didn't. I said, "You know, it looks to me like it could be an old Indian burial mound." Jerry always was turned on by Indian lore. He couldn't wait to check it out. "Where did you see this?" he asked. I said, "It's only a hundred yards down the road on the right. Let's go check it out." I drove to the spot and pointed it out to him. I said, "It sure looks like a grave to me." He couldn't get out of the car fast enough. Jerry carefully removed the ferns and stopped abruptly when he spotted the feathers on my arrow. I'll never forget his remark, "You bastard, when did you shoot this buck?" He liked to use the word bastard. I explained that the buck had been trying to get into my Pinto and I had to shoot him. Jerry was in shock. I was pleased. I'd repaid him for last year's dunking.

Comments from Jerry Anderson

Most of my systems are still jogging along, but my memory is starting to walk. It is difficult to recall the exact date Bob Munger walked into my small archery shop in Grand Ledge, Michigan, but I can remember exactly what he said. "I'm going bow hunting in Alaska with Fred Bear for Polar bears, and I need you to show me how to shoot a bow." I agreed, and casually inquired, "When are you leaving?" His reply said a lot about the man who has since traveled so many continents in Fred Bears' footsteps. "Tomorrow." It wouldn't have been quite so bad, but he was a hell of a slow learner. His lessons and practice finally did pay off in a few years and a thousand arrows later, when he drew down on an unsuspecting Cape buffalo, broadside, at forty yards. The fact that the arrow flew four feet to the left of the rib cage and severed the jugular is nowhere to be found in the *Pope and Young* book.

I could write an entire volume of my experiences covering twenty-five years in the bush, snow, water, and camps with Munger, including one five-year stretch when we took unscheduled turns at saving each other's ass.

The rewarding values of hunting with Bob and Fred are really found in the fringe benefits so unknown to those who carry the anti-hunting placards. The trophies, missed shots, close calls, and far away places fade when compared to rituals of swapping philosophies, experiences, and lies about the chase. Many nights I could hardly wait to exit my blind and return to camp where Fred was about to hold court. Sometimes the historical verbage would assume the nature of a debate. The Bear version, and the Munger version, and you knew that somewhere in the middle crouched the truth, hoping to be discovered.

I am not a writer, but I am an appreciator of life, its challenges and rewards. Because of these two characters, my longevity has probably been shortened by twenty or thirty years, but I wouldn't trade the shared experiences. Except maybe the time they dragged me through the swamp and I acquired the incurable fungus, or the box of goose heads and guts, gift wrapped in the mail, or . . .

Jer. Anderson

BEAR ARCHERY
Subsidiary of Kidde, Inc.
KIDDE

Fred B. Bear
Chairman

Rural Route 4
4600 S.W. 41st Boulevard
Gainesville, Florida 32601
904-376-2327

August 18, 1982

Mr. Robert Munger
General Delivery
Gould City, Michigan 49838

Dear Bob:

In spite of a rather severe winter following a light crop of acorns, the deer herd at Grousehaven seems to be larger than ever and it becomes imperative that something be done to reduce the herd to range carrying capacity.

I have been chosen to chair a committee to come up with the answer to this problem. Following several rather stormy sessions we think that we have a course of action that will produce the desired results.

It has been decided to hunt the area with bow and arrow and we are now in the process in rounding up volunteers who might be willing to sacrifice themselves for this most distasteful task.

The purpose of this letter is to ask if you will give of yourself in this hour of dire need? If so, you would fit nicely into a group who have already pledged for the period of October the 12th through the 22nd.

It is fully realized that much is being asked of you and we will understand if your answer is no.

Most humbly,

Fred

dg

P.S. Have sent the same invitation to Jerry and included Mike. Also writing to Ed Bilderback to see if he can come and bring a few tons of herring.

No Audubon meeting. There was a death in the family and Bill could not make the Les Line date.

Fred Bear

Bob Munger

American Broadcasting Company

330 AVENUE OF THE AMERICAS · NEW YORK, N.Y. 10019

LT 1-7777

ABC SPORTS, INC.
PLEASE REPLY TO:
THE AMERICAN SPORTSMAN
354 WEST 54ᵗʰ STREET
NEW YORK, NEW YORK 10019
(212) 765-2020

January 23, 1967

Mr. Bob Munger
224 S. Cochrane Avenue
Charlotte, Michigan

Dear Bob:

This is just a note to tell you that the Alaska Polar Bear
show, in which you played such an instrumental part, will be airing
on January 29th, 1967 at 4:00 p.m., Eastern Standard Time, on ABC-Tv.

As Producer of the series, my greatest wish is that I could
get out on every location and meet all of you who are responsible, by
your personal contributions, to the success that this show has
experienced, but unfortunately, I cannot. I would just like to say
that although we never had an opportunity to meet personally, I
appreciate all you've done for our series under the producership of
Burr Smidt and hope that you'll enjoy the show.

With best regards,
THE AMERICAN SPORTSMAN

Lorne Hassan
Producer

LH:ss

CLIFF ROBERTSON

April 29, 1985

Mr. Robert S. Munger
3222 Elmwood Beach Road
Middleville, MI 49333

Dear Bob:

What a delightful surprise to hear from
you after lo these many moons.

I often think of our intrepid crew on
that damn ice pack and how we all
managed to huddle close together with
bonds of fellowship and mutual dis-
respect for the "Great White Hunter"
Helmericks.

I was sorry to hear that Fred is not in
the best of health. Please give him
my very, very best. I'm sure that a
little fresh air, some good friends, a
small hunt, a large crew and a pretty
lass along the way would cheer him up.
Tell him I can supply the beer!

Glad you are on the mend from your heart
operation and trust life is treating
you better. I'm so sorry we didn't get
a chance to see each other in Grand
Rapids, but I only just received your
letter today via the producers.

Thanks again and happy hunting.

As always,

August 4, 1986

Mr. Robert Munger,
General Delivery
Gould City, Michigan   49838

Dear Bob:

The Bear Bowhunting Academy will again be conducting
seminars at Grousehaven in October and this is to advise
that once more you have won a scholarship for this
semester.

Our faculty has been most attractively enhanced this year.
Astronaut and Space Shuttle Commander JOE ENGLE, will
continue his quest for a Pope-Young buck, along with Ben
Lee, World Champion turkey caller and Whitetail authority,
plus my hunting companion of many hunts, Bob Munger, who
won the bedroom snoring competition last year and did a
good job of keeping me honest at story telling time during
evening cocktails.

Immediately following, last year's Grousehaven activities,
our Records Chairman, Bill Boyer, came up with some
astonishing findings, one of which was that 15 arrows were
shot for each deer taken.   Bill, our host, was greatly
concerned about this situation and appointed a committee to
study the problem. They came up with the conclusion that
the targets were too small or the distance too far or both.
Bill, being a man with a reputation for getting things
done, went into action and immediately doubled the ration
of winter deer feed and offered a choice of clover and
alfalfa plus the standard timothy. Pellets were also added
along with a broad range of vitamins.

I spoke with Bill by phone several days ago and he tells me
that the deer are already nearly twice their normal size
and felt that the take should double this year.

Robert Munger
Page Two
August 4, 1986

To silence some critics that the tree stands were too high
or too low , you will now find your stand at ground level.
Push the button to your desired height and our robot takes
over up to 40 feet. For those who like to shoot at high
flying turkeys or low flying geese, there are several
stands that go to 100 feet (oxygen and parachutes are
provided at this elevation).

To ease the monotony during hunting, the blinds will be
equipped with product samples along with catalog, price
list and order pad. If the deer - bear - turkey and
squirrel activity does not allow for order writing, just
sign your name and Charlie Smith will be glad to write your
order.

Looking forward to having you with us.

                    Fred Bear -
                    Head Tracker

Bill Boyer (OWNER OF PROPERTY)   Bob Munger (Very Famous)
Honorary Chairman   Head Honcho

Charlie Smith (PRES. OF Bear ARCHERY) Ben Lee
Coordinator   (CAMP Boss)   Turkey Consultant

Hap Fling (SALES MGR.)   Tom Jennings Bow MFGR
Jaeger   Bow Stringer

                    Joe Engle
                    Skinner

            TED NUGENT - Rock Star
            NOISE MAKER
            AND DINNER MUSIC

February 17, 1987

Mr. Robert Munger
P.O. Box 1853
Anna Maria, Florida 33501

Dear Bob:

Have only just received your letter regarding your upcoming
book on Fred Bear. You may quote the following:

«Fred Bear is one of the most memorable characters I have ever
met. He is, in truth, bigger than life -- in truth, bigger than
the animals he has hunted with bow and arrow. I had the occasion
to travel up into the Arctic for the television special «The American
Sportsman». We were some 200 miles northeast of Point Barrow,
not far from the Defence Early Warning System, the United States'
most northern radar facility. The idea at the time (1965 --
prior to the ban on polar bear hunting) was to see if Red could
complete his hunting litany with a huge polar bear trophy. We
spent some two weeks on the ice flows awaiting the polar bear
to come to us! Seal oil had been spread around the camp to
attract the polar bears. It was risky business but, needless
to say, Fred ultimately got his bear. During that time, we
had snow blizzards, white-outs and a recalcitrant supply plane
to contend with. But not once did Fred ever complain! He
is a man of delightful good humour and infinite patience. I
will treasure the memory of those two weeks fully as much as
Fred treasures his well deserved trophy».

Sincerely,

Cliff Robertson

CR:jg

P.S.   Bob, I have no photos to supply you -- however, Fred
may have -- you might ask him. Best wishes on the
book.

Ritz-Carlton
1228, rue Sherbrooke Ouest
Montréal, Québec, Canada H3G 1H6
Tél (514) 842-4212   Telex 05-24322

MY FRIENDS, FRED BEAR AND BOB MUNGER
by Bert Klineburger

I first met Fred Bear in Anchorage, Alaska. The year was about 1958.

In those days I was spending about half my time in Alaska. Two years earlier my brothers and I had started the first taxidermy receiving station for our company, Jonas Bros. of Seattle (now Klineburger Bros.), in Anchorage. Hunting was really starting to open up and more guides were getting into the business. We, too, were expanding into the fur trading business with trappers and Eskimos, and manufacturing these skins into fur garments.

That great guide Eldon Brandt and I were hunting for world record moose. In 1961 we found it, and also, the year before, the Number Two trophy.

It was a thrill for me to meet a great man like Fred. He was already becoming a legend and on his way to taking more trophies in his lifetime than any other archer.

We kind of got plastered in Fred's hotel room that night in Anchorage, and he suggested that I go hunting with him. I told him I had to work when the weather was bad and hunt with Eldon when we could fly.

I often regretted that I did not hunt with Fred. He was doing his with bow and arrow and my hunting was with rifle, and I felt that the two would not mix. In those days I was thinking mostly about the North Country, and places like Africa, India, China, Afghanistan and Russia were only distant dreams. Little did I realize that one day I would hunt them all.

I got to meet and know a bunch of great archers through Fred. These included Glenn St. Charles of Seattle, Bud Grev, and a man who was to become a lifelong friend, Bob Munger.

Fred, too, was thinking "North," so we were to meet often as he passed through Seattle and Anchorage on his way to his many great adventures in Alaska and Canada. As our hunting adventures grew, so did a great friendship. This friendship still goes on today, and I enjoy visiting with Fred at any chance I get to meet him.

When we got together we always had lots to talk about. Fred went to India for the first time the same year that I did—1963. That first trip could have been with Fred, but it was not to be. Even so, we sure had even more stories to swap the next time we got together.

Fred also hunted Uganda. I was part of the opening of Uganda to hunting, and Fred was the first archer to hunt there. We had to get him a special permit to hunt with bow and arrow. The Africans thought he was crazy to hunt with a bow and arrow, the same primitive weapons that they used in their hunting. They had seen the powers of the rifles and wondered why this crazy man came from so far away to hunt with his brightly colored arrows rather than a big, loud rifle.

I know Fred went on to hunt Mozambique and other parts of Africa. So did I. This gave us even more to talk about when we got together. Quite often, fair amounts of booze were consumed at these meetings, and Bob Munger was often with us. Bob was himself a fine bow hunter and took much game from all over the world. Brigitte and I have enjoyed a long friendship with Bob and his wife, Phyllis.

A friend of ours, Tony Sulak, had purchased an island in the San Juan group in Washington State. He chose a great time to buy this island, as the Japs had just bombed Pearl Harbor and the US government was setting up big guns along the Straits of Juan de Fuca to bust the Japs if they came along the Straits in order to attack Boeing Aircraft and the Bremerton shipyards. Tony probably made a good deal on a beautiful island located just below the Canadian border. Tony had built a beautiful lodge and a boat house on the island, and as he was getting older, he suggested we get a group together to buy the island. Well, we did, and Bob Munger was one of our principal organizers on the deal. We spent many wonderful days hunting on the island and digging for clams or fishing the nearby waters with the Mungers. Later, the island was sold and those enjoyable times were over, but the friendship remained.

Bob continued to hunt around the world, and I always remember the time I had just returned from hunting Asiatic buffalo on Giant Marajo Island in the mouth of the Amazon River in Brazil. I told Bob, "You and Fred Bear should go hunt these!" Well, they did go hunt the buffalo and both got fine specimens after a long, tough hunt.

This was a rough hunt under terrible conditions. It was hotter than hell, and wet. I always remember that Bob told me, "The most enjoyable thing we had to talk about each evening, as we drank gin in hot, muddy water, was to cuss Bert Klineburger for sending us down here!"

I guess when all is said and done, it's the good friends and good times that really count. I really appreciate the memories of the good times we had and being able to call Fred and Bob my friends.

XIX

Banter, Tall Tales and Plain Talk

The Snowshoe Rabbit Hunts

I was in Grayling during the month of March one spring going over some business problems with Fred. We finished around 4 o'clock and Fred asked if I'd like to shoot a Snowshoe rabbit with a bow. I jumped at the opportunity and Fred fixed me up with a bow. We went to his house where he came up with two pair of snowshoes.

The snow was about thirty inches deep in the swamp directly behind his house. He marked out the plan of attack, using a stick in the snow. He pointed out the spot where I should go, down to the end of the swamp, and said that he thought he could drive the rabbit to me. I floundered through the deep snow and brush to where I judged the spot was and took my stand. In a few minutes I heard Fred let a yelp out of him like a beagle. I readied myself in a shooting position. I could see a little trail in the snow

341

that the rabbit used. The yelping grew louder and soon I caught a glimpse of the snow-white rabbit heading my way. He stopped about twenty feet from me and I let fly with my arrow. Somehow I managed to center him and he flopped over. I was quite proud of the shot I had made and couldn't wait till Fred came along.

Fred looked at the rabbit and in a disgusted voice said, "Oh shit! you shot the wrong rabbit!" He had me sputtering for a moment. I had expected a congratulatory comment on my shot. Fred laughed and said that's just about what you could expect for a beginner.

The next winter when I was living in Hawaii, Fred mailed me a copy of the *Michigan Out of Doors* magazine. The cover had a colored picture that Fred had taken of me proudly holding my rabbit.

The following year Fred called me to be a part of the program that he was putting on for all of his sales staff in April at the factory. I went up to Grayling in time to have lunch with him. He told me the show that evening was for a group of game wardens he had invited as his guests. We had a couple of hours to kill before the sales meeting and Fred suggested that we stage another rabbit hunt. I said I'd like to, but I thought that the rabbit season was closed. He thought no one would bother us on his property, behind his house, so I agreed and we went over to his house where he equipped me with a bow, arrows and snowshoes. He was not taking his bow and I asked him why. Fred responded, "I'm going to be the driver and you can be the shooter." I still thought, as we started for the swamp, that it was funny he didn't take his bow in case I missed my shot.

The snow was about two feet deep. Fred suggested that I go to the north end of the swamp which runs out to a main blacktop road. I had not gone far when I caught a glimpse of something shining in the sunlight beyond the thick cedar trees ahead. I stopped and took a better look. It didn't take me long to discover that it was a long whip antenna like the ones on game wardens' cars. It was about one hundred fifty yards away and I could make out a suspicious looking dull green car parked on the side of the road.

I rammed the bow under the snow and the arrows along with it. Plodding to the spot where Fred had told me to take my stand I arrived as a game warden stepped out from behind a large spruce tree. "What are you doing?" he asked. He hadn't noticed that I had no bow. "I'm picking mushrooms," I said. "What the hell are you doing?" The warden snickered as he realized Fred's plan had backfired. Later I found out that Fred had a spot on the wall where he had planned to nail the rabbit's hide, so the game wardens knew I was hunting rabbits out of season. Nice guy!

A Short Drive

It seemed that Fred and I had a knack for getting each other in trouble. I was a snowmobile dealer and Fred told me that he would like to buy a Ski-doo. We'd used them in one of the ABC films above the Arctic. I delivered the snowmobile to his home in Grayling, but he was away, so I left it in the yard next to the garage. Upon his return, he hopped on the machine, gave it a crank, promptly ran into a tree about forty feet away, and broke his ankle. This put him on crutches for the better part of two months. I was not a big hit with his wife. I'm told the machine left the next day.

Bears on the Loose

Another time he called me wanting to borrow my life-size mounted Alaskan Brown Bear. Fred had a bear like mine which he had sent to Los Angeles for a sports show. There was another show in Wisconsin at the same time and Fred needed a bear for display there. I normally don't loan my bears out as they are quite fragile, expensive and irreplaceable. But for Fred, I'd do it. He turned me over to one of his salesmen for shipping instructions. I crated up five hundred pounds of bear standing nine feet tall and six feet wide and sent it on it's way.

About ten days later I got a phone call from a guy in some little town in Wisconsin who wanted to know why in hell I had sent him a big bear in a crate. He said it had been setting out in his field for several days. After a few frantic calls to Grayling and Wisconsin I learned that the bear had been delivered to the wrong guy and in the wrong town. A salesman was sent out with a truck to pick it up. That's the last time I loaned my brown bear out, even to Fred.

Fred also had a life-size fiberglass bear that he used as an advertising attraction. It was about eight-feet tall and was bolted to a six-foot cement platform at the entrance of The Bear Mountain Resort where his museum was located. One night it disappeared. When the police were alerted, a state-wide search was put in operation for the missing bear. The bear was located finally in a ditch in southern Michigan over two-hundred miles from Grayling. It was returned and bolted back into place, only to be stolen again a few months later. This time it was found in Lansing about one hundred fifty miles away.

Fred's Big Sting

The night watchman in Fred's plant informed him that someone had broken into the warehouse the night before and taken a number of bows. Fred suggested setting up a trap to apprehend the culprits, suspecting they might return. That night the night watchman caught several teenagers coming through the window, from the outside, carrying the stolen bows. It seems that they had wanted to exchange them for lighter-weight models, as they were unable to pull the heavy bows they had taken the night before.

Famous Trout Fisherman

Fred has the reputation around Grayling for being quite an expert fly fisherman. Fred loves to fish for big trout after dark, during the Mayfly hatch. This story is his most exciting experience.

It seems that Fred had located a big trout feeding on a bend in the stream near a log jam. He had hooked into the fish on two previous occasions and was determined to keep after him till he caught him. On this particular night as he cautiously approached the hole, he could hear the "sloop!" sound of the big trout taking a Mayfly on the surface. He spent several minutes positioning himself so he could lay his fly in the right spot on his first cast.

Timing is the most important factor in catching one of these large feeding trout. A person can count between the times the fish comes up and takes a fly, and knows exactly when he will feed again. That's when you lay the fly on the water.

Fred tested the feeding fish three times by counting. Then at the precise time he laid his fly near the log where the trout was feeding. As his fly hit the water there was a splash and Fred's rod was nearly jerked from his hand. Fred had put an extra heavy leader on so the fish couldn't get away. He fought the huge fish frantically for several minutes. When he reached for his landing net, it wasn't hanging from it's strap—it was on the roof of his car. Fred battled the fish for several more minutes and wondered how he was going to land it.

At this moment he heard the brush crack and saw the silhouette of another fisherman in the pale moon light. Fred called to him, to come over and give him a hand. Fortunately he had a net and volunteered to net Fred's fish. Fred directed the other fisherman to where he was going to try to lead the trout in and they both positioned themselves for the landing. The fish made one more run toward the log jam, but he was tiring and Fred was able to turn him back, toward the man's net. The guy carefully slipped the net under the splashing fish, turned on his flashlight and to their surprise, there was a frightened muskrat clawing to get out of the net.

Fred Bear Day

Chuck Kroll, Fred's son-in-law, called me about a tribute to be paid to Fred by the city of Grayling. Many celebrities came from all over the state of Michigan for the gala event. The Chamber of Commerce plans included several bands and a motocade, with the Guest of Honor, Fred, and his wife Henrietta riding in a long convertible limo. Speeches of high praise followed at the high school auditorium.

When my turn came I tried to make Fred uncomfortable by telling the story of our first meeting when we lost our arrows with our names on them, on private rifle hunting club land.

All went well and Fred was presented many cherished gifts. I had to leave right after the program, as I had flown up from home and wanted to get back before dark. The next day Fred called to thank me for coming up and being on the program. He said that the committee was well organized, and did a bang-up job. After everyone left, Fred and his wife had to walk home a half mile away. The only thing overlooked was a ride back home. Fred said, "I guess someone in town doesn't love me."

The Big Bird

In 1968 after listening for two years to people who wanted to make love with Fred's company, Fred and I met the suitor, to whom we eventually sold the company at the airport in Grayling. The Victor Comptometer company had contacted Fred and wanted to send a man to take a look at the plant. Fred called and wanted me to fly up and join him to greet the Victor Comptometer agent and take him on a tour of the plant and museum. Fred said, "we'll take my station wagon which has ample room for his luggage."

It was a cold bleak winter day in January and it started to snow as we arrived at the airport. This is a military airbase used primarily in the summer by the Michigan National Guard. In the winter, it is almost abandoned. As weather worsened, we wondered whether a a single engine or perhaps even a small twin-engine plane could land with such heavy snow squalls.

Suddenly we were startled to see a huge plane appear in the blowing snow. It quickly disappeared out of sight to the east. Fred said that it must be a National Guard plane, even though they don't normally come here in the winter.

After a few minutes, the huge plane broke out of the snow cloud again, its landing gear and breaking flaps were down. It was a B111 twin jet equipped for eighty passengers. When it taxied towards our car, we caught a glimpse of the name on the plane—Victor Comptometer. Fred and I were both in a state of shock. As eight passengers emerged from the plane, Fred finally caught his breath and said, "My God, Bob, what'll I do, offer to trade them the plane even up for the plant?"

A Most Humble Man

Ben East, a popular sports writer for the *Outdoor Life* magazine in the 1960s told me that Fred was the hardest guy he ever had to interview. He related that, when he questioned Fred about an exciting hunt, Fred would say, "Ben, there really wasn't much to it, the bear came along, I shot him, he fell down and that's about it." Ben said, "How in the hell can you make a story out of that?"

Not only was Fred humble about his own exploits but he had the highest regard for his favorite guide, Ed Bilderback. Many times I have heard Fred say that his Alaskan Brown Bear guide was the greatest all-around bow hunter he had ever hunted with. Ed could call almost any animal and sneak up on them. Plus he's the most fantastic shot with a bow or gun Fred had ever seen. They threw away the mold after they made Ed. He's a going machine. Fred said, "He moves faster than a piss ant on a burning stick."

Twisted Facts

Last fall I was amused by a bow hunter whom I met in the upper peninsula of Michigan. I spend part of each year, in a trailer on a beach, near a small village in a remote and primitive spot south of Gould City on the shore of Lake Michigan. I doubt if one hundred people live there and the post office is smaller than a one-car garage. It just so happened that I went into town to pick up my mail on opening day for the black bear season. It was pouring rain. As I went in the post office and shook the water off my parka, I looked up into the eyes of a guy dressed in camouflage gear. We passed the time of day and started griping about the weather. He told me that he had been looking forward to this day for months. He said he had sat in his stand until he got soaked and cold, and decided to bunch it for the day. He looked a miserable, dripping mess, standing in a pool of water that had dripped off of him.

He was hungry to tell someone about his problems. He said he was using a rifle but that he used to hunt with a bow. I asked him what kind of a bow he had. He said, "Well, I've got a Browning, now, but my favorite was a Bear bow." He told me that after old Fred died, they sold his company to Brunswick and since then the bows haven't been worth a shit. Fred liked this story so much that he made me tell it several times at our hunting camp last fall.

Good Fortune of Health

Fred and I often have talked of our good fortune to be blessed with fairly good health during our lifetimes. Yes, even hunters have to worry about their health. We both reflected on the fact that each of us was able to make these hunts at a time in our lives when we were physically able to stand it. You can't climb mountains in a wheel chair. Fred and I have always agreed that having good health put us in a position where we could compete with most of the hunting clan. We are great believers in the remark that 10% of the hunters usually take about 90% of the game—same thing goes for fishing. Fred's physical condition always amazed me. I don't mind admitting that I had one hell of a time paddling my short legs to keep up with a guy fifteen years my senior. I have often complained that his legs were six inches longer than mine.

I used to jog off-season in the 1960s to ready myself for the next hunt. In those days joggers were a rarity, so people looked at you as if you were out of your mind. Jogging did help my wind though. I could keep up with Fred on the steep climbs, but he left me in the dust on the flats. We were lucky, very lucky not to be struck with something that would have prompted us to discontinue our endeavors.

Now in our waning years, it's a different story. Fred has emphysema and is on oxygen twenty-four hours a day. At eighty, he still goes to his office daily, still a sharp thinker having retained his sense of humor. He's had to back off on the hunting some but spent a month this past season helping others harvest their buck up at Grousehaven in Michigan.

As for myself, I'm no pillar of strength, but I'm not a frail weakling either. I have survived two open heart surgeries. I go at my own speed. I fly fish. I hunt out of a treestand but I have cranked my compound down to my size (Fred says he won't use a compound because it's an old man's bow) and I'm just damned lucky to be any place!

Another thing we have discussed many times is just what a hunting experience is worth. We, of course, can tabulate the travel expenses, the guides, etc., but the real value is the personal satisfaction, relaxation, and therapy of a super hunt with a special friend. I don't think this can ever be converted into dollars and cents. I have done many things, seen a good part of the world and peeked behind the velvet curtain. How much is that worth?

About the Author

My early days of hunting started when I was eight years old in the southern part of Michigan. On my first hunt I was only an observer, accompanying an older friend of mine who rode me on the crossbars of his bicycle out into the country to hunt pheasants. His success in getting the first game I had ever seen taken made a mark on my mind for a lifetime.

In the later years, I was taught the fundamental of bird hunting by my father. There was no big game in our area and it was many years before I went on my first deer hunt in the northern part of the state. I was seventeen, in high school at Charlotte and was taken by a friend, an old time deer hunter, on Thanksgiving Day to Baldwin, Michigan, where I shot my first buck with a rifle. In 1940, I was introduced to hunting with a bow and arrow by my good friend Bill Graham.

In 1951, I met Fred Bear, while hunting in northern Michigan, who drastically changed my life and hunting style.

My first big game hunt was in 1954 when I joined some of my friends on a hunt in the Canadian Rockies in the Provence of Alberta. I failed to take any big game on my first big game hunt with my bow and arrow, but I learned of the fun the others were missing by using a gun.

In 1956, I went to Kodiak Island for an Alaskan brown bear. I was obliged to take my trophy with a rifle having lacked the hunting skills of getting close to the game. Had I known then what I have learned during the years from my expert teacher, Fred Bear, my walls would probably have many more trophies. I cannot stress strong enough the importance of the skills one acquires when using a bow and arrow, which helps in other types of hunting.

Nine years passed before I teamed with Fred Bear on the first polar bear hunt in the Arctic. From this point on hunting became more on a professional level.